Strategies for Improving Patient Care

Interdisciplinary Case Studies in Health Care Redesign

Strategies for Improving Patient Care

Guide to Clinical Resource Management
Mickey L. Parsons
Carolyn L. Murdaugh
Thomas F. Purdon
Bruce E. Jarrell

Interdisciplinary Case Studies in Health Care Redesign
Mickey L. Parsons
Carolyn L. Murdaugh
Robert A. O'Rourke

Strategies for Improving Patient Care

Interdisciplinary Case Studies in Health Care Redesign

Mickey L. Parsons, RN, MN, MHA
Organizational Consultant
Tucson, Arizona

Carolyn L. Murdaugh, RN, PhD, FAAN
Professor and Associate Dean for Research
College of Nursing
University of South Carolina
Columbia, South Carolina

Robert A. O'Rourke, MD, FACP, FACC
Charles Conrad Brown Distinguished Professor
in Cardiovascular Disease
Professor of Medicine
The University of Texas Health Science Center
San Antonio, Texas

GOVERNORS STATE UNIVERSITY
UNIVERSITY PARK
IL 60466

AN ASPEN PUBLICATION®
Aspen Publishers, Inc.
Gaithersburg, Maryland
1998

Library of Congress Cataloging-in-Publication Data

Parsons, Mickey L.
Interdisciplinary case studies in health care redesign/
Mickey L. Parsons, Carolyn L. Murdaugh, Robert A. O'Rourke.
p.   cm.—(Strategies for improving patient care)
Includes bibliographical references and index.
ISBN 0-8342-0970-5
1. Health services administration.   2. Reengineering (Management)
I. Murdaugh, Carolyn L.   II. O'Rourke, Robert A.
III. Title.   IV. Series.
RA971.P275   1997
362.1'068—dc21
97-21500
CIP

Orders: (800) 638-8437
Customer Service: (800) 234-1660

About Aspen Publishers • For more than 35 years, Aspen has been a leading professional publisher in a variety of disciplines. Aspen's vast information resources are available in both print and electronic formats. We are committed to providing the highest quality information available in the most appropriate format for our customers. Visit Aspen's Internet site for more information resources, directories, articles, and a searchable version of Aspen's full catalog, including the most recent publications: **http://www.aspenpub.com**
    Aspen Publishers, Inc. • The hallmark of quality in publishing
    Member of the worldwide Wolters Kluwer group.

Editorial Resources: Jane Colilla
Library of Congress Catalog Card Number: 97-21500
ISBN: 0-8342-0970-5

Printed in the United States of America

1   2   3   4   5

TABLE OF CONTENTS

CONTRIBUTORS

Anne M. Bolger, MSN
Senior Vice President, Hospital
 Operations
Northwestern Memorial Hospital
Chicago, Illinois

Edward G. Brooks, MD
Assistant Professor
Department of Pediatrics
Children's Hospital
The University of Texas Medical
 Branch at Galveston
Galveston, Texas

Marcia A. Colone, PhD, MSSW
Director, Case Management
Northwestern Memorial Hospital
Chicago, Illinois

Jean G. Crane, BSN, MS
Manager, Healthcare Information
 Consulting Services
First Consulting Group
Chicago, Illinois

Terese Lynch Donovan, RN, MS
Neonatal Clinical Nurse Specialist
Department of Nursing

John Dempsey Hospital
University of Connecticut Health
 Center
Farmington, Connecticut

Martha Gunther Enriquez, RN, MS
Vice President
University Medical Center
Tucson, Arizona

**Robin G. Fleschler, MSN, RNC,
 CNS, Perinatal NP**
Outcomes Manager, Women's
 Services
St. Luke's Episcopal Hospital
Houston, Texas

Pamela Garrison, MSPH
Vice President
First Consulting Group
Los Angeles, California

Clayton Gillett, MBA, MHA
Clinical Roadmap Team Coordinator
Group Health Cooperative of Puget
 Sound
Seattle, Washington

Alan Golston, MD
Co-Chair, Heart Care Roadmap Team
Director, Medical Consultant Services
Group Health Cooperative of Puget
    Sound
Tacoma, Washington

Robert D. Gordon, MD
Professor of Surgery
Woodruff Health Sciences Center
Emory University School of Medicine
Director, Liver Transplant Program
Emory University Hospital
Atlanta, Georgia

Anne Horbatuck, RN, BSN, MBA
Nursing Manager, Surgery and
    Staffing
Department of Nursing
John Dempsey Hospital
University of Connecticut Health
    Center
Farmington, Connecticut

Susan Houston, PhD, RN
Director of Outcomes Measurement
    and Research
St. Luke's Episcopal Hospital
Houston, Texas

**Leanne Braden Hunstock, RN,
    MBA, MEd, CS, CNAA**
Patient Care Executive Consultant
APM Management Consultants, Inc.
San Francisco, California

Robin E. Johnson, MBA
Director, Population-Based Planning
    and Improvement
Group Health Cooperative of Puget
    Sound
Seattle, Washington

**Karlene Kerfoot, PhD, RN, CNAA,
    FAAN**
Internal Consultant
Memorial Healthcare System
Houston, Texas

Courtland G. Lewis, MD
Associate Professor, Orthopaedic
    Surgery
University of Connecticut Health
    Center
Farmington, Connecticut

Karen Livingston, APRN, MS, ONC
Acute Care Nurse Practitioner in
    Orthopaedics
Department of Nursing
John Dempsey Hospital
University of Connecticut Health
    Center
Farmington, Connecticut

Rosemary Luquire, PhD, RN
Senior Vice President
Chief Nursing Officer
Chief Quality Officer
St. Luke's Episcopal Hospital
Houston, Texas

Nanette E. Martorell, RN, CPN
Case Manager
Department of Outcomes, Evaluation,
    and Nursing Research
Children's Hospital
The University of Texas Medical
    Branch at Galveston
Galveston, Texas

Beverly A. Massey, BSN, RNC
Program Manager, Case Management
The University of Texas Medical
    Branch at Galveston
Galveston, Texas

Rebecca McKee-Waddle, RN, MSN
Clinical Coordinator
Medical Services
Emory Hospitals
Atlanta, Georgia

Kenneth J. Moise, Jr., MD
Professor of Obstetrics and
 Gynecology
Baylor College of Medicine
Houston, Texas

**Carolyn L. Murdaugh, RN, PhD,
 FAAN**
Professor and Associate Dean for
 Research
College of Nursing
University of South Carolina
Columbia, South Carolina

Mary D. Naehring, RN, CPHQ
Associate Director, Aston Clinics
University of Texas Southwestern
Director, Medical Services
University of Texas Southwestern
 Health System
Dallas, Texas

Michael E. Newmark, MD
Clinical Associate Professor
Baylor College of Medicine
Associate Chairman
Department of Neurology
St. Luke's Episcopal Hospital
Neurologist
Kelsey Seybold Clinic
Houston, Texas

Debbie Olson, MSG, MPA
Senior Consultant
First Consulting Group
Los Angeles, California

**Gloria J. Opirhory, RNC, CNAA,
 PhD**
Associate Vice President, Operations
Associate Hospital Director
Director of Nursing
John Dempsey Hospital
University of Connecticut Health
 Center
Farmington, Connecticut

**Robert A. O'Rourke, MD, FACP,
 FACC**
Charles Conrad Brown Distinguished
 Professor in Cardiovascular Disease
Professor of Medicine
The University of Texas Health
 Science Center
San Antonio, Texas

Robin S. O'Toole, RN, AAM, MSHA
Director, Clinical Resource
 Management
Inpatient Services
The University of Texas Medical
 Branch at Galveston
Galveston, Texas

Mickey L. Parsons, RN, MN, MHA
Organizational Consultant
Tucson, Arizona

**Suzanne S. Prevost, RN, PhD,
 CCRN, CNAA**
Director, Outcomes Evaluation and
 Nursing Education
Associate Professor
The University of Texas Medical
 Branch at Galveston
Galveston, Texas

C. Joan Richardson, MD
Professor and Vice Chair
Department of Pediatrics

Director, Division of Neonatology
Medical Director for Clinical
    Affairs
Chief of Staff
The University of Texas Medical
    Branch at Galveston
Galveston, Texas

Marilyn R. Sanders, MD
Assistant Professor, Pediatrics
Division of Neonatology
University of Connecticut Health
    Center
Farmington, Connecticut

William L. Sheats, MPH
Practice Director
First Consulting Group
Alpharetta, Georgia

Carl Smith, MD
Associate Medical Director
Crawford Long Hospital
Atlanta, Georgia

Susan L. Smith, RN, PhD
Director, Clinical Outcomes
    Assessment
Emory Hospitals
Atlanta, Georgia

Dona E. Stablein, BSN, MBA
Specialty Master
First Consulting Group
Bethesda, Maryland

**Jana S. Stonestreet, RN, PhD
    Candidate, CNAA**
Chief Nursing Executive
Methodist Healthcare System
San Antonio, Texas

Dorothy Teeter, MHA
Vice President
Clinical Planning and
    Improvement

Group Health Cooperative of Puget
    Sound
Seattle, Washington

Alice F. Vautier, RN, EdD
Associate Administrator for Patient
    Services
Chief Nursing Officer
Emory Hospitals
Atlanta, Georgia

Anthony E. Voytovich, MD
Professor of Medicine
Chief of Staff
Department of Medicine
University of Connecticut School of
    Medicine
Farmington, Connecticut

Michael M. Warren, MD
Chief, Division of Urology
Deputy Director of Health Services
Texas Department of Criminal Justice
The University of Texas Medical
    Branch at Galveston
Galveston, Texas

Vivian West
Senior Manager
First Consulting Group
Los Angeles, California

Anne W. Wojner, MSN, RN, CCRN
President
Health Outcomes Institute, Inc.
The Woodlands, Texas
Assistant Professor of Clinical
    Nursing
School of Nursing
University of Texas at Houston
Houston, Texas

Charles Clagett Yaney, MPPM
Senior Associate Consultant
APM Management Consultants, Inc.
San Francisco, California

FOREWORDS

Health care is experiencing what other businesses learned long ago—that the delivery of services must be cost-effective, customer focused, and high in quality. The practice of medicine, once confined to individual physician practices and hospitals whose goal was to fill beds, has been radically altered by competitive cost-cutting market forces. Consequently, health care has evolved into an interdependent triad of insurers, physicians, and hospitals constrained by a capitated-payment system. Along with this corporatization, a plethora of management consultants have launched reengineering to solve operational efficiency problems and achieve cost-effective delivery of services. However, *reengineering* is considered by some to be a euphemism for downsizing. This is probably accurate with respect to hospitals, especially if critical processes are not changed to enhance operational efficiency and effectiveness. One result of cost reduction has been dissatisfaction with the impersonal treatment patients have experienced in the redesigned hospital environment. Administrators cannot forget that a business focused on satisfying customer needs will be successful. However, in many situations, particularly in academic medical centers, the patient asks: "Who is my doctor and where is my doctor?" Such questions reveal the confusion and mixed missions of academic centers that struggle with the changing health care market and their role in it. What is our business? What will it be, and what should it be? Who is the customer? Many businesses, particularly in health care and in academic medical centers, are unsure of the answers. But if they are unable to answer, how can they deliver a strategy for success? For those health care organizations that are struggling to be "reborn," it is important to realize that becoming more efficient without becoming more effective is not a formula for long-term success.

Interdisciplinary Case Studies in Health Care Redesign by Parsons, Murdaugh, and O'Rourke is a practical guide for process redesign that can achieve organizational effectiveness in line with institutional strategy. This book provides a framework for reestablishing effective service to the ultimate customer: the patient. As a medical professional, I have personally worked with Ms. Parsons and have witnessed her effectiveness in redesigning processes in an academic medical center. True process redesign as presented in this book will take organizational efficiency to the effective outcome of consumer satisfaction.

John B. Sullivan, Jr., MD, MBA
Chief Medical Officer
University Physicians/University Medical Center
Associate Dean for Clinical Affairs, College of Medicine
University of Arizona Health Sciences Center
Tucson, Arizona

A fiscally responsible health care system with substantiated quality results—this must be the goal for all health care providers today. To deliver care efficiently and effectively, we must shift our focus from a task-oriented, departmentally focused care delivery system to a health care system that is seamless and characterized by operational and clinical processes that offer quality care at lowest cost. By upending the system and redesigning it through study and analyses of core processes, service is improved, quality is maintained, and cost is reduced.

Interdisciplinary Case Studies in Health Care Redesign is a comprehensive and exciting effort to enable the reader to do just that. It is comprehensive in that it contains principles, guidelines, and examples of all the major approaches to the complex process of system redesign—total quality management, continuous quality improvement, case management, critical pathways, outcome management, and integrative information systems. It is exciting in that it emphasizes that no single approach or process is the ideal or particular standard for all organizations. While local and regional benchmarking is imperative, each organization must study and analyze its own processes and determine its own "best practices."

Although there is no single or best approach, these authors have made an outstanding contribution to the single most important endeavor in health care today by highlighting six functions common to all successful redesign efforts. The first of these is the centrality of the communication process. Communicate every day about the effort and the project.

The intensity of the commitment required to support and maintain the effort is a second commonality of redesign projects. The commitment from the administrative level is absolutely mandatory for success and requires a tremendous amount of time and effort to make the process of redesign work and to force the collaboration that must happen. As in all interdisciplinary efforts, contributions from every member of the team are needed and are important, but physician collaboration and commitment is a sine qua non.

Focus on process is a third characteristic and commonality of all redesign efforts. Processes are identified by describing and defining all activities leading to a desired outcome. Processes—clinical and operational—are the basic building blocks in any quality improvement endeavor, and all are open to scrutiny. Increasingly, we must look at processes related to disease management in an enrolled population and processes related to the cross-continuum of care management. By reducing variation in practice of a process, improved quality at lower cost is achieved.

Monitoring of the project on a continual basis is not only an inherent part of the process; it is vital to the enterprise. The constant monitoring of the characteristics of the target population enables the process of establishing "best practices" in a critical pathway or other structured care methodology. The critical pathway itself must be monitored to see if outcomes have been achieved within designated time frames. And then, most important, variance monitoring is vital to ascertaining the worth of the "best practice." It is not good enough that outcomes are satisfactory; if there is any way that the process can be shortened or be made more efficient, we must do that.

Effectively creating a case for change is a fifth commonality of successful redesign efforts. A host of economic, technologic, societal, and humanitarian trends are mandating change in today's health care system. Change is occurring—rapidly, often discontinuously, and with unrelenting ferocity. Creating a case and a need for change is the responsibility and challenge facing health care leaders. It is not accidental that the authors of so many case studies in this book begin their tale by stating that they started with a particular disease management category because not only was it a high-volume or high-cost diagnosis-related group (DRG) but the staff, physicians, the entire team were particularly interested in it. High interest is reflective of need, and when there is a felt need to resolve a problem, the process of change flows much more smoothly. It is paramount that organizers recognize high interest and capitalize on this interest in the change process.

The last commonality—seamlessness—is critical to successful redesign efforts. If processes, care, and, most important, information systems are not integrated horizontally and vertically, the best redesign efforts will be ineffective and unsuccessful. Seamlessness as a concept will expand beyond the walls of all existing health care organizations and will ultimately result in information system tools such as the birth-to-death patient record.

Redesign with emphasis on effective outcomes speaks to the necessity for a major research focus for clinical practice. For many years, researchers have pleaded the case for research-based clinical practice. Although not redesign's primary purpose, all redesign efforts are perforce based on scientific methodology. The case studies in this book present one of the greatest cases ever for the value of scientific methodology in patient care.

The authors of this book are to be commended for sharing with us a practical, innovative, and timely presentation of approaches to dealing with the revolution in health care. The changes noted in this book are only a beginning. The process revolution occurring in health care delivery organizations will have a tremendous effect on the education of all future health professionals. Health care administration and finance programs will also feel the repercussions. Not only will the education of physicians, nurses, and allied health personnel need to keep pace with the current changes, but if it is true to the mission of education, it should lead and prepare for even more changes in the future.

Marlene Kramer, RN, PhD, FAAN
Consultant
Health Science Research Associates
Reno, Nevada

PREFACE

The most important subject in health care today is maintaining quality while reducing costs. Following downsizing and the reduction of extravagance in work processes, organizations are challenged to transform their operating and clinical processes to respond to the ongoing driving forces of change in health care. This book describes approaches to operational redesign and clinical process redesign and provides examples and case studies from the field. The pragmatic examples are intended to assist health care professionals in redesign.

The introduction discusses the most significant trends influencing the health care industry and introduces societal and humanitarian forces that necesssitate redesign. It discusses a new mental model of work that should emerge as care is redesigned operationally and clinically across the continuum.

Chapter 1 begins Part I, "Operational Redesign." Effectively creating the case for change is critical to engaging all the leaders and staff in the organization in the creative redesign process. Examples of analyses needed to create a case for change are presented.

Chapter 2 discusses the structure and team processes that are instrumental in planning and implementing the redesign, as well as the organizational communication that is critical to success. Examples are also provided.

The purpose of Chapter 3 is to provide a framework for core process redesign. A practical framework is delineated. Application of the framework is described, using the inpatient care process. Chapter 4 describes the redesign planning for an inpatient and perioperative process and discusses the types of operational analyses that are needed as well as design team recommendations.

Part II of the book, entitled "Approaches to Clinical Process Redesign" (Chapters 5–16) includes organizationwide program descriptions and clinical case studies. Clinical redesign projects that are occurring in hospitals in various stages of managed-care evolution are described. Two known leaders in stage 3, represented by consolidation of the market, that are now moving toward stage 4, hyper-competition, are Crawford Long Hospital of Emory University, including Emory University Hospital and Clinics, and St. Luke's Episcopal Hospital. Both hospitals describe how their organizational systems of quality improvement embody process improvement and clinical redesign. The University of Texas Medical Branch at Galveston and the John Dempsey Hospital at the University of Connecticut Health Center have not yet reached stage 3, and their market can be described as a loose framework. Their clinical case studies are excellent examples of the type of multidisciplinary redesign necessary in managed care. Both organizations share their planning for more comprehensive programs that reflect their stage of market-place development.

Part III discusses the information system support that is essential for effective operational and clinical process improvement and redesign. An overview of an information support system is provided in Chapter 17. Two clinical case studies are reviewed: an organization that is redesigning care for a specific group of patients (Chapter 18) and an HMO that has implemented population-based care (Chapter 19). Both are in stage 3 markets.

Finally, Part IV (Chapter 20) discusses the individual and organizational impact of constant change in the health care environment, as well as the new kinds of leadership, management structures, and roles that such change requires. Strategies for organizations to thrive in the new age of process management are introduced.

ACKNOWLEDGMENTS

First and foremost, special thanks to our families and friends for their support and encouragement. The contributors and committed staff at these health care organizations deserve special recognition. Several individuals played key roles in coordinating content for the book, including Jana S. Stonestreet, Karlene Kerfoot, Gloria J. Opirhory, and Alice Forsha Vautier. Their expertise and assistance are greatly appreciated. Serving as a pathfinder in redesign in one's own organization is never easy, and it is commendable that they share their work from which we may learn.

Special recognition is due to our special editorial coach, Carmen Warner. She never stops supporting those who are trying to go "where no one else has been before." She is a special gift to us.

Our executive secretary, Lynn Davis, also deserves special recognition. Her excellent organizational skills have helped make this book a reality.

INTRODUCTION

The Quest To Strengthen and Redesign Our Organizations

Mickey L. Parsons and Carolyn L. Murdaugh

Objectives

1. To provide an overview of the most significant trends influencing the health care industry.
2. To discuss societal and humanitarian forces that necessitate redesign.
3. To describe the emerging new mental model of work.

The purpose of this introduction is to provide an overview of trends that are mandating change in the health care industry. These trends are economic, technological, societal, and humanitarian. An emerging mental model of work to replace the traditional view is also described.

SIGNIFICANT TRENDS IN THE HEALTH CARE INDUSTRY

The health care industry, along with all other businesses and organizations, is being challenged by its environment. The key phenomenon of this environment is rapid and constant change. Anticipating and reacting to this unrelenting change and creating the necessary changes to ensure that the organization survives and thrives are the responsibilities of the industry leaders.

Recognizing key trends and developing business approaches have become a necessity for leaders in every industry. Two upheavals are altering the essence of business and affecting every person and organization in the world. The first upheaval is the business reality of globalization: the local economy is no longer driven by the region. Employment and industry in small communities are affected by business development throughout the world, and this new competitiveness has brought major challenges and opportunities. An excellent example of such a challenge was recently reported in a *Wall Street Journal* article comparing the cost of employee health expenses for each automobile produced by American versus Japanese automakers. A significantly higher cost of greater than $1,000 per automobile for General Motors makes it more difficult for the American product to compete in a worldwide economy.[1] American businesses, to be successful in a cost-driven, price-competitive, global economy, will require changes in the delivery and costs of health care services that will in turn require rapid changes in health care systems.

The second upheaval is the revolution in information technology and accelerating rate of technological progress. It is now possible for immediate developments to be known worldwide. People can know more about the world than about their neighborhood. The speed of technological change forces people to learn entirely new ways to communicate with one another and to produce products. The speed with which innovations are communicated heightens the worldwide tension to adapt to or create the next wave of change.[2]

Hammer describes the forces for change as unrelenting global competition and ever more powerful and demanding customers.[3] Because these forces are combined with persistent problems of high cost and variable quality and service, the health care industry is in what feels like an earthquake. "At the epicenter of this earthquake is the American hospital."[4] Of all these organizations, the academic medical center (AMC), with its tripartite missions of education, research, and patient care, is in the most perilous position. The 20 to 25 percent higher cost of AMC care places extraordinary demands on the redesign of patient care delivery so that the position of leadership that AMCs define as essential to their missions can be maintained. The redesign of patient care delivery is only the first step in this health care revolution. It naturally follows that as the delivery system changes, education must change, as well as research. Indeed, the earthquake is only beginning.

SOCIETAL AND HUMAN FORCES NECESSITATING REDESIGN

Concomitantly, the health care industry faces challenges not seen in other industries. It is recognized increasingly that societal issues and trends have more to do with health status than the health care delivery system. The results of the escalation and incidence of violence in our communities, drug use, teen pregnancy, and smoking are intense utilization of acute care services and high costs to society. Changing family dynamics place demands on the health care system. For example, it is estimated that 40 percent of American children will be born into single-parent families by the year 2000. The fastest-growing cause of death among young people is automobile accidents, and for males between 17 and 44 years, the most frequent cause of death is AIDS.[5] At the other end of the age spectrum is the increasing proportion of the population that is elderly and the rise in longevity and chronic illness. The U.S. Census Bureau estimates that 40.1 percent of the U.S. population will be 65 years or older by the year 2010.[6]

Also, at least 48 million people in the United States are uninsured or underinsured. Given the corporatization of health care and the increasing number of publicly traded companies on the stock market with concerns about shareholder profit, almost 20 percent of the American population appears to be forgotten. Repeatedly, voters and government have rejected health care as a right and have refused to implement forms of national health insurance. It is proposed that the key reason to redesign the health care delivery system is to meet unmet demand. Hammer notes that reengineering concerns growth in the long term but that without redesign in the short term to maintain a competitive position, growth is not possible.[7] For health care providers who have been propelled into the frighteningly and maddeningly competitive business world, no greater humanitarian rationale to drive redesign would seem to be needed. At the same time, in the different economic paradigm of nationalized health service, a major acute care trust north of London, England, has embarked upon an organizational redesign project for inpatient, outpatient, and emergency care with just that goal: to meet unmet demand (M. Lowe-Lowri, Chief Executive, Peterborough Hospitals NHS Trust, Peterborough, England, personal communication, 1996).

The second key reason for health care providers to redesign the delivery of patient care is to establish the new system of care. The industry must transform itself from a hospital system to a health care system. Shortell et al. state that a major paradigm shift is required to move the focus from acute inpatient care to the continuum of care, from treating illness to maintaining and promoting wellness, and from caring for individuals to being accountable for the health status of defined populations.[8] As the success criteria change to the number of covered lives in the system and to the provision of care at the most appropriate level, clinicians must join together to standardize operational and clinical processes to offer quality at the lowest cost. For clinicians and the lay public, the national variations in clinical care and costs from communities across America documented in the *Dartmouth Atlas* serve as dramatic examples to drive redesign.[9] Only by radical redesign of the system and its components to create a seamless delivery system will current dollars be saved while permitting health care systems to remain competitive and to grow to provide tomorrow's services to even larger numbers of the American population.

AN EMERGING MODEL OF WORK

The phrases "standardize operational and clinical processes for top quality at the lowest cost" and "radical redesign to create a health care delivery system" sound too commercial to some health care providers. For the business world as well as the health care industry, process management as a theoretical approach to organizational design is new. Deming's pioneering work in Japan after World War II has been the basis for quality improvement, process analysis, and incremental process improvement.[10] Hammer, as the leading reengineering theorist in organizational design, defines *reengineering* as the radical redesign of business processes for dramatic improvement.[11] Quality improvement and reengineering are described as complementary in process redesign.[12] They are both essential and must be ongoing for organizational success.

Process is the difficult aspect. Today's organizational leaders were educated and worked in the era of scientific management, when jobs were simplified and role functions were organized in silos. The focus was to maximize each function, with no emphasis on how the functions fit together in a process. The result was simple jobs and complex processes with many "hand-offs." The predominant mental model of work in scientific management and the resulting organization of work make it difficult to think about work as a process. Hammer defines a process as a complete end-to-end set of activities that together create value for a customer.[13] The goal in radical redesign is to create simple processes that lead to more complex jobs.

Clinicians need to become process centered. They must learn new ways to provide patient care to be able to understand new mental models of work and work design. Senge defines the creation of mental models, one of five "learning disciplines," as "reflecting upon, continually clarifying, and improving our internal pictures of the world, and seeing how they shape our actions and decisions."[14] The practice of inquiry and reflection is essential to begin to look at the world in a new way. Only then will a second "learning discipline," systems thinking, become useful. Wheatley and Kellner-Rogers describe "organizing-as-process rather than organization-as-object" in their systems view.[15] Effective process redesign, whether incremental or radical, requires a systems perspective to look at the whole—core business processes, subprocesses, and clinical processes—within an evolving new mental model.

Quality improvement, continuous improvement, operations improvement, clinical process advancement, clinical resource management, outcomes management, value enhancement, reengineering, and redesign are all related. Terminology varies for different organizations. However, improving quality and service while decreasing cost are the three primary criteria for successful redesign. One useful example of terminology is as follows[16]:

- *Value Enhancement Teams (VETs)* focus on quality, outcomes, and cost-effectiveness for specific diagnosis, procedures, and population issues.
- *Continuous Improvement (CI) Teams* improve current processes based on data and customer feedback.

- *Reengineering Teams* work to redesign processes to achieve dramatic improvements in performance, such as cost, quality, service, and timeliness.

In this book, *operational redesign* encompasses the redesign of all processes in the provision and support of patient care to improve quality and service and to reduce cost. *Clinical process redesign* describes the restructuring of patient care according to a procedure or diagnosis to maintain or enhance quality and reduce cost. As managed care begins to dominate a marketplace, it is essential that clinical process design focus on the continuum of care.

CONCLUSION

The radical changes in the financing of health care dramatically demand redesign in the health care industry. Global economics has the greatest influence on the creation of new health care organizations that must address financial and societal needs. The unmet need of the millions of Americans who are underinsured or uninsured must become a primary rationale for enduring the pain of redesign in the short term. As organizational competitiveness is ensured, services should be able to grow to meet the unmet demand. New mental models will continue to emerge that, along with systems thinking, will change our view of work from the scientific management perspective to the new view of work as a process.

NOTES

1. R. Blumenstein, "Seeking a Cure: Auto Makers Attack High Health-Care Bills with a New Approach: They Treat the Providers Like Other Suppliers, Try To Help Them Cut Costs: The UAW Is Going Along," *Wall Street Journal,* 9 December 1996, A1, A4.

2. A. Mandl and D. Sethi, "Either/or Yields to the Theory of Both," in *The Leader of the Future: New Visions, Strategies, and Practices for the Next Era,* ed. F. Hesselbein et al. (San Francisco: Jossey-Bass Publishers, 1996), 257–264; W. Steere, "Key Leadership Challenges for Present and Future Executives," in *The Leader of the Future: New Visions, Strategies, and Practices for the Next Era,* ed. F. Hesselbein et al. (San Francisco: Jossey-Bass Publishers, 1996), 265–272; W. Bridges, "Leading the De-Jobbed Organization," in *The Leader of the Future: New Visions, Strategies, and Practices for the Next Era,* ed. F. Hesselbein et al. (San Francisco: Jossey-Bass Publishers, 1996), 11–18.

3. M. Hammer, *Beyond Reengineering: How the Process-Centered Organization Is Changing Our Work and Our Lives* (New York: HarperCollins Publishers, 1996).

4. S. Shortell et al., "Reinventing the American Hospital," *Milbank Quarterly* 73 (1995): 131.

5. T. Porter-O'Grady and C. Krueger Wilson, *The Leadership Revolution in Health Care: Altering Systems, Changing Behaviors* (Gaithersburg, MD: Aspen Publishers, Inc., 1995).

6. C. Snow, "One-Stop Shopping," *Modern Healthcare* 26, no. 48 (1996): 32–37.

7. Hammer, *Beyond Reengineering.*

8. Shortell et al., "Reinventing the American Hospital."

9. J. Wennberg and M. Cooper, *The Dartmouth Atlas of Health Care* (Chicago: American Hospital Association, 1996).

10. M. Walton, *The Deming Management Method* (New York: G.P. Putnam's Sons, 1986).

11. Hammer, *Beyond Reengineering,* xii.

12. Ibid.

13. Ibid.

14. P. Senge et al., *The Fifth Discipline Fieldbook: Strategies and Tools for Building a Learning Organization* (New York: Doubleday, 1994), 7.

15. M.J. Wheatley and M. Kellner-Rogers, *A Simpler Way* (San Francisco: Berrett-Koehler, 1996), 38.

16. *Change Update 1996: Ohio State University Hospitals Publication for Staff and Volunteers,* June 1996, 1–4.

PART I

Operational Redesign

Part Editors

Mickey L. Parsons and Carolyn L. Murdaugh

CHAPTER 1

Creating the Case for Change for Redesign and Selecting the Approach

Leanne Braden Hunstock and Charles Clagett Yaney

Chapter Objectives

1. To describe key analyses that must be performed to create a case for change.
2. To describe methods to set quality, cost, and service goals.
3. To discuss the strengths and weaknesses of approaches to redesign.

A compelling and meaningful reason to redesign must first be established to facilitate project momentum and direction. The case for change must be communicated to all stakeholders, both internal and external. The reasons for undertaking such a comprehensive program must be outlined. Additionally, assessments are necessary to determine cost, service, and quality targets for the redesign project and to select an appropriate redesign approach.

The focus of this chapter is to describe key analyses that must be performed to create a case for organizational change or action; to describe methods to set quality, service, and cost goals; and to discuss the strengths and weaknesses of approaches to operational and clinical core process redesign.

KEY ANALYSES FOR CREATING A CASE

Operational and clinical process redesign must be data driven; the project's actions and efforts should be guided by relevant, comprehensive information. Information that must be analyzed to obtain an organizational profile includes

- overall structure and performance
- financial operations
- clinical operations
- market position
- business relationships with physicians
- key operational processes

Overall Structure and Performance

Evaluation of overall structure and performance creates the case for change because the information provides an overview of organizational performance at the beginning of the project from which subsequent progress may be measured. Key insights are gained from an assessment of organization structure and performance when the following questions are answered:

- Is the organization's management structure conducive to supporting dynamic and extensive operational and clinical process redesign?
- How does the organization compare to peers?
- Is the organization's technology well integrated and supportive of clinical operations?

Several types of analyses provide insight into the above questions, including an assessment of span of control, staff interviews, and change readiness surveys.

Span of Control

A span-of-control analysis is a method to measure the amount of management required to supervise staff. Span of control is assessed as follows:

1. Identify all of the organization's full-time equivalents (FTEs) by job title or position.
2. Assign all of the job titles to two categories: management and staff.
3. Create a ratio of staff to management.

An example of a span-of-control analysis is provided in Exhibit 1–1.

The ratio developed in step 3 of span-of-control analysis enables one to understand the organization's structure prior to redesign. To provide other insights into the organization's structure, several variations of this analysis can be performed by changing the categories of management and staff to other categories of department or function, such as direct caregiver and support staff (Exhibit 1–2). In both span-of-control analyses, the higher the number, the more personnel who are involved in either directly working or providing services rather than coordinating or managing activities. Generally, the higher the ratio, the leaner the organization.

Exhibit 1–1 Span-of-Control Analysis: Staff-to-Management Ratio

Job Title	FTEs	Job Category
CEOs	1	Management
CFOs	1	Management
Managers	25	Management
Supervisors	50	Management
Clinical and technical staff	723	Staff
Clerical staff	200	Staff
Total	1,000	
Total Management:	77	
Total Staff:	923	
Total:	1,000	
Span of Control:		
Ratio of Staff to Management =	12.0	(923/77)

Staff Interview and Surveys

Early in a redesign project, input from a large cross section of staff begins to identify key areas of potential improvement, major process obstacles, key communication needs, and organizationwide expectations. Face-to-face interviews provide direct contact with staff and an ability to expand and clarify questions. However, interviews are labor intensive and may not be possible given the number

Exhibit 1–2 Span-of-Control Analysis: Caregiver-to-Support Staff Ratio

Job Title	FTEs	Caregiver/Support
CEOs	1	Support
CFOs	1	Support
Managers	25	Support
Supervisors	50	Support
Clinical and technical staff	723	Caregiver
Clerical staff	200	Support
Total	1,000	
Total Support:	277	
Total Caregiver:	723	
Total:	1,000	
Span of Control:		
Ratio of Caregiver to Support Staff =	2.6	(723/277)

of personnel in an organization. A more efficient strategy is to interview a representative sample while collecting other information with a written survey. Written surveys are impersonal and potentially less specific to an individual area of expertise. However, they are objective and can be efficiently used to gauge organizational attitudes. Additionally, the ability to provide anonymity to respondents allows for more candid responses. Whatever method used, the results should be communicated to key persons in the organization in a timely fashion.

Change Readiness Survey

A change readiness survey assists in designing communication and provides insight into important trends in the organization in terms of ability and willingness to change. Change readiness surveys are potentially more useful if they are administered separately from the initial staff interviews. The change readiness survey should gauge the organization's ability to adapt to new structures and processes and the level of attraction of the potential redesign changes. In a change readiness survey, staff respond to written statements that measure an organization's adaptability to change and the potential attractiveness of the redesign state.

Examples of statements that assess adaptability to change include:

- The organization can make significant changes in operations.
- Leadership is ready to make significant changes.
- Staff trust leadership to guide changes to the organization.
- Staff is ready to make significant changes.
- Leadership trusts staff to make changes.
- Leadership trusts staff to implement changes.
- Decisions are made efficiently in this organization.

Examples of statements that assess the attractiveness of the redesigned state include:

- Changes in the health care industry will provide opportunity to my organization.
- After redesign, my position in the organization will be enhanced.
- A redesigned organization will improve service.
- A redesigned organization will improve quality.
- A redesigned organization will improve cost.
- Changes made in the redesign process will most likely be fair.

These statements are not comprehensive and can easily be modified. Staff are asked to respond on a scale that indicates their degree of agreement or disagreement with the statement. The results can then be displayed as shown in Figure 1–1. The scatterplot shows that the organization has a high adaptability to change and moderate to low attraction to a redesigned future.

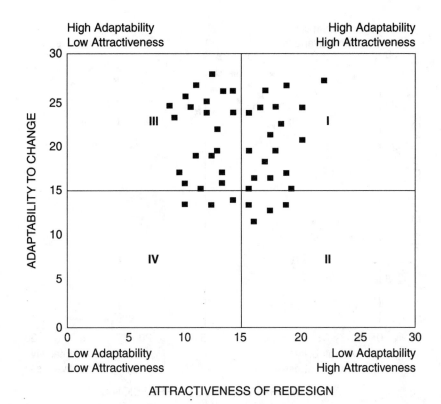

Figure 1–1 Scatterplot of Change Readiness Survey Results. Courtesy of APM, Inc., San Francisco, California.

The analysis can be performed separately for administration, management, and staff. For example, if management and administration are clustered in quadrant I (high attractiveness of redesigned future, high adaptability to change), while line staff are in quadrant III (low attractiveness of redesigned future, high adaptability to change), the redesign project plan should reflect these differences (Figure 1–2). Communication is critical to improve the staff's attraction to a redesigned organization.

Organizational Performance Assessment

Organizational performance assessment involves benchmarking, or analyzing how the organization operates compared to peers, including both competitors and best-practice institutions. Such an assessment provides insight about how the or-

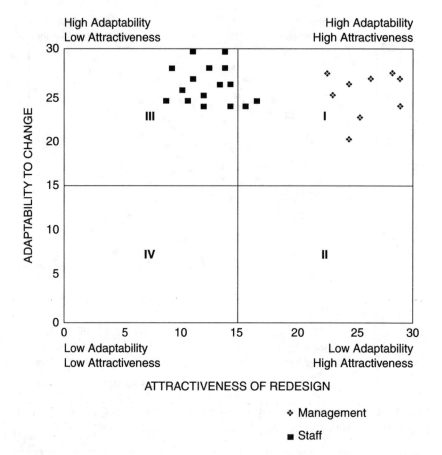

Figure 1–2 Scatterplot of Change Readiness Survey Results. Courtesy of APM, Inc., San Francisco, California.

ganization should operate with changes such as an increase in managed-care activity and allows the organization to develop and set quality, service, and cost targets.

High-Level Benchmarking. High-level benchmarking, which uses metrics relevant to the overall institution, helps the organization understand its overall position in the market. A common benchmark for overall organization performance is total costs per adjusted patient day. An adjusted patient day is calculated as follows:

Total Patient Days ÷ (Inpatient Gross Revenue ÷ Total Gross Revenue)

Adjusted patient days allow for differences in outpatient volume.

Meaningful variations include categorizing costs as patient care services costs (including all inpatient nursing activities), ancillary costs, and administrative costs (including all general and financial services). An example of high-level benchmarking with these cost categories is in Figure 1–3. The exhibit compares a hospital to two competitors and two best-practice institutions. One hospital spends more money on administrative costs than competitor A and both best-practice institutions. In the example, our hospital has higher costs in all three areas. If data are collected during different time periods, all costs should be inflation adjusted. If data are used from different geographic areas, labor costs should be wage adjusted.

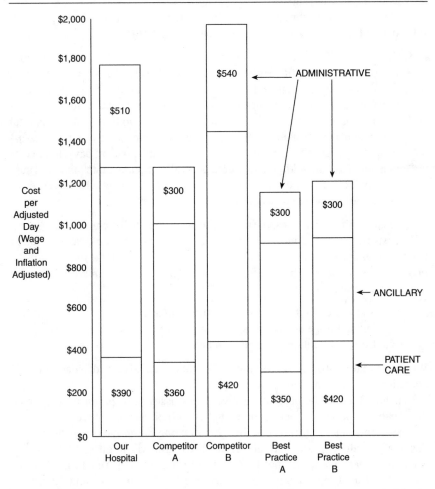

Figure 1–3 High-Level Benchmarking. Courtesy of APM, Inc., San Francisco, California.

Benchmarking at this level is helpful to communicate overall performance. However, this type of benchmarking does not provide the detail needed to understand where the cost of operations can be improved. Furthermore, service and quality levels are not considered by this method of benchmarking.

Departmental Benchmarking. In departmental benchmarking, operations are examined at a more detailed level. Departmental benchmarking identifies specific areas for improvement, helps set targets for clinical and process redesign teams, and provides quantitative support for information generated from other sources, such as interviews and surveys.

The general process for departmental benchmarking is to obtain two pieces of information for each department and comparable institutions:

1. *Total controllable costs:* costs that the department directly controls, including salary and benefits, supplies, professional fees, and other direct costs. These costs do not include depreciation, interest, and other overhead allocations. An alternative to using direct costs is using productive hours.
2. *Relevant unit of service:* the primary department volume that drives total departmental controllable costs. Generally, if volume increases, total departmental costs are expected to increase. For example, patient days drive costs in a nursing unit. Additional volume generally requires more labor and supplies, which are the primary costs in nursing departments. However, costs per unit of service may decrease.

Hours per unit of service can be used as an alternative to benchmarking controllable costs per unit of service. Generally, productive hours should be used rather than paid hours. Productive hours are controllable and are not a function of the organization's benefit policy. Using productive hours to benchmark is advantageous for several reasons:

- Productive hour data are generally easily available.
- Inflation and wage adjustments are unnecessary.
- Data from different time periods can be used.

While useful for initial analysis in productive hours, actual costs of a department's operations are not considered.

Benchmarking at the department level helps assess cost performance, which then enables a project to focus on potential opportunities for cost reduction. Nevertheless, one should proceed cautiously in drawing definitive conclusions from this analysis alone. Costs may not be reported similarly in all institutions. For example, benefit costs may not be accounted for at the department level in the hospital you are using to compare cost performance. Additionally, units of service may not be reported similarly across benchmarked institutions. For example, one institution may count a 30-minute respiratory procedure as a unit of service, while another counts a 15-minute procedure as a unit of service. The departmental benchmarking analysis should therefore be only one component of broader analyses used to determine cost reduction targets in clinical and process redesign. In Figure 1–4, nursing unit costs per patient day for one hospital are compared to those of two competitors and two best-practice hospitals.

Skill Mix Analysis

Another significant contributor to costs of an organization is the level of skill used to provide services. While using all senior medical technologists in the lab may provide a level of comfort that the job will be performed correctly, a more appropriate match of skill level to actual tasks performed could yield significant savings. To analyze skill mix, productive hours and productive payroll dollars need to be identified by each job title within a given department. Job titles must then be grouped together. For example, RN I, RN II, RN III, RN Per Diem I, and RN Per Diem II should be grouped together as "RN." Productive hours and dollars for the groupings should be calculated and meaningfully displayed. The pie chart in Figure 1–5 is one way to communicate the results of a skill mix analysis.

Financial Operations

Understanding the financial strength of the organization assists in assessing the magnitude and timing of the needed change. Benchmarking helps define the organization's opportunity to achieve external levels of performance. However, it

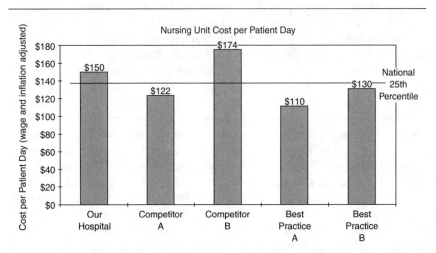

Figure 1–4 Department-Level Benchmarking

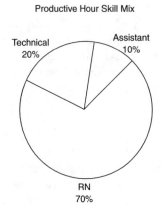

Productive Hour Skill Mix

Technical 20%

Assistant 10%

RN 70%

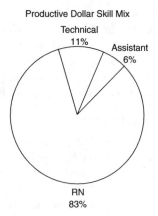

Productive Dollar Skill Mix

Technical 11%

Assistant 6%

RN 83%

Figure 1–5 Skill Mix Analysis

is also important to know the financial status of the organization. For example, the organization's levels of profitability must be known to assess whether the organization is able to invest in people and technology, maintain adequate capital investment, continue making strategic investments, and, most critically, remain solvent.

To determine the ability to meet the internal needs of the organization, a financial pro forma should be prepared. Several options exist to prepare pro formas, varying in the degree of complexity. This chapter will describe a simple income statement method. More detailed cash flow and balance sheet projections may be necessary depending on the needs of the redesign project.

A baseline income statement needs to be developed to project income. The most recent fiscal year or current budgeted income statement may be used. For each category of expense, three changes must be forecast: volume, inflation, and productivity. For example, suppose salary expense in a base year is $100. In subsequent years, salary cost may increase, labor costs may increase because of higher salaries, and productivity may change. In our example, assume that volume is expected to increase 5 percent, costs are expected to increase 2 percent, and productivity is expected to improve 2 percent. Under these assumptions, salary expenses will increase to $105: $100 (base) × 105% (volume) × 102% (costs) × 98% (production). Performing this exercise for each income statement item will yield projections for the next year. This process is repeated for additional years. Usually three years is an adequate base for financial analysis. (See the example of a budget plus two years projected in Table 1–1.)

Table 1–1 Budgeted and Projected Income Statement for Years 1999–2001 (in Millions)

	Budgeted 1999	Change Due To			Projected 2000	Change Due To			Projected 2001
		Volume	Inflation	Productivity		Volume	Inflation	Productivity	
NET PATIENT SERVICE REVENUE	$150,000	1%	0%	0%	$151,500	1%	0%	0%	$153,015
OTHER OPERATING REVENUE	$10,000	1%	2%	0%	$10,302	1%	2%	0%	$10,613
TOTAL REVENUE	$160,000				$161,802				$163,628
EXPENSES									
Salaries and Wages	$48,000	1%	4%	1%	$49,915	1%	4%	1%	$51,906
Employee Benefits	$9,000	1%	4%	1%	$9,359	1%	4%	1%	$9,732
Supplies	$20,000	1%	4%	2%	$20,588	1%	4%	2%	$21,193
Professional Services	$8,000	1%	6%	0%	$8,565	1%	6%	0%	$9,169
Purchased Services	$7,000	1%	6%	0%	$7,494	1%	6%	0%	$8,023
Bad Debt Expenses	$10,000	1%	5%	0%	$10,605	1%	5%	0%	$11,247
Other Expenses	$25,000	1%	5%	0%	$26,513	1%	5%	0%	$28,117
Depreciation and Amortization	$15,000	1%	0%	0%	$15,150	1%	0%	0%	$15,302
Interest	$8,900	0%	0%	0%	$8,900	1%	0%	0%	$8,989
TOTAL EXPENSES	$150,900				$157,089				$163,678
EXCESS OF REVENUE OVER EXPENSES	$9,100				$4,713				$–50

Clinical Operations

A clinical process redesign project must also analyze how patients are treated by the system clinically. This will enable the organization to understand the types of patients who are entering the system and how those patients are managed. Key clinical variables that help make the case for change are length-of-stay profiling by physician and diagnosis-related groups (DRGs), utilization, and selected analysis of patient care operations.

Length-of-Stay Profiling

Length-of-stay (LOS) profiling can be performed with two methods: (1) comparing LOS by DRG to published metrics and (2) making comparisons among institutional physicians. For example, mean LOS can be calculated for all patients who were admitted to the system in the past year. This can be compared to Medicare's published geometric mean average LOS (GMALOS) found annually in the *Federal Register*. Additionally, one can compare institution physicians to each other. Combining the two profiles produces compelling results, as observed in Figure 1–6, in which LOS varies almost two days between physician A and physician E. LOS profiling provides insight into overall utilization of patient days. However, patient day patterns vary significantly due to patient populations and complicating factors that may not be captured in summary DRG statistics. Also, the profiles do not consider costs, although the assumption is that LOS is highly correlated with overall patient costs through the volume-to-cost relationship discussed previously.

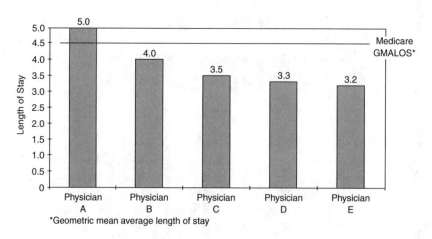

Figure 1–6 Length-of-Stay Profiling for DRG 000

Utilization

To get an accurate picture of clinical operating performance, costs also need to be considered. The level of sophistication of an institution's cost-accounting systems determines whether this analysis can be straightforward or cumbersome. In many modern institutions, clinical cost-accounting system cost per case by service or attending physician can be obtained. If the system is not capable of supplying this information, patient charges may be used. Costs can then be extrapolated using a cost-to-charge ratio for the hospital. An example of utilization profiling is shown in Figure 1–7. Utilization analysis provides meaningful insight into costs relative to physician practice patterns. However, the analysis may not adequately reflect different patient characteristics (age, psychosocial needs, comorbidities) that may need to be taken into account in patient costs.

Patient Care Operations

Because patient care labor costs are a large component of clinical operations, it is helpful to analyze these costs in the clinical and ancillary areas. By analyzing the drivers of patient care costs, the potential areas of greatest benefit for redesign can be determined. The components or drivers of patient care costs include the following:

* Personnel systems
  1. ratio of management cost to productive nonmanagement cost
  2. management structure
  3. premium-pay practices such as overtime, on call, callback, holiday, shift and weekend differentials, and bonuses

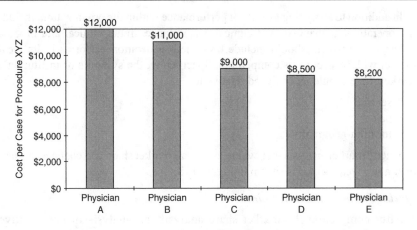

Figure 1–7 Utilization Profiling: Cost Per Case by Physician

  4. role evaluation
  5. work force composition
  6. skill mix
  7. staffing and scheduling practices
  8. mix of regular staff to part-time staff
  9. minimum staffing levels
- Operating performance
  1. productivity performance/hours per unit of service
  2. actual productive cost per unit of service
  3. staffing-to-demand performance
  4. effectiveness and satisfaction with clinical processes and systems based on interviews and surveys
     a. documentation
     b. medication administration
     c. patient transportation
- Demand
  1. census variation by patient care unit
  2. patient population
  3. patient turnover
  4. patient acuity

Benchmarks from best-practice performance should be used as much as possible to evaluate the magnitude of change possible in the personnel system, operations, and demand.

Market Position

In addition to analyzing aspects of performance within the organization, including operational, financial, and clinical performance, initial clinical and process redesign assessment should include how the organization performs in its local market with respect to its competitors. Specifically, the system's or institution's market share should be analyzed relative to

- service
- payer
- location/geography

A general market analysis that evaluates overall market share and changes in share over a two-year period is shown in Figure 1–8.

Market Strength of Service Lines

After completing the market share analysis, an analysis of comparative strengths can be performed. General favorable market characteristics for service

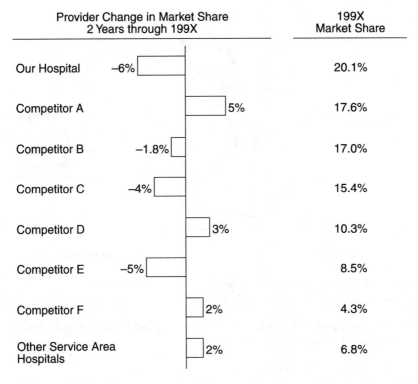

Provider Change in Market Share 2 Years through 199X	199X Market Share
Our Hospital −6%	20.1%
Competitor A 5%	17.6%
Competitor B −1.8%	17.0%
Competitor C −4%	15.4%
Competitor D 3%	10.3%
Competitor E −5%	8.5%
Competitor F 2%	4.3%
Other Service Area Hospitals 2%	6.8%

Figure 1–8 Market Share Analysis

lines should be determined. These characteristics may include physician, payer, and patient satisfaction with the service line; the image of the service line in the community; scope of services offered; and technology used. After the favorable market characteristics are identified, top service lines can be compared. Quantitative data should be gathered so that an institution's performance can be meaningfully compared to that of its competitors. The radar graph in Figure 1–9 compares one hospital's cardiology service line to its major competitors on five characteristics. The graph shows that improvements are needed in both payer and physician satisfaction and community image.

Business Relationships with Physicians

Even in highly penetrated managed-care markets, hospitals rely on their relationships with physicians to provide volume. However, the nature of the relationship is more complex, because external contracting relationships add an additional

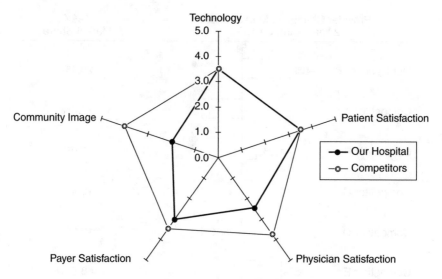

Figure 1–9 Market Strength Analysis for a Cardiology Service Line

---

dynamic dimension. Therefore, it is important to analyze the hospital's business relationship with admitting physicians.

General Physician Profiling

General characteristics of the medical staff should be reviewed, including the number of physicians who are board certified, percentage of admissions from physicians who have full privileges, group practice characteristics, and most frequent admitting physicians. The analysis should also evaluate the strength of physician loyalty to the institution or system. For example, if information is available for admitting physicians, the number of patients who are admitted to other competing hospitals should be obtained. An example of a physician admitting analysis is shown in Table 1–2.

Physician Interviews

After general physician profiling is complete, the top 10 to 15 admitting physicians (or the number of physicians representing at least 50 percent of admissions) should be interviewed. The interview should seek to answer the following questions:

- How does the physician feel about the quality and service at the institution? In nursing? Ancillaries? Administrative and support services?
- Does the physician admit patients to other hospitals? How do they compare in terms of service and quality?

Table 1–2 Physician Profiling

Physician	Specialty	Board Certified	Privilege Status	Admissions		Admissions to Other Hospitals
				Number	%	
Physician A	OB/GYN	Yes	Full	939	5%	125
Physician B	Family Medicine	Yes	Full	892	4%	150
Physician C	Internal Medicine	Yes	Full	848	4%	250
Physician D	OB/GYN	Yes	Full	805	4%	10
Physician E	Internal Medicine	Yes	Full	765	4%	None
Physician F	Internal Medicine	Yes	Full	727	4%	100
Physician G	OB/GYN	Yes	Probationary	690	3%	100
Physician H	Neurology	Yes	Full	656	3%	None
Physician I	Urology	Yes	Full	623	3%	None
Physician J	Internal Medicine/Cardiology	Yes	Full	592	3%	125
Other				13,145	63%	
Total				20,682	100%	

- What are the strengths of local area hospitals? How does the institution compare to local hospitals?
- What drives the decision to admit a patient to a specific hospital?

Interviews should be kept to a maximum of 30 minutes and summary, and anonymous results should be provided to participants. An analysis of results from physician interviews is shown in Exhibit 1–3.

Exhibit 1–3 Physician Interview Results

I.   How do you rate our hospital's quality? Our competitors?

| | *Percentage of Respondents* | |
	Our Hospital	*Our Competitors*
High	90%	80%
Medium	9%	15%
Low	1%	5%

II.   How do you rate our hospital's service? Our competitors?

| | *Percentage of Respondents* | |
	Our Hospital	*Our Competitors*
High	85%	90%
Medium	9%	6%
Low	6%	4%

III.   What are our hospital's key strengths?

| | *Percentage of Respondents* | |
	Our Hospital	*Our Competitors*
Good staff	70%	60%
Good physicians	91%	84%
Strong service lines	76%	88%
Good technology	90%	70%

IV.   What are key reasons to choose to admit to a hospital?

	Percentage of Respondents
Payer requirements	80%
Patient preferences	75%
Physician preferences	60%
Service offerings at hospitals	90%

Key Operational Processes

To begin laying the groundwork for the clinical and process redesign teams, key business processes (*core processes*) should be analyzed. These processes are shown in Exhibit 1–4 along with indicators of their breakdown.

Analysis of core processes helps assess how "things" flow through the systems in an institution: patients, laboratory results, paper, orders, and so forth. The concept of core processes is discussed in detail in subsequent chapters. This chapter focuses on the initial analysis of key core processes. By analyzing how a process currently works, one can begin identifying redesign opportunities. One method to analyze core processes is process mapping.

Process Mapping

Process mapping involves diagramming important steps in a process and establishing relationships between those steps. Symbols are used to represent the various steps, or the sequence, of the process being analyzed. A list of common symbols can be found in numerous business books. By arranging the symbols, one can begin to analyze relationships between the steps. Questions to ask about the process map include:

- Are the steps duplicative or redundant?
- Are the steps overly complicated or confusing?
- Do the steps involve redundant checks and rechecks?
- Are the steps in the right sequence?
- Are the steps necessary?

Exhibit 1–4 Core Processes and Indicators of Their Breakdown

Core Process	*Indicators of Process Breakdown*
• Admitting the patient	• Admission to any bed regardless of staffing availability, staff capabilities
• Treating the patient	• Frequent treatment delays
• Providing ancillary tests and procedures to an inpatient	• Inability to provide results in a timely manner
• Providing ancillary tests and procedure to an outpatient	• Inability to compete with independent outpatient providers
• Discharging the patient	• Discharges occurring late in the day
• Billing the patient	• Inaccurate, incomplete bills resulting in long payment delays

An example of a process flow chart that separates value-added and cost-added activities can be found in Figure 1–10. The example provides a work flow analysis of radiology and shows how the symbols are effectively used in the flow diagram.

Summary

The information described above will assist in defining the quality, service, and cost goals of the redesign project. Quality and service goals can be derived from the staff and physician interviews, clinical operations analyses, and core process analyses. Customer surveys also provide useful information for quality and service goals. Cost goals can be identified with the benchmarking information, which sheds light on the potential to achieve cost improvements. Financial analyses provide a picture of the internal financial needs of the organization in terms of timing and amount, and this information is also used in setting cost goals.

Regardless of the information used to determine the goals of the organization, the objectives of the redesign project should include

- meeting and/or exceeding service and quality levels of competitors in the market
- achieving best-practice levels of performance
- providing services at competitive prices
- generating sufficient income to maintain current investments
- generating sufficient income to continue strategic investments

APPROACHES TO OPERATIONAL AND CLINICAL REDESIGN

After completing the relevant analyses and determining the quality, service, and cost goals, a redesign project approach must be selected. One should consider the results of the analyses before selecting the approach to benefit fully from the insights gained from the collected information. While numerous approaches exist for clinical and core process redesign, they can be classified by two basic schemes

1. organizationwide versus departmental approaches
2. functional versus core process approaches

Organizationwide versus Departmental Approaches

Organizationwide Approaches

An organizationwide approach is used when the organization wants to redesign efforts across the entire organization. It offers several benefits:

- The whole organization is involved; all opportunities to achieve cost, service, and quality gains can be addressed.

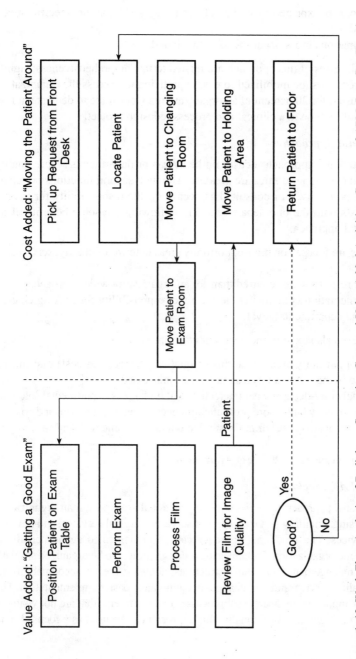

Figure 1–10 Work Flow Analysis of Radiology, Separating Cost- and Value-Added Activities. Courtesy of APM, Inc., San Francisco, California.

- Everyone is expected to participate and play a role, so no specific area is singled out.
- Participation across departments is facilitated.

The weaknesses of this approach are related to its comprehensiveness: significant resources must be mobilized to ensure participation across the organization. It is not unusual for 20 percent of an organization's work force to dedicate at least 20 percent of its time to a clinical and process redesign project.

Departmental Approaches

A departmental approach focuses on key areas or departments where quality, service, and cost opportunities are greatest. Although several functions or departments may be involved or consulted as necessary, the responsibility for making changes rests with the one department. The following are some benefits of the departmental approach:

- Efforts are focused on high-opportunity areas in terms of quality, service, and cost.
- Fewer resources are required than for an organizationwide approach.
- Implementation is facilitated because the responsibility for making changes is at the departmental level.

Weaknesses also exist in the departmental approach:

- High-opportunity areas (in terms of quality, service, and cost) that did not surface in the initial analyses may not be addressed.
- Minimal cross-departmental interaction will limit cross-departmental solutions, which typically have more profound influence on quality, service, and cost.
- Departments may feel unfairly singled out and become resistant to change.

Functional versus Core Process Approaches

Functional Approaches

A functional approach focuses on major functional areas within an organization, such as nursing, ancillary services, support services, surgical services, and environmental services. The functional approach can be implemented departmentally or throughout the organization. It enables the redesign project to be organized similarly to existing management and control structures, allowing greater accountability for making quality, service, and cost changes and ultimately easier implementation. This approach is applicable to discrete subprocesses in departments that are not visible in other areas or functions. Additionally, this approach can be used as a focused redesign effort to break down independent subprocesses of core processes. The disadvantages of this approach are similar to those of the departmental approach.

Core Process Approaches

A core process approach focuses on key business processes. For example, admitting a patient involves multiple functions, including nursing, environmental services, patient financial services, medical records, physicians, and other stakeholders. Any one of these functions can severely affect the admission process. For example, the admission cannot occur smoothly if

- nursing does not have the staff
- the patient cannot be transported to the bed
- environmental services cannot prepare the room
- patient financial services cannot obtain financial authorization for the patient visit
- medical records cannot locate old charts
- the physician cannot be contacted

Therefore, all these functions must be addressed in the admitting process. The multiple functions involved will ensure participation of all involved in the process. Weaknesses of a core process approach are similar to those of the organizationwide approach:

- Large requirements of time are needed to participate in the process.
- The potential for lack of participant ownership and involvement in the process is greater.
- Consensus regarding solutions is more difficult as a result of diverse membership. The problems may be seen as the responsibility of "other" departments or functions.

The core process approach is discussed in depth in Chapter 3.

A useful matrix that describes the strengths and weaknesses of the approaches can be seen in Figure 1–11. Several organizing decisions must be made when deciding which approach to use:

- How much participation can the organization dedicate?
- How much change can the organization afford? Will this meet the financial needs of the organization?
- Who will lead the teams? How much representation from different departments and functions will be available?

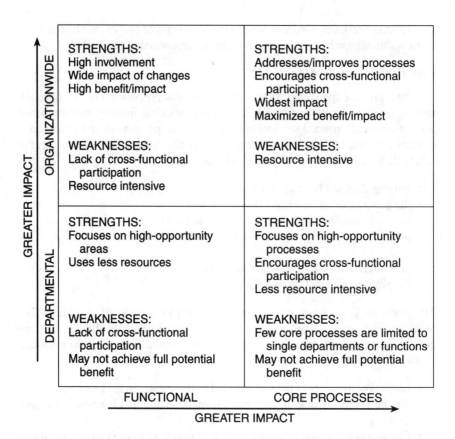

Figure 1–11 Comparison of Approaches to Operational and Clinical Redesign. Courtesy of APM, Inc., San Francisco, California.

CONCLUSION

A clinical and process redesign project should consider the strengths and weaknesses of the varying approaches prior to determining which one is most suited to the specific needs of the organization. The decision should be driven by the data collected initially to create the case for change. Answers to the following questions will facilitate the choice of a redesign approach:

- Is the organization ready to change? Are participants ready to engage and participate in the process?
- What is the magnitude of the change required? Is the organization refining current practices or trying to perform a major turnaround?

- What is the timing of the change? Does change need to happen immediately, or are the changes expected to occur over a period of time?
- How is the market changing, and what are the implications for the organization?
- How will staff react to changes? How will physicians react to changes?

After a case for change has been created, organizational goals are established, an approach is chosen, and the stage for redesign is set.

CHAPTER 2

Structure and Team Processes To Plan Redesign

Leanne Braden Hunstock and Martha Gunther Enriquez

Chapter Objectives

1. To describe an overall structure for redesign.
2. To describe how to develop a process redesign team.
3. To discuss the communication process in redesign.

The organizational structure of the redesign effort is critical to the smooth running and successful outcome of a complex and comprehensive change process. The successful redesign project requires broad participation by diverse constituencies and stakeholders. To accommodate many participants in a complicated undertaking, the structure must be sound, yet agile and flexible.

The complexity of hospital operations is reflected in the current organizational structure that supports daily operations. The policy and executive level includes the governing body and executive staff who ensure that the organization meets its mission within the context of a strategic plan and vision that is guided by their values. The administrative level consists of executive staff who develop an operating structure that enables the organization both to execute its strategic plan and to meet its financial and operational performance objectives. The operating level is organized by departments and services that carry out the mission and meet the strategic goals within financial parameters. The medical staff structure operates parallel to the hospital governing, executive, and operating structures. Ideally, the medical staff structure integrates with the hospital structure through representation at all levels. Likewise, the organizational structure for the redesign effort should reflect a compatible yet streamlined structure that facilitates and enables the decision-making process that will shape the selection, design, and implementation of the redesign initiatives.

This chapter has three objectives:

1. To describe an overall structure for a redesign process in a hospital and detail the structure and operating mechanics that guide the overall effort. Hammer and Champy describe the ideal participants as process owners, insiders, outsiders, and stakeholders.[1] The roles and responsibilities for each participant and team member will be described within the context of his or her position within the structure.
2. To describe how to develop a process redesign team.
3. To discuss one of the most critical elements of the redesign effort, communication. The lack of an appropriately executed communication strategy and plan will significantly hinder the success of complex change efforts. In redesign efforts, communication must be sensitive to the organization's culture, reflect understanding of the organization's concerns, acknowledge organization members' fears and anxieties, and anticipate the organization's need for information in terms of timing. The manner in which an organization proposes to keep the staff informed of planned changes is critical to helping the staff understand and accept why the organization has chosen to redesign. Likewise, the manner in which the message is delivered is crucial in developing the kind of caring and supportive environment that is required to make redesign successful.

ORGANIZATIONAL STRUCTURE FOR REDESIGN

Separate Organizational Structures for Redesign and Operations

It is important to devise a structure for the redesign effort that is separate from the current operating structure. The existing operating structure is likely to be overtaxed in terms of managing day-to-day activities. The charge and nature of the redesign teams require concentrated and sometimes intense focus to produce radical results that reach beyond incremental changes. Most organizations are inundated with projects, plus long- and short-term initiatives. Existing operating project and committee structures are not adequate to manage the redesign process unless initiatives are reprioritized.

The organization should inventory all current initiatives and assess both their validity and their value with respect to the current strategic priorities. If redesign is determined to be consistent with the strategic priorities and necessary to achieve both short- and long-term objectives, then the organization must make redesign a high priority. Redesign in a hospital bureaucracy will require the devotion and persistence of the entire organization to achieve and maximize results.

Organizational Levels

The organization structure for the redesign process consists of three levels, as illustrated in Figure 2–1. The highest level is the *executive group,* usually a steering committee or existing committee that reflects the appropriate membership. The steering committee is the decision-making level for the overall redesign effort.

The second level is *support.* The steering committee has a subcommittee or support level that includes the project support team and the communications, change management, and human resources subcommittees. These subcommittees provide specialized support to the steering committee and the process redesign teams in addition to managing the specialized areas of change management and communications within the organization throughout the redesign process.

The third level is the *process team.* The process redesign teams are charged with the redesign of selected processes.

An optional fourth level is the *subprocess* or *subteam* level. This level is used when the core process is too large or complex for a single group or team to manage all components of the process for redesign. For example, a core process of providing ancillary services to the patient involves ordering, producing, and delivering an ancillary service. Each of these activities is a component of the larger core process and might be considered for a subprocess team. An alternative method is to examine all activities related to a particular ancillary service such as pharmacy. The process redesign team may then consider those activities that other ancillary services share with pharmacy that could be consolidated or enhanced through redesign, such as purchasing or supply procurement or documentation.

Actively Involving Leadership

Champy states that the newest responsibility of leadership is to "explain what's going on. To everyone."[2] It is desirable, if not imperative, to align the leader of the organization with the leadership of the redesign effort both functionally and manifestly. The achievements of the redesign effort are influenced by the direct and active involvement of the executive leadership staff in the steering committee, the communications subcommittee, and the process design teams. Leadership's lack of visible, active inclusion and participation in the process will dilute the results and heighten the organization's resolve to resist change. Leadership cannot effectively sit on the fence waiting to see the outcome before getting involved; nor can it participate only to disempower the participants or thwart forward movement. Champy notes that "we must dramatically improve business results, now, and do it while earning the hearts and minds of our people. To make things still more difficult, 'now' has no traditions, no precedents, no time tested formulas. Now has never been seen before."[3] Leadership commitment and participation is perhaps the most important factor in successful redesign. The leader of the organization should be a strong force on the steering com-

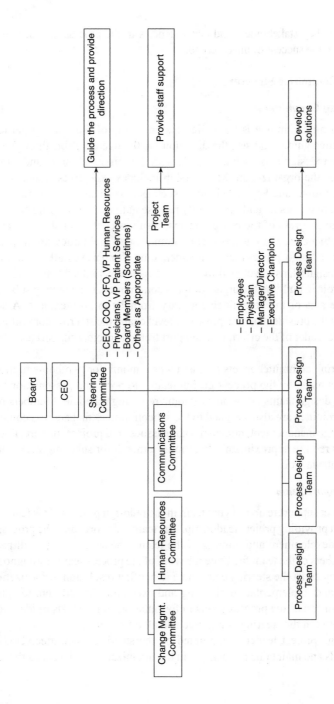

Figure 2–1 Organizational Structure for Redesign. Courtesy of APM, Inc., San Francisco, California.

mittee. Enlist key stakeholders and constituencies in the process, and secure their investment in the success of the outcome.

Redesign Committee Structure

The Steering Committee

The steering committee is the policy-making body of the redesign structure. The committee guides and sets the direction for the overall effort through alignment of the redesign approach and goals with the mission, vision, and strategic objectives of the organization. Membership includes executives responsible for hospital operations and key stakeholders such as physicians, administrators, employees, board members, and community representatives. The steering committee monitors the progress of the process teams, resolves conflicts between teams or other constituencies, and ensures that communication and policy are in place to support the redesign process and implementation. It approves all recommendations and design plans developed by the process teams and subteams. Members play a key role in building the organization's commitment to achieving substantial results. The size of the committee can vary from 10 to 20 members. A senior executive at the president or vice president level chairs the steering committee and is the visible leader of the effort, with support from the project support team leader (project leader).

The steering committee meets at least twice a month for two hours to monitor the progress made by the process design teams. Reports and presentations from the process design teams occur on a periodic reporting schedule. Members of the steering committee are also assigned to the subcommittees that address communication, change management, human resource issues, and project support. The subcommittees require approximately four hours a month for subcommittee meeting time and outside work.

Project Support Team

The project support team is a vital team in the redesign process. This team plays a key role in providing project leadership. The team helps organize the process and guides the development and training of the teams, the subteams, and all participants. Members of the team facilitate the work of the process teams throughout the project. They assist the steering committee in conflict resolution, prioritization of initiatives, and implementation planning and execution. In addition, the project support team assists the process teams in formulation and analysis of ideas and is a liaison between the steering committee and all other entities.

A redesign project leader is appointed by the steering committee. This individual builds and maintains momentum in the organization and ensures that coordination exists between the steering committee members and the other groups and committees. The role of the project leader is to provide overall leadership and to oversee and ensure quality and integrity of the process in terms of analysis, assumptions, and decision making. The project leader and project support team facilitate the smooth flow of information throughout the organization. The project support team members are selected for their knowledge of operations and clinical or analytical expertise. The team drives the redesign process by helping design the approach, manage the logistics, and facilitate process design teams. The typical size of an organization's project team is 6 to 10 employees. Outside consultants are members of the project support team and bring additional specialized expertise. In most cases, the team members relinquish their regular roles within the organization to devote full-time energy to the redesign project. The willingness to dedicate full-time staff to any redesign effort demonstrates the organization's commitment to the project. Often the team members go into the role with the risk that the job they leave may be eliminated when they are ready to return up to two years later.

Communications Committee

The communications committee is a subcommittee of the steering committee that oversees the creation and implementation of a communications strategy. The communications committee coordinates an intensive and comprehensive communications program that will keep constituents well informed with reliable and timely information. The importance of communication and the details of developing the communication plan are discussed later in this chapter.

The membership of the communications committee consists of approximately 8 to 10 individuals from the steering committee, the project support team, the communications department, and employee representatives. This committee is responsible for the development of a short-term and a long-term communication strategy that will be tailored to employees, patients, medical staff, and the community. The charge of the subcommittee is to maintain a high level of visibility for the redesign effort and to ensure that information from credible sources is presented throughout the process to manage the anxiety of change.

The communications committee meets approximately once a week for one to two hours during the planning phase in order to have a communication plan ready to implement immediately prior to staffing of the process design teams. A clear understanding of the objectives, the rationale, and the process of redesign is required. Following the initial organizationwide communication blitz, regular updates through a variety of mechanisms and vehicles are necessary. Approximately four to five hours per month are required to plan and, in some cases, to deliver the communication personally.

Change Management Committee

The change management committee focuses on the cultural aspects of the change process and assists the organization in adjusting to the transitions accompanied by a change of management. Membership includes representation from the major constituencies of the organization. Six to eight members who are appointed by the steering committee participate in an organizationwide assessment of readiness for change. The assessment determines the agility of the organization with respect to the depth and speed of change potentially tolerated by the organization. Information is obtained through interviews with leadership, medical staff, employees, payers, and other community constituencies. Other methods of assessment such as surveys and focus groups may also be used to obtain the necessary information. Change management committee members have backgrounds in interviewing, employee assessment, employee relations, or management and receive training prior to the active assessment activities. If a member does not have the needed skills, training is provided. Analytical skill and the ability to synthesize and analyze the assessment data are valuable contributions to the committee.

The initial organizationwide assessment process is quite time consuming and requires full-time effort from at least half of the committee membership for an intense period of three to four weeks. Following the assessment, up to 60 hours may be required to analyze the data for presentation in a conclusive format.

Human Resources Committee

The human resources committee is responsible for developing and recommending a well-articulated personnel policy to ensure that disruption to employees is minimized during and as a result of the redesign effort. Various analyses are completed relative to the work force and the impact of role redesign, role shift, and displacement or reduction in force. Attrition analysis is useful, because the historical rate of attrition for the institution is analyzed to project future attrition rates and areas of highest attrition. Policy recommendations are made to the steering committee about reduction in force policy, early retirement, seniority and benefit issues, and issues relating to organized labor relations. Displacement issues and retraining needs and opportunities are also assessed by the committee.

Members of the human resources committee are usually the human resources executive, the patient care executive, and management representatives from ancillary and support areas and the large clinical and patient care areas most likely to be affected by redesign changes. The committee is supported by one to two members of the project team and is closely linked to the change management committee. It meets weekly early in the effort, less frequently during the design phase, and with increased frequency when the changes are actually implemented.

Process Redesign Teams

The process redesign teams, or design teams, are the center of the redesign effort. The teams are charged with analyzing the current core process, understanding the process outcomes, and then redesigning new, more efficient and effective ways to accomplish the outcomes. Ideally, the new designs should reduce duplication, streamline the process, involve fewer people, and accomplish the outcome of the process with greater effectiveness and customer satisfaction at a lower cost.

The ideal members of the design teams are best described as process owners, insiders, outsiders, and stakeholders.[4] To maximize accountability and link the design with the highest probability for successful implementation, the process design team is led by a process owner. The process owner is an executive or senior-level manager who will be accountable after redesign. Ideally, the leader or leaders of the team are also members of the steering committee. In a hospital, medical staff participation at the team leadership level is imperative to provide the perspective of key stakeholders and to assist in communicating the new design to medical staff. The process owner's responsibility is to ensure that redesign is a team effort. Process owners motivate, encourage, and advise the team and buffer them from the negativity of workers in the organization who resist change. Process owners "take the heat from the organization so that their teams can concentrate on making redesign happen."[5] Insiders currently work within the process being redesigned and are involved with various functions of the process.[6] They may not be familiar with the entire process but are able to add a dimension of clarity to functional aspects of the process. Outsiders do not work in the process and bring objectivity to the redesign effort. They are expected to question the process steps and the redesign. The ratio of insiders to outsiders should be no more than one outsider to three to five insiders.

The design team needs to be large enough to include the right insiders and outsiders but small enough to develop momentum, focus, and commitment. If the team is too large or the core process too broad, the team should be broken down into "subteams" (see Chapter 3). The team meets for two hours two to four times per month for the first four to six months to analyze the current process and redesign the new process through many iterations. The team may need to increase the meeting frequency if momentum is lost through less frequent meetings, absent members, or failure to complete work that is to be done outside of the team meetings.

Membership selection should combine voluntary and directed efforts. Exhibit 2–1 describes the qualities of a good design team member. Volunteers who are interested in process redesign may be of great value in terms of motivation but may come with rigid predetermined ideas of what the "answer" is. The most effective way to include volunteers is to solicit both volunteers and nominees. Creative,

Exhibit 2–1 Qualities of a Desirable Design Team Member

- Leadership
  - Highly regarded by peers, superiors, and subordinates
  - Willing to question and challenge
  - Seeks consensus
- Commitment
  - Maintains a positive attitude toward work and others
  - Can be a team player
  - Takes pride in high-quality work
  - Has shown a commitment to the values and mission of the organization
  - Takes responsibilities seriously
    a. will attend meetings and meet deadlines
    b. will perform work in assigned groups
- Communications
  - Can listen nondefensively
  - Actively participates in group discussions
- Substance
  - Perceived as credible in his/her own area
  - Can think globally about an issue
  - Can be focused and persistent, detail oriented, and thorough
  - Can be creative, innovative, and realistic

Courtesy of APM, Inc., San Francisco, California.

innovative, or otherwise qualified outsiders and insiders are suggested without volunteering. The project team and the process owner or leader(s) should interview the volunteers and nominees to explain the expectations and commitment required and select the most qualified in light of their attributes. The project team works closely with the process redesign teams as facilitators and support personnel. The process team interfaces with the steering committee through the project team. When updates, recommendations, and final plans are proposed to the steering committee, the design team is present to discuss their design.

Incorporating Stakeholders into the Design Process

Stakeholders are those individuals, departments, or constituencies who have a vested interest in either the current or the new process design. They may be employees whose jobs will change as a result of the new design, customers of the process, or suppliers to the process. It is important for the design team to consider the implications and ask the stakeholders for feedback as they progress through the design process.

Incorporating stakeholder input is accomplished by first identifying potential stakeholders and determining their expectations and concerns about the new design. Stakeholder input is valuable to determine problems with the current process that exceed the perspective of the design team. It is also important to keep stakeholders involved by selecting their feedback into the design process. This involvement can break down resistance and avoid problems that occur when stakeholders perceive that the process was designed in a vacuum by a small elite group.

Documenting the Process

A useful format for documenting the redesign effort is to describe it in the context of the "cycle for improving performance" adopted by the Joint Commission on Accreditation of Healthcare Organizations (Joint Commission).[7] The elements of the Joint Commission's performance improvement cycle are as follows:

1. *Design* a function or process based on a clear objective, goal, or purpose.
2. *Measure* the performance of the function, creating an internal database that is used to measure performance over time.
3. *Assess* comparative information to identify opportunities for improvement and setting priorities.
4. *Improve* on the basis of priorities, design, test, and implement improvements and innovations.
5. *Design/redesign* evaluation of the improvements and innovations may lead to further redesign or new design of the process or function.

The Joint Commission framework assists a health care organization to demonstrate and illustrate its compliance with the Joint Commission standards as well as to document the change process within the organization.

PROCESS REDESIGN TEAM DEVELOPMENT

Developing a cohesive yet innovative team from a diverse group of people who may have never worked together or who have worked at opposite ends of a process is essential, because the group must become a team progressing toward a common goal in a short period of time. Although there is a strong focus on the task at hand, the quality of the product is dependent on the ability of the members to address issues in a challenging and thought-provoking manner while preserving the willingness to reach the goal. Scholtes describes four stages of team growth:

1. *Forming:* the process of moving from individual to team status
2. *Storming:* the realization that the task is different from and more difficult than what the members imagined
3. *Norming:* the acceptance of the team and its norms
4. *Performing:* diagnosing and solving problems, implementing changes[8]

Recognition that each team usually progresses through these stages of development will assist the facilitator and leaders to understand and guide the team until it begins to produce the objective and fulfill its purpose. A team charter assists the team to focus on its charge, purpose, and expected outcomes. An example of a charter for a design team is illustrated in Chapter 3, Exhibit 3–5. Ground rules are developed by the team to guide its interactions in meetings and during the course of its work.

Guiding principles are the operating parameters that guide the work and decisions made by the team. Some guiding principles for redesign might include the following:

- The mission and strategic goals will guide the process.
- Communications will be fair, open, honest, and timely.
- Concerns about the change process will be recognized and addressed.
- Approved ideas will maintain or enhance outcomes, satisfaction, and service levels.
- There are no hidden or predetermined solutions.
- Employees will be encouraged and supported to challenge the status quo to enhance services.
- All ideas and recommendations will be reviewed and treated with respect.
- Multidisciplinary, multilevel teamwork is vital to the success of the process.
- Interdepartmental cooperation and participation is critical.
- Employees will be involved in the formulation and implementation of changes affecting their departments.
- Key stakeholders will participate in all levels of redesign.

Orientation and training are important activities for the design teams to focus on in the first meetings. Or the organization may choose to orient and train all teams at the same time on a processwide blitz. Orientation should focus on an overview of the redesign project and the project structure and should clarify why the organization is undergoing change. The case for change should be reviewed as well as the goals of redesign. This is an opportunity for team members to get acquainted and to understand why they were selected and their collective purpose. Training should focus on the tools needed to redesign. For example, the following topics should be included in the team training:

- Problem-solving process
  1. structuring themes
  2. gap analysis
  3. brainstorming
- Techniques for improving processes
  1. work simplification: streamlining activities, eliminating redundancy and rework

   2. managing demand for work and using the appropriate level of resources to meet the need

   3. restructuring where work is done through centralization and/or decentralization

   4. aggregation and organization of demand

   5. cross-training and expanding the skill set of workers

   6. matching skill sets of the worker to the work

   7. leveraging technology through the use of automated tools and processes

   8. "make versus buy" analysis to determine the relative cost benefit of producing versus purchasing goods and services

   9. work elimination through analysis of value of specific activities

- Analytical tools
  1. process flowcharting
  2. cause-and-effect analysis
  3. skill mix analysis
  4. turnaround time analysis
  5. staffing to demand analysis
- Developing recommendations

If orientation and training are accomplished in a processwide blitz, the first time a design team convenes should be a "kickoff" meeting. Otherwise the "kickoff" begins with the orientation and training noted above. If the team has been oriented and trained, the "kickoff" meeting is the first meeting where team members have the opportunity to meet each other; review the charter, the process scope, the goals and expectations, and the work plan (see Chapter 3); and establish their ground rules. In addition to the agenda above, it is helpful to have one or two icebreaker or group participation activities to help the members get acquainted and an activity to help members begin to think creatively. It is recommended that the orientation training and "kickoff" occur close together in time to gain and sustain information and momentum and move quickly through the formation stages of team development.

Successful Strategies and Tips

The following success tips in project structure and team development are based on our own experience:

1. Include key constituents in the structure on all teams and committees.
2. Communicate every day in every way about the effort and the project.
3. Structure the project so that executive leaders are accountable for the outcome and implementation of changes.
4. Make leadership changes prior to redesign.
5. Orient team members early, and train just in time during the design process.

6. Interview potential design team members by two or more project team members. Resist the inclination to select on the basis of prior knowledge.
7. Develop a firsthand relationship with the design teams and the steering committee through frequent updates and presentations.

The project structure is key to the smooth assessment, planning, design, and implementation of changes to work flow and operations. Thoughtful and careful selection of participants is as important as the structure itself.

THE COMMUNICATION STRATEGY: PLAN AND PROCESS

Because redesign unleashes many changes, the art of selling it to reluctant buyers will become the organization's greatest challenge. Communication is a creative way to send a message so that people both understand and embrace the concept and ideas of redesign and respond positively to the messages.[9] Communication is critical to establish clear direction for any organization that is in transition. It provides a way to be in touch, joined with others, and to express and transfer ideas, feelings, and thoughts.[10] If it is authentic, it also brings people together into a community, listening, responding, confronting, asserting, and disputing, engaged in a perpetual process of change.[11]

Designing the Communication Plan

Given the impact of the changes that will occur as a result of redesign, part of planning for success includes developing a plan to communicate the planned changes. The communication plan sets the objectives, implications, training requirements, and progress reports of the planned changes. In addition, it gives detail about the key message, the message timing, and the frequency of the communication.[12] Before designing the communication plan, it is important to assess and analyze how the organization has received messages or changes in the past. This analysis helps to determine the best approach for successful communications.

The first step is to develop guiding principles for communication in your organization. Decisions are made about what to communicate, whom to communicate to, and when to communicate. Some organizational guiding principles are as follows:

- Communication is essential to the success of the redesign project.
- Communication is the responsibility of the entire organization.
- Communication will occur in a timely manner and will be clear, consistent, and concise.
- Communication approaches will be tailored to respond to the different needs of the staff and the message.
- Communication approaches will include opportunities for two-way communication.

These guiding principles demonstrate a commitment on the part of the organization to develop a plan that will keep everyone informed of all changes. A communication plan commits the organization early in the project to ensuring that everyone is kept current. More important, these guiding principles set the pace for what everyone in the organization can expect in the potential turbulence of redesign.

Once the guiding principles are in place, decisions are made about what is to be communicated. Many organizations will appoint a communication czar or a communication committee. This person or group of persons assumes responsibility for development of the communication plan prior to the start of the redesign effort. This czar or committee must work closely with the leadership (administrative) team to ensure support for the plan. Preferably, the czar or chair of the communication committee should be a member of the administrative team, because the link between the two groups is critical to the success of any and all types of communication.

Implementing the Communication Plan

Before the project actually begins, individual meetings should be held with key stakeholders and critical functional leaders in the organization. Key constituencies such as physicians and potentially the medicine, pharmacy, and nursing deans in academic medical centers should also be considered for specific preproject communication. A retreat should be scheduled with the administrative and management team to announce the program officially. In addition, a letter may be sent to everyone in the organization from the CEO/president to introduce them to the redesign project. The letter should include specific factors that have influenced the organization to help everyone understand. Exhibit 2–2 is an example of a letter that may be sent to everyone in the organization.

The next step is to schedule organizationwide meetings or a redesign "kickoff" meeting, led by the CEO/president, to introduce the concept of redesign formally. The case for action is presented during this meeting. A simple one-page handout or fact sheet is also important to have available so that everyone can further understand what redesign is and why the organization is redesigning processes.

Once the redesign kickoff is communicated and some information has been disseminated about the organization's case for action, smaller group or department meetings should be scheduled to discuss redesign in two parts: "What is it?" and "How will it be done?"

- Part 1:
  1. What the organization is trying to do
  2. Why the organization is doing this
  3. How important our mission is to our patients and our community
  4. How fortunate the organization is to have this opportunity to redesign while not in crisis

- Part 2:
  1. What the organization is going to do
  2. What is going to happen during the assessment phase of the project
  3. What is expected to happen over the next 18 to 24 months of the project
  4. What is needed from the employees/staff

Exhibit 2–3 shows a script for both part 1 and part 2 of the meetings. It is recommended that the meetings are scripted to ensure that the same information is disseminated to everyone. Slides provide a visual presentation of each of the key points. Exhibit 2–4 is an example of a handout that can be provided to meeting attendees.

After the first round of communications, the planned timeline for the phases of the redesign project and the proposed communication for each phase need to be communicated to all. This includes the information on the organizations compared (these are the hospitals that have been selected for benchmarking on the basis of similarities of size, acuity, type of organization, geographic location, services offered, etc.), the core processes that have been selected (these are described early in

---

Exhibit 2–2 A Staff Letter Announcing Redesign

Dear Staff Member:

A rapidly changing health care environment is challenging health care providers across the country to reexamine the way they deliver health care. Our organization is no exception. In addition to changes in our local market, changes being proposed by Congress may contribute to significant organizational losses over the next few years. However, we must turn this threat into an opportunity, an opportunity for our organization to be a leader in our community to set the standard for quality care, customer satisfaction, and efficiency. We believe that we can be successful in our efforts, but we will need your help.

Our organization is embarking on an exciting Redesign Project. What does this mean? It means we will be starting over! We will be looking at new ways of delivering care, new ways of doing our jobs, and new ways of meeting our customers' needs. Each of you is an expert, and we will need you to be involved, be supportive, and, more important, be prepared for change.

The project will start soon. There will be more information about redesign coming over the next few weeks. Look for it, and ask questions and give us your ideas. Your challenge is to dare to be different and be caring. Together, we can all make a difference.

Sincerely,

CEO/President

Exhibit 2–3 A Script for Staff Meetings on Redesign

Part 1 (10 Minutes)

What are we trying to do?

Transform the organization into the best hospital in the eyes of our community and customers.

- Be the leader for health, wellness, and caring.
- Improve quality, improve customer satisfaction, and increase profitability.
- Have the organization identified as the best employer in the city in the eyes of our staff.
- Lay the groundwork for survival given the current economies in health care.
- Provide patient care in a seamless and efficient manner.
- Eliminate unnecessary tasks and redesign jobs.
- Remove the work that has no value to the customer.
- Create breakthroughs in performance.

Why are we doing this?

- Changing health care industry.
- Economics!
- Current market in the immediate area.
- Because we have to!
- Need to keep up with local competition.
- We can't afford to work the old way anymore.
- Way things are done worked at one time, not anymore!
- We have a firm belief that we want, need, and must change to achieve our mission, vision, and values.
- Without this commitment, the organization will fail to exist.

How important is our mission to our patients, our community, and our staff?

- Tells our patients and the community what our unique purpose is that sets us apart from others.
- Mission needs to be aligned with what our customers want.
- It is the only reason we exist.
- Helps our employees understand clearly what we are here to do.

How lucky we are to have this opportunity:

- The redesign process will allow us to be the leader in our community to set the standard for quality care, customer satisfaction, and efficiency.
- We (the staff) have the opportunity to direct our future, to be the drivers of change.
- Because we currently have a positive bottom line, we can afford to plan our strategy. If it were negative, our strategy would be just cuts and more cuts.
- The opportunity gives us promise in an otherwise gloomy business environment.

continues

Exhibit 2–3 continued

- We will eliminate the daily frustrations all of us have experienced in trying to get our jobs done.
- Remember, with change comes opportunity.

Part 2 (10 Minutes)

Here's what we're going to do:

- Start over!
- Identify inefficiencies and service issues.
- Streamline our efforts, our processes, our systems.
- Review everything; there will be no sacred cows.
- Break the rules, question everything.
- Think "out of the box," be radical.
- Break down the barriers between departments.

Here is what is going to happen over the next 2 months during the assessment phase:

- Assess the market and the organization's infrastructure.
- Develop a work plan and communication plan.
- Define core processes and allocate department costs and resources to core processes.
- Assess current information systems and technologies in relation to identified core processes.
- Benchmark processes and departments against local and national competitors.
- Select a couple of processes to focus on in the first phase.

Here is what we expect to happen over the next 18 months:

- Redesign core processes identified in the first two months.
- Identify infrastructure changes.
- Monitor implementation and evaluate changes.
- Communicate.
- Develop new human resources policies as needed.

Here is what we need from you:

- The patient needs to be the focus of everything we do.
- We need you to be ready for change.
- We need you to be open-minded.
- We need you to commit yourself to the organization and redesign.
- Provide excellent customer service.
- Give us ideas for improvement.
- Identify inefficiencies in your area and outside your area.
- Don't be afraid to question the purpose of your tasks. Ask yourself, "Why am I doing this?" If it doesn't make sense (add value to the customer), speak up!
- Never say, "It's not my job." If something needs to be done, and you can't do it, find someone who can.
- Join us in a cooperative team effort; break down department barriers and walls.

Exhibit 2–4 A Staff Meeting Handout on Redesign

REDESIGN

WHAT IS IT? WHAT DOES IT MEAN?

A formal (book) definition of reengineering is: the fundamental re-thinking and radical redesign of an entire business (that includes business processes, job definitions, organizational structures, management and measurement systems, values, and beliefs) to achieve dramatic improvements in critical measures of performance, such as cost, quality, service, and speed.

In simple terms, redesign just means **starting over!**

WHAT ARE THE GOALS OF REDESIGN?

1. improvement in customer satisfaction
2. improvement in quality
3. improvement in profitability
4. a methodology to continue redesign after the consultants are gone
5. a continuous change environment

WHY ARE WE DOING THIS?

AT A NATIONAL LEVEL:

- Health care costs continue to increase, yet overall reimbursement is decreasing as more patients shift into HMOs.
- If we consider the inflation factor of 5 percent and the decrease in reimbursement, and if we stay on our current path, we will lose money and eventually close our doors. It is predicted that as many as one third of the nation's hospitals could close, over time, under the managed-care system.
- Proposed Medicare cuts could cost the organization millions of dollars.
- HMOs are reviewing patient outcomes of selected DRGs, by health care institution, along with cost, in order to determine affiliation.
- Case management of high-risk patient populations is becoming the norm to facilitate clinical outcomes, utilization of resources, continuous improvement opportunities, and program development.

AT A LOCAL LEVEL:

- The area has the highest penetration of HMOs for comparable cities of its size in the country.
- 21 percent of the organization's patients are already enrolled in HMOs, and this number has doubled over the last three years.
- The organization is already 20 to 25 percent more costly than our local competition (taking into account our teaching mission) and 31 percent higher than other community hospitals (adjusted for our level of acuity).
- The longer we delay, the more our services will cost in relation to our competition. In addition, the competitor is already planning to reduce by another $20,000,000.

continues

Exhibit 2–4 continued

- Our competitor announced that it has merged with another entity to form the largest statewide network of hospitals. There are three major advantages for them: economies of scale, streamlining operations, and increasing their competitive presence.

WHAT HAVE BEEN OUR CURRENT EFFORTS?

- We have "tried" to contain costs and have ended up with across-the-board budget cuts over the past five years due to $10 million bottom-line problems. In other words, blanket cuts are not the answer.
- Continuous improvement alone cannot solve the problems when we may see only a 5 to 10 percent increase in efficiency.
- "Slash and burn" or "downsizing" will end up costing us in the end because we will still have the same workload with less staff. This will cause staff burnout and turnover. We need to eliminate work that does *NOT* add value to the customer.

WHO IS GOING TO DO THIS?

- Redesign Steering Committee
- Redesign Core Team
- Core Process Teams
- Service Teams
- Consultants

WILL THIS AFFECT ME? WHAT CAN I DO?

- Redesign *will* affect everyone.
- Remember that the patient *must* be the focus of everything we do.
- Start thinking about the patient flow. What happens to the patient when he/she enters the system, and how does each of your services come in contact with the patient.
- We need to focus on processes, which are groups of tasks that together create value for our customer. To do this, we need to forget about departments and functions.
- Prepare for dramatic changes that will be improvements, and prepare to continue to change in the future.
- We are not guaranteed a lifetime of employment. We must continually earn our keep in a value-added fashion.
- Work will be eliminated and streamlined; this may result in work redesign and/or possibly layoffs.
- We will do away with much of the tracking, reconciliation, duplication of effort, and micromanaging due to increased accountability.
- The organization needs to empower you, the staff. You will need to be accountable and responsible to your teams.
- Empower to be positive, to create positive change, not to impede!

continues

Exhibit 2–4 continued

HOW WILL WE DO THIS?

A plan will be developed to do the following:

1. Plan, assess, set goals
2. Examine processes
3. Identify opportunities
4. Redesign the clinical and operational processes
5. Implement

WHAT IS THE TIMELINE?

2 to 3 months: laying the foundation

- confirmation of mission, vision, and values
- assessment of key operating processes
- human resources policies
- process team organization

2 to 3 months: redesign of priority operational and support processes

- medication administration
- documentation
- patient flow
- admitting
- discharges

2 to 3 months: reconfiguring operations

- redesign of hospital departments to meet overall goals
- redesign of support systems

6 months: implement

- implementation of organizational structure
- process implementation

Chapter 3), and the department allocations that are the potential opportunities for savings; the strategic and organizational goals; other benchmarking information; the financial target setting for each core process; the development of human resources policies, if needed; and the fast-track redesign.

Once the communication plan has been developed and shared with everyone, the selection of members for the various process teams begins. In the meantime, it is important to continue to keep everyone updated on the progress of the project, the proposed next steps, and any decisions. This next level of communication can be maintained through a variety of methods, including staff meetings; newsletter articles; one-page flyers; messages on paychecks, bulletin boards, TV monitors, and "table tents" in the cafeteria and/or lounges; open forums with management; displays in public areas; electronic mail; voice mail; and an information phone line to answer questions and concerns. Exhibit 2–5 is an example of an overall matrix communication plan that identifies the types of messages to be delivered and the audience. Both oral and written communication are included in the plan. The communication plan must make provisions to personalize communication as much as possible to reduce misunderstandings, promote trust, and communicate the right message in the right way.[13]

Strategies for Successful Communication

Communication is critical when an organization is undergoing major fundamental changes. The changes will often lead to fear, anxiety, disbelief, fear of layoffs, and an active rumor mill that can all impede communications.[14] The success of a redesign project is highly dependent on how well everyone accepts and supports, or "buys into," the concept of changing.

All of the change that occurs in an organization can be managed effectively through good communication. All leaders and team members need to be effective

Exhibit 2–5 A Communications Plan

	Communications Plan							
	ORAL				**WRITTEN**			
Audience	Rap Session	Discussion Sessions	Department Meetings	Voice Mail	Monthly Newsletter	Regular Weekly Newsletter	"Bright Idea" Posters	Idea Notebook in Divisions
Employees	4	8	20		10: Sent in paycheck	All public areas	All public areas	Updated after every steering committee
Managers and Supervisors	4	8	20	Updated regularly	10: Sent in paycheck	All public areas	All public areas	meeting
Physicians			18			Mailed to 800 physicians	All public areas	Updated after every steering committee meeting
12-Person Communications Committee		• Nurses • Health and Education Marketing • Marketing				• Public Relations • Other Staff		

Courtesy of APM, Inc., San Francisco, California.

communicators to spare the organization turmoil and anxiety through the transition. The following 10 pointers facilitate successful communications:

1. *Segment your audience.* This is important to do because the impact of redesign will be different for each group.
2. *Use multiple channels of communication.* These include but are not limited to talks, articles, videos, and phone messages.
3. *Use multiple voices.* CEO/president, directors, managers, peers, etc.
4. *Communicate clearly.* Remember the four Ps—purpose (why redesign), process (how we will do it), progress (how it's going), and problems (admit failures, stress lessons learned, and move on).
5. *Communicate, communicate, communicate.* Repetition is important; it matters and it works.
6. *Honesty is the only policy.* Truth is better than fear. Some information is better than none. If a mistake is made, admit it; if you don't know, acknowledge it; and if something is painful, face it.
7. *Use emotions, not just logic.* Communicate passion, be enthusiastic, and, more important, be sincere.
8. *Communicate to heal.* Understand and share people's fears. Redesign affects real people with real lives, and it causes pain.
9. *Communicate tangibly.* Find experiential ways to convey information; use gimmicks whenever possible.
10. *Listen, listen, listen.* Communication is a two-way street. It is important to have feedback and to offer people an opportunity to voice concerns.[15]

Poor or inadequate communication can cause damage to an organization that will be difficult to repair. No level of effort will prevent all problems from occurring, but many can be prevented through a well-designed communication plan, especially when the organization is undergoing major change.

CONCLUSION

The current organizational structure within a hospital is already overtaxed and should not be used to design and implement a redesign project. A separate structure provides the levels of input necessary for success. This chapter describes the redesign structure necessary to the development of process redesign teams. The communication plan, a critical component, has also been detailed.

NOTES

1. M. Hammer and J. Champy, *Reengineering the Corporation: A Manifesto for Business Revolution* (New York: Harper Business, 1993).

2. J. Champy, *Reengineering Management: The Mandate for New Leadership* (New York: Harper Business, 1993), 39.

3. Ibid., 7.

4. Hammer and Champy, *Reengineering the Corporation.*

5. Ibid., 109.

6. Ibid.

7. Joint Commission on Accreditation of Healthcare Organizations, *Framework for Improving Performance: A Guide for Nurses* (Oakbrook Terrace, IL: 1994).

8. P. Scholtes et al., *The Team Handbook* (Madison, WI: Joiner Associates, 1994).

9. M. Hammer and S. Stanton, *The Reengineering Revolution* (New York: Harper Business, 1995), 136.

10. D. Costello-Nickitas, *Quick Reference to Nursing Leadership* (New York: Delmar Publishers, 1997), 81.

11. Champy, *Reengineering Management,* 128.

12. Costello-Nickitas, *Quick Reference,* 81.

13. Ibid., 81.

14. Hammer and Stanton, *The Reengineering Revolution,* 137.

15. Ibid., 142.

CHAPTER 3

A Framework for
Core Process Redesign

Leanne Braden Hunstock and Carolyn L. Murdaugh

Chapter Objectives

1. To describe elements of the change process that facilitate successful redesign.
2. To discuss the flow framework as a model for core process redesign.
3. To present a case study that applies the flow framework in a redesign project.

Despite recent innovations in health care delivery, such as patient-focused care and operational restructuring, health care organizations have not yet achieved success in the delicate balance of cost, service, and quality outcomes. The goal of patient-focused care is to shift the structure of health care operations from a fragmented, overly specialized, bureaucratic delay–prone model to a new paradigm that focuses on the patient's perspective and fundamental needs.[1] Such a shift requires major leadership commitment and fundamental changes in health care organizations.

Restructuring the operations that directly support patient care has had an enormous influence on the inpatient setting. Operational restructuring is well accepted as a strategy to reduce costs and improve service. However, the transition to cross-trained multiskilled workers, a multidisciplinary team of professionals, and cross-functional departments with a nursing skill mix change is indeed radical and a challenge to implement. This chapter describes the evolution of performance improvement through redesign. First, elements of the change process that are necessary for successful redesign are overviewed. Following a historical overview of redesign, a model for core process redesign that incorporates the flow framework is provided that will assist a design team to identify and understand core processes and their various dimensions. The chapter concludes with a case study that describes how to apply the framework to an inpatient redesign project as a method to organize and structure the multidimensional activities into flow dimensions.

ELEMENTS OF SUCCESSFUL CHANGE

Health care reform has mandated radical changes in how patient care has traditionally been delivered. However, change has not always been successful in redesign efforts because it threatens the stability of the status quo. Change can be positive because new opportunities for providing quality, cost-effective care are created. Because change is inevitable and necessary for survival in today's health care environment, elements that promote successful change have been identified.

First, the change process involves a series of steps or phases that should not be skipped or ignored. Eliminating or ignoring steps in planning and implementing change shortens the initial process, while contributing to the possible failure of the change because valuable aspects are missed. A useful model that builds on Lewin's three-stage model of unfreezing, moving, and refreezing focuses on steps in planned change.[2] First, the organization must establish a need for change. Successful change efforts occur when a sense of urgency or crisis is conveyed.[3] Specifically, the organization must be convinced that the change is urgently needed on the basis of market demands, revenues, or growth. Without a sense of an urgent need for change, it is difficult to move people out of their comfort zones into uncharted waters. Second, a change relationship must be established between the organization and a change agent, either a consultant or consultant group or a powerful coalition of leaders within the organization who will lead the change. Change efforts often fail because of lack of strong leadership at the top and a change agent to guide and support the redesign efforts. A strong leadership coalition linked with persons who have expertise in the process is a necessary element in successful change. This leadership-change team will develop the vision that clarifies the direction in which the organization needs to move and formulates the strategies to achieve the vision. Third, appropriate and accurate data must be collected to assist in diagnosing the changes needed. Data provide the evidence needed to make a case for the change as well as information on which to base redesign efforts. An organization's data can also be compared to that of successful organizations or national databases to help make a case for the needed changes. Reliable and valid data change enable agents to make decisions on facts rather than anecdotal information.

Fourth, systematic planning is necessary prior to implementing any change. Planning for implementation includes communicating the vision or the proposed direction of the organization and engaging others to participate in the change efforts. All channels of communication should be used to proclaim the vision, including group meetings, individual meetings, and newsletters. Communication must be ongoing throughout the change process. All information about the proposed change must be shared with everyone who will be affected.[4] Every department must play a role in the planning process by articulating its role in the change. Departmental input helps eliminate some of the obstacles to change, as once employees understand the vision and the need for change and have contributed input into the change process, they believe that their ideas and concerns are valued. Employee input generates empowerment or feelings of control over the change process.[5] As a result, there is less likelihood that the efforts will be undermined. Employees within all departments should be encouraged to be creative in the planning process and to think about nontraditional approaches for changing the organization. Innovative ideas and approaches should be rewarded. Detailed attention to the planning process is essential to ensure that the necessary structure and processes are in place prior to implementing the change.

Next, the planned change should be implemented by qualified persons who have been prepared to implement the change within the organization. The more persons who are prepared to implement the change, the more likely it is that the implementation will be successful. Persons who are qualified to execute the change assist in removing obstacles to implementation, because they understand the organizational culture and have been prepared as change agents for the organization. Ongoing reward systems need to have been established to serve as incentives as well as to compensate employees for their roles in the change process. The change should be implemented in short-term phases with easily observable outcomes so that employees will remain committed over the long term.

Last, the success of the change must be evaluated, and new planned change efforts should be implemented if necessary, based on the results of the evaluation. Evaluation is required to assess if the desired outcomes have been met. Time frames for evaluation of the change as well as significant outcomes of the change in terms of cost, service, and quality should be established during the planning stage and adhered to if at all possible. Evaluation is often forgotten in the health care setting, because everyone is too busy implementing the change. However, data obtained in the evaluation process are critical to understand the consequence of the change efforts within the organization. The case study at the end of this chapter provides examples of application of successful elements of the change process

HISTORICAL PERSPECTIVE

In the early 1980s, performance improvement efforts focused on incremental changes and centered on the principles of total quality management and the reintroduction of assistive personnel to the nursing and patient care areas. The mid-1980s brought performance improvement into departmental operations with emphasis on efficiencies to reduce costs through increased productivity and a decrease in patient length of stay. In the early 1990s, performance improvement efforts emphasized systems restructuring and gains in efficiency through stream-lining processes. Current redesign examines the fundamental drivers of the prob-lematic, inefficient, expensive, and ineffective systems as well as outcomes. Man-aging demand by controlling access to high-cost services and reducing variance in provision of services is a significant lever to meet cost, service, and quality out-comes in today's competitive managed-care markets.

Many organizations have implemented performance improvement initiatives in an attempt to meet constantly changing market demands and costs of managed care while trying to meet higher expectations for service and quality. Core process redesign in health care is a method to examine the total operations and provide a structure for the organization and the medical staff to align their efforts to meet collective goals. Exhibit 3–1 describes the evolution of performance improvement through redesign in health care organizations over the last decade.

Hammer and Champy define *reengineering* as the fundamental rethinking and radical redesign of an organization and its operating systems to achieve dramatic improvements in critical contemporary measures of cost, quality, service, and speed.[6] Reengineering dramatically improves operating effectiveness by focusing on a set of customer-oriented business processes. *Core process redesign* is the redesign of es-sential and fundamental processes that can be described by a specific beginning point or initial activity and an end point or final activity. The *core process* encompasses activities, tasks, and work steps that, when performed in a particular manner, produce a new mechanism to accomplish the activity. The core processes within a business operation intertwine to produce the primary product or service of the organization. In health care, for example, an essential hospital function is admitting a patient. The activity of admitting the patient comprises numerous subprocesses—activities or tasks such as scheduling, registering the patient, and assigning the patient to a bed. Through core process redesign, the admitting process may be radically changed by eliminating, streamlining, reorganizing, reassigning, or omitting subprocesses.

A MODEL FOR CORE PROCESS REDESIGN

Identification of core processes in the health care organization requires an ex-amination of each task or activity in the context of its relationship to the primary recipient or beneficiary, which in most cases is the patient. Examination of opera-tions in terms of core processes requires a cross-departmental and cross-functional view. Each process definition takes into account the many contributors and the interface of various functional areas across the organization. The core processes should be mutually exclusive and collectively exhaustive to eliminate ambiguity and omission. Identifying, quantifying, and organizing the core processes for the initial phase of the redesign process occurs in three steps. The fourth step is the design process itself.

Exhibit 3–1 Evolution of Performance Improvement and Redesign in Health Care Organizations

WORK SHIFTING	OPERATIONAL RESTRUCTURING	WORK TRANSFORMATION	CORE PROCESS REDESIGN
Work activity or tasks are shifted to helpers to complete.	Work is redesigned to consolidate roles and move tasks into a new and different configuration.	Work is realigned around care complexity and optimal patient flow.	Work is fundamentally redesigned according to current and targeted clinical resource utilization.
• Tasks are delegated to a nurse extender. • Nurse supervises extender. • Some efficiency is gained. • Work is functional. • Work and organization are hierarchical.	• Work is supervised and delivered as close as possible to the patient. • Multidisciplinary team plans and delivers outcome-based care. • Service is enhanced. • Cross-training produces efficiencies.	• Patients are aggregated according to clinical resources consumed. • Work that does not add value is eliminated. • Processes are simplified to support restructured care delivery system: i.e., admission, discharge, transfer, supply, distribution, and documentation. • Patient's experience across the continuum is streamlined.	• Best-practice clinical resource utilization patterns drive demand for work. • Core processes are redesigned according to demand characteristics. • Job roles are built based on core process and clinical care imperatives. • Processes that manage demand for services are developed.

Courtesy of APM, Inc., San Francisco, California.

- *Step 1:* Define core processes and subprocesses. Each core process consists of subprocesses or activities that when combined in a linear or integrated fashion create the larger core process (Exhibit 3–2).
- *Step 2:* Determine allocation of resources dedicated to each core process from every department. To benchmark best practice by core process, resources must be reallocated and redistributed proportionately to all of the applicable core processes. An example of how resources are reallocated to core processes by department is given in Table 3–1.

Exhibit 3–2 Step 1: Identify Core Processes and Subprocesses

Core Process	Subprocesses
Treat the Patient on an Emergent Basis	• planning staff resources • prioritizing procedures • identifying patient room • providing emergency care • interfacing with the clinics • triaging patient • registering the emergency room patient • providing emergency air care • coordinating and providing patient transport • providing urgent care • maintaining regulatory compliance
Admit the Patient on a Nonemergent Basis	• scheduling • registering patients • assigning beds • providing nonemergency air care • maintaining regulatory compliance • performing preadmit assessment • coordinating with physicians • assessing the patient financially • interfacing with the clinics

Perform and Schedule Patient Ancillary and Diagnostic Procedures (Inpatient and Outpatient)	• taking orders off charts
	• scheduling and performing:
	  –laboratory tests
	  –radiology procedures and tests
	  –other procedures and tests
	• collecting and processing specimens
	• coordinating with physicians
	• providing results to patient and care providers
	• procuring and dispensing medication
	• planning staff resources in support and ancillary departments
	• interfacing with the clinics
	• maintaining regulatory compliance

Provide Resources for Patient Surgical Procedures (Inpatient and Outpatient)	• scheduling and performing surgery and recovery • coordinating with physicians • interfacing with the clinics • maintaining regulatory compliance

continues

Exhibit 3–2 continued

Core Process	Subprocesses
Provide and Manage Clinical Treatment to Patient	• managing clinical resources • managing patient cases • developing and applying clinical pathways/algorithms

Serve the Patient in Room	• providing patient care unit activities:
	  –assessing the patient
	  –planning and evaluating care
	  –documenting clinical data
	  –administering medications
	  –assisting with activities of daily living
	  –educating patient and family
	  –delivering nutritional services
	  –communicating with physician
	  –performing other unit-based procedures
	• coordinating care and facilitating care plan
	• coordinating transportation
	• preparing and cleaning room
	• interfacing with the clinics
	• delivering ancillary clinical services
	• aggregating patients
	• planning and scheduling staff
	• maintaining regulatory compliance

Discharge the Patient	• obtaining physician discharge order • planning and executing patient discharge • interfacing with the clinics • preparing the patient for discharge • teaching patient to continue care after discharge • communicating to continuum of care providers • maintaining regulatory compliance
Bill the Patient	• coding/billing (patient and/or payer) • collecting payment • maintaining medical and financial records • obtaining physician documentation • maintaining regulatory compliance

continues

Exhibit 3–2 continued

Core Process	*Subprocesses*
Provide Appropriate Environment for the Patient, Visitor, and Staff	• directing patients through plant • maintaining physical plant and equipment • communicating (e-mail, voice mail, mail, etc.) • retailing (cafeteria, gift shop, etc.) • performing technology management • maintaining patient rights and relations • providing a caring environment • maintaining employee wellness • educating employees • conducting plant management • ensuring patient, visitor, and staff safety • maintaining regulatory compliance
Ensure Patient Wellness	• performing preventative care • administering home health • providing wellness education and services to patients and community • maintaining regulatory compliance
Manage Patient Care Staff and Resources	• hiring and training staff • maintaining regulatory compliance • training residents, nursing students, other health care professionals
Provide Patient- and Non–Patient-Related Supplies, Materials, and Equipment	• acquiring patient supplies/materials • maintaining regulatory compliance • ensuring that supplies/materials are readily available at the point of service(s)
Plan for and Monitor Patient Activity	• tracking and summarizing data from service to patients (finance, information services) • maintaining regulatory compliance • planning for patient needs (capital investment) • attracting patients (contracting, enrolling, marketing)

Courtesy of APM, Inc., San Francisco, California.

Table 3-1 Core Process Resources Allocation

1 Define Processes	2 Determine Resources by Department									
	Inpatient Nursing	Nursing Admin.	ER	OR	Laboratory	Radiology	Physical Medicine	Admitting	Admin. Service	Respiratory
Admit and treat the patient on an emergent basis	X		X						X	X
Admit the patient on a nonemergent basis	X								X	X
Schedule procedure for patient								X	X	
Perform patient ancillary/diagnostic procedure	X		X	X	X	X		X		X
Provide resources for patient surgical procedure	X			X	X	X	X			X
Provide clinical treatment to patient	X			X	X	X	X			
Serve the patient in room	X	X		X	X	X	X		X	X
Discharge the patient	X	X			X	X			X	X
Bill the patient								X	X	
Provide appropriate patient, visitor, and staff environment	X	X	X							
Ensure patient wellness	X	X								X
Hire and schedule patient care staff and resources		X							X	X
Provide patient- and non–patient-related supplies and materials	X				X	X				
Total expense by core process									X	X

3 Establish Cost Targets

Courtesy of APM, Inc., San Francisco, California.

- *Step 3:* Sum the departmental allocations by core process. Compare the totals to the expense benchmark allocations if the goal is to identify cost reduction targets by core process.
- *Step 4:* Establish design teams, and assign targets for quality, service, and cost. The mission of the design teams is to redesign core processes to meet quality, service, and cost goals. The number of teams needed is determined by the following factors:
  1. Strategic alignment of mission, vision, values, and economic imperatives of the organization
  2. Level of available expertise in core process redesign to plan and lead the effort and implement complex change
  3. Size of cost reduction target in terms of percentage compared to best practice and benchmarks
  4. Time frame in which results are expected
  5. Availability of high-performance individuals to participate in the design process
  6. Amount of time participants can spare to participate in the design process
  7. Availability of analytical resources
  8. Rate at which the organization can embrace and incorporate change
  9. Relationship of the organization with the attending medical staff
  10. Degree to which current operational systems and processes are convoluted and fragmented

Alternatively, the 13 core processes defined in Exhibit 3–2 may be consolidated and organized in fewer core processes with different elements and a broader scope. For example, core processes related to the multiple direct care services may be combined into one core process, inpatient clinical services (Table 3–2). The combined groups facilitate the design process by decreasing the number of teams that may be needed.

THE FLOW FRAMEWORK

The redesign and rethinking of existing systems and processes requires a conceptual framework that examines the fundamental levels of a core process and organizes the design process. The flow framework (Figure 3–1) enables one to examine the issues related to a core process within three dimensions of flow. The three dimensions of flow that all work processes share are (1) patient or customer flow, (2) process flow, and (3) personnel flow. Often, only one or two dimensions of flow are considered in process redesign, limiting both insight and the impact of redesign work to a single dimension. The three-dimensional flow perspective enables the design team to isolate a particular subprocess of the core process and to

Table 3–2 Core Process Groupings

Core Process	Concept	Begin Point	End Point	Outcome
Inpatient clinical service	Integrates and facilitates the treatment of the patient; comprises diagnostic and therapeutic services that generate a plan of care for patients in an effort to improve the patient's condition	Initial MD order to admit to inpatient hospitalization	Patient ready for discharge; inpatient episode complete	An effective hospital stay; a patient who is ready for discharge
Outpatient and wellness services	Process of providing diagnostic, therapeutic, and preventative care and procedures not requiring overnight hospitalization	Request for services, including physician orders, payer or individual request	Reporting results to requester	Healthy community; utilization of inpatient intensive services is reduced
Patient/information flow	The movement of patient and related information through the hospital environment; emphasis is on maximum patient convenience and comfort, high levels of accuracy, and access to patient-specific data	Initial information received regarding the payment	Settled account	Settled account; coherent and timely medical record
Physical resource management	Process of delivering products and nonclinical services, ensuring that the right physical resources are in the right place at the right time for the right price	Identified need for goods or services	Delivery of needed goods or services	Suitable environment in which to operate; accessible timely supplies and coordinated services

continues

Table 3–2 continued

Core Process	Concept	Begin Point	End Point	Outcome
Human resource management	Process of developing and assisting in the realization of the hospital's mission and the attainment of its business vision by ensuring that the right people with the right skills are in the right place at the right time for the right price	Identification of the employee attributes that will support the organization's culture, mission, vision, values, and strategic plan	Career pathing	Effective, affordable work force
Strategic leadership	Understanding strategic priorities and aligning available resources with them, then measuring performance of the strategies and resource alignments	Understanding corporate direction	Measuring performance	Resources allocated for optimal performance against strategic goals

Courtesy of APM, Inc., San Francisco, California.

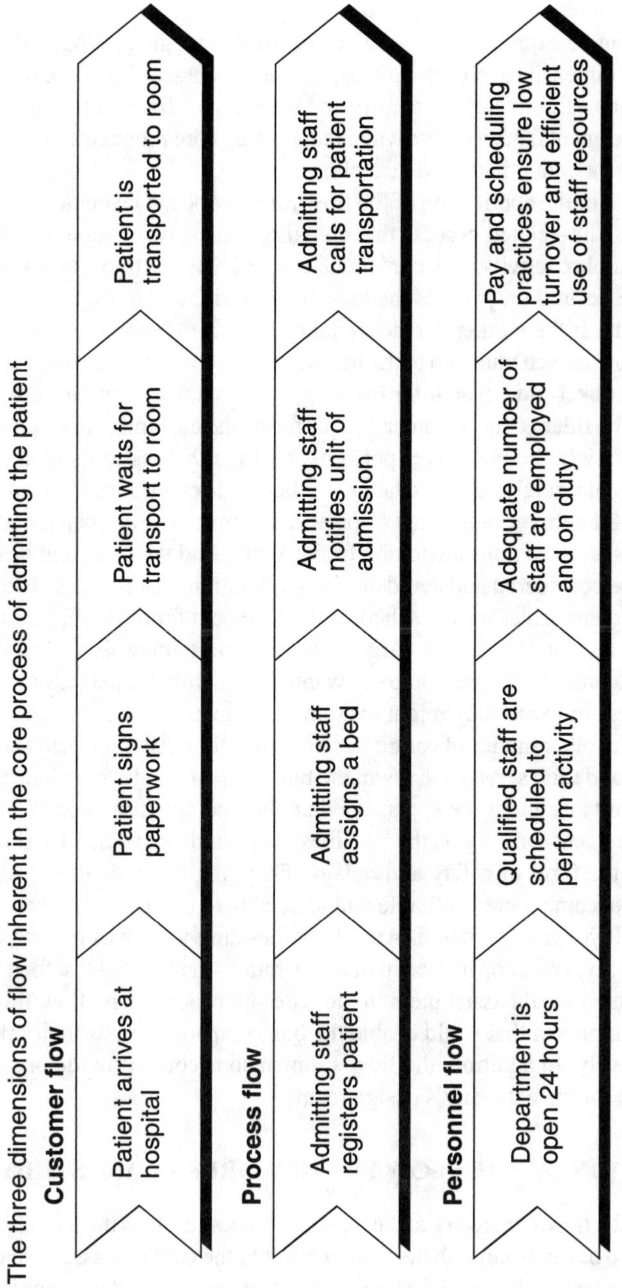

The three dimensions of flow inherent in the core process of admitting the patient

Customer flow

Patient arrives at hospital → Patient signs paperwork → Patient waits for transport to room → Patient is transported to room

Process flow

Admitting staff registers patient → Admitting staff assigns a bed → Admitting staff notifies unit of admission → Admitting staff calls for patient transportation

Personnel flow

Department is open 24 hours → Qualified staff are scheduled to perform activity → Adequate number of staff are employed and on duty → Pay and scheduling practices ensure low turnover and efficient use of staff resources

Figure 3–1 Flow Framework. Courtesy of APM, Inc., San Francisco, California.

consider the activity from a focused, detailed point of view. At the same time, the subprocess can be examined from the perspective of its integration with and impact on other dimensions, core processes, and subprocesses. The three dimensions of flow provide a framework to identify and solve issues from an interdisciplinary and interdepartmental perspective when redesigning core processes that span multiple departments, functions, and disciplines.

An example of the application of the flow framework can be demonstrated with a non–health care–related process that contains at least two people engaged in a relatively complex activity. The core process, in this case, is transporting someone to work. The desired outcome is the arrival at the right address, on time, safely, and affordably. If the worker decides to take a bus from home to work, he or she will need know the schedule, go to the bus stop at the correct time, wait for the bus, board, buy a ticket, ride, watch for the stop, and disembark the bus at the designated stop. The rider is the customer and performs the customer flow. The process flow is the activity the bus driver performs to drive the bus to its planned stops through the route, safely and on schedule. Inherent circumstances that are outside the control of the driver may delay or prevent the process from being completed. These factors, such as nonfunctioning traffic lights, bad weather, and heavy traffic, need to be considered and avoided when redesigning the process. The personnel flow is the bus driver's work schedule, replacement for days off, pay, training, competency, and job satisfaction. Any of these variables may also affect the quality of the outcome. If the bus company wanted to capture 60 percent of the commuter business in town, they might examine how their service, cost, and quality compared with other modes of commuter transportation. After an analysis of other similar transportation services in town, the bus company might conclude that they were less profitable and more expensive than their competition, because they operated at 60 percent capacity on the bus lines, and that they had quality and service problems in the form of safety and delays. They might decide to redesign their operation to become more profitable and to be able to contract with large companies for employee transportation. After hypothesizing what was driving the high cost, low quality, and poor service in their operation, they would test their hypotheses. The results would assist them in the redesign process. The flow framework provides an approach that could enable the bus company to view their operations comprehensively. In addition, the flow's dimensions could provide organization and structure for the company's design teams.

APPLICATION OF THE FLOW FRAMEWORK: A CASE STUDY

Applying the flow framework to the inpatient process enables the interdisciplinary design team to navigate through the complexities of the core processes and organize redesign efforts into subteams of a larger process design team. An example that occurred at a 250-bed academic medical center demonstrates application of the framework. The inpatient process team was one of 12 core process design teams launched in a comprehensive redesign effort. The inpatient team's charge was to redesign the core process of serving the patient in the room. Membership of the inpatient design team consisted of members from all departments and services, including the academic medical services that supported the inpatient services. The team was led by the vice president for patient care services, a nurse, and a faculty physician. Design team methodology was outlined in a high-level work plan (Exhibit 3–3) that served as a general guideline for the design process. The work plan included a time frame, assignments, and desired process team outcomes.

Exhibit 3–3 Inpatient Design Team Work Plan

Week	*Process Design Team Outcomes*
0	• Discuss proposed membership • Set up meeting times for team and leader meeting • Review and provide training needed
1	• Team ground rules • Team charter, purpose, goals, and expectations • Roles and time commitment • Process definition (inputs, outputs, boundaries, intersections, etc.) • Problem statement (current state/future state/gap analysis) • Brainstorm hypotheses/drivers/impediments/issues • Discuss work plan • *Assignment(s):* Team: Stakeholder needs assessment, process improvement ideas; two principles for inpatient care delivery (Core team: Group hypotheses)
2	• Review stakeholder assessments • Review interview/focus group and survey data • Vision of future state of inpatient process • Principles for future state • Hypotheses about high-opportunity areas (key subprocesses) from week 1 • Initial list of analyses to test hypotheses • Discuss subgroup configuration around key focus areas • Discuss subgroup principles • *Assignment(s):* Process flowcharting of key subprocesses, additional hypotheses, process improvement ideas, stakeholder input/feedback
3	• Discuss flowcharts' key blocks, key control points re: problem statement • Finalize subgroups/goals/principles

continues

Exhibit 3–3 continued

	• Brainstorm service objectives
	• Review analysis/data collected to date
	• Review process improvement ideas to date
	• Identify and stage further analyses
	• *Assignment(s):* Data collection, analysis, idea generation, stakeholder input/feedback
4	• Subgroups meet
	• Review principles and goals
	• Review analyses
	• Identify further data needs/analysis
	• Brainstorm solutions and ideas
	• *Assignment(s):* Data collection, analysis, stakeholder input/feedback, idea generation
5–12	• Subgroups meet and process team meets
	• Solution development/evaluation
	• Review analyses
	• Identify further data needs/analysis
	• Solution development in focus areas
	• Redesign process to achieve goals/vision
	• Identify further analyses (if needed)
	• *Assignment(s):* Evaluation/development of specific solutions
	–Describe idea/solution
	–Quantify cost/service impact
	–Identify/quantify service/quality improvement targets
	–Communicate with key stakeholders
	–Develop implementation plans

Courtesy of APM, Inc., San Francisco, California.

Several sources of data were collected and analyzed by the redesign project team and consultant team prior to the initial meeting of the design team. (Such analyses are described in detail in Chapter 1.) Results of analysis of baseline data provided benchmarks for the targets set for the team by the steering committee. (See redesign organizational structure in Chapter 2.) In the first team meeting, the foundation was laid for the work of the group by defining the scope of the core process, which included the concept description, the "begin point" or initial activity in the process and the "end point" or final activity in the process, the desired output, the major activities or subprocesses, and the boundaries and intersections with other core processes. Exhibit 3–4 shows the elements of the scope of the inpatient core process. A team charter was written that described the charge or mission of the team in terms of the purpose, goals, and measurable objectives. The

Exhibit 3–4 Inpatient Process Scope

Concept	The inpatient process is a dynamic process in which patient treatment is planned, facilitated, and implemented.
Begin Point	Initial MD order relative to inpatient hospitalization.
End Point	Patient ready for discharge; inpatient episode complete.
Main Output	An effective hospital stay; a patient who is ready for discharge; an improved patient condition.

Major Activities/ Subprocesses	• Patient care activities
	  –assessing the patient
	  –collecting/charting patient information
	  –administering medications
	  –assisting patient in ADLs
	  –educating patient activities
	  –delivering nutritional services
	  –coordinating transportation
	  –communicating with team members
	• Interfacing with clinics
	• Psychological interventions
	• Planning and scheduling staff
	• Patient placement/aggregation
	• Regulatory preparation/compliance
	• Order processing

Intersections and Boundaries	• Admitting process • Discharge process • Billing process • Managing human resources • Clinic process • Monitoring process • Emergent process • Ancillary process • Surgical process • Wellness process • Materials, supplies, equipment process • Environment process

Courtesy of APM, Inc., San Francisco, California.

charter is shown in Exhibit 3–5. Ground rules for group process, member roles, and team etiquette were also determined at the initial meeting. The work plan was discussed, and brainstorming sessions lasted for one hour. The purpose of brainstorming was to generate possible hypotheses for the drivers of high cost, low

Exhibit 3–5 Inpatient Process Team Charter

Purpose:
- Redesign the process of serving the patient in the room in order to meet service, cost, and quality goals that will enable the organization to meet competitive demands.

Goals and Objectives:
- Provide high-quality care to all patients.
- Improve process and patient flow through the inpatient units in such a manner as to enhance patient and staff satisfaction, thereby enabling care to be rendered in a more efficient and effective manner.
- Reduce variation in processes across departments.
- Lower the cost of providing each patient's care in the inpatient process.
- Achieve a total of $X amount in cost reduction by July 1, 199X.

Major Activities:
- Identify and analyze drivers of high cost, low quality, and poor service.
- Reaggregate patients on the basis of utilization of resources and services.
- Redesign key subprocesses identified as high-opportunity drivers.
- Redesign roles built around reengineered processes.
- Redesign management structure to support new processes.

Courtesy of APM, Inc., San Francisco, California.

---

quality, and poor service in the organization. No holds were barred in this process. The premise is that the redesign triumvirate of cost, quality, and service must be as carefully balanced in the health care environment as in any industry that serves the populace. In health care, however, the balance is more delicate, with potentially more serious repercussions. Quality is the foundation that balances service and cost in a dynamic, interdependent relationship. The relationship of cost, quality, and services is represented in Figure 3–2.

The hypothesized drivers of high cost, low quality, and poor service began to reflect all the issues in the systems and the processes in the organization that were perceived to be problematic for staff, patients, families, and the community. The issues were not new. However, resistance to resolution was ongoing in the traditional approaches of quality improvement teams and restructuring. Approximately 30 hypotheses were generated in the initial session. Framing issues in the context of the drivers of high cost, low quality, and poor service enabled the team to begin to think about and identify hypotheses that could be validated through analysis of the data. The issues were then grouped by the team facilitators into the three dimensions of flow. These flow dimensions became the framework to break down the core process into subprocesses and then differentiate the design team's work by subteam.

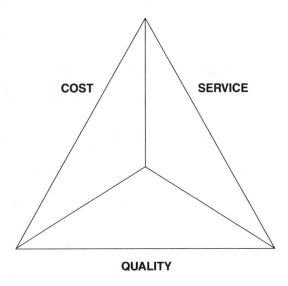

COST   SERVICE

QUALITY

Figure 3–2 Quality, Cost, and Service Triumverate. Courtesy of APM, Inc., San Francisco, California.

The design team members interviewed process stakeholders to validate the team's views of the issues and hypotheses. The stakeholders represented anyone in or associated with the organization who had played a role in the core process. This group included other staff, patients, physicians, visitors, and families. Vision and guiding principles were developed to assist the team in its decision making during the next three design meetings. The vision and guiding principles were developed by a subgroup and are shown in Exhibit 3–6. The subteams were organized, and the activities of each subteam were incorporated into a work plan (Exhibits 3–7 through 3–9).

Outcomes identified for each subteam became levers to meet established targets in terms of cost, quality, and service. *Levers* are subprocesses or activities that require redesign in order to redesign the broader core process effectively. The levers specifically addressed areas that were barriers to efficient and effective functioning within the core process. An overview of the inpatient process structure outlining levers, analysis, and stakeholder data that the subteams considered relative to each subteam's objectives appears in Table 3–3. Levers were linked to each other within a flow dimension and to other levers in other flow dimensions. As a result, the redesign of some levers needed to precede the redesign of others. For example, the patient aggregation model, which was part of the work of the patient flow team, needed to occur before the personnel flow team configured the

Exhibit 3–6 Inpatient Process Design Team's Vision and Principles

---

Vision
- To provide our patients and their families with quality hospital care delivered in a compassionate, cost-effective manner that satisfies the needs and expectations of all our customers.

Guiding Principles
- To do the right thing, for the right reason, by the right person, the right way at the right cost
- To be a leader in patient care, education, research, and appropriate use of advanced technologies
- To improve constantly by evaluating and adopting new ideas and processes
- To value and appreciate all members of the team

Courtesy of APM, Inc., San Francisco, California.

---

health care teams to deliver direct patient care and developed staffing guidelines. However, the personnel flow team could meanwhile work on other aspects of the process, such as scheduling and pay practices. The impact of the care model in terms of staffing guidelines was dependent on the amount of process improvement and streamlining that was designed by the process flow team. All teams were

---

Exhibit 3–7 Inpatient Process Design Team's Work Plan for Patient Flow Subteam

Outcomes	• Optimal bed mix
	• Patient aggregation by resource consumption similarity
	• Criteria-based patient placement
	• Appropriate levels of care and patient placement
Impact	• Reduced transfers
	• Reduced census variability by unit
	• Appropriate utilization of each level of care
Timing	• 4 weeks
Analyses	• Patient placement study/level-of-care resource utilization study
	• Census variation study
	• Patients waiting for bed study
	• Chart review/data identifying patient movement and flow
	• Adult and pediatric patient flowchart

Courtesy of APM, Inc., San Francisco, California.

Exhibit 3–8 Inpatient Process Design Team's Work Plan for Process Flow Subteam

Outcomes	• Interdisciplinary documentation • Streamlined documentation • Streamlined order processing
Impact	• Integrate clinical documentation/flow • Reduce time spent in documentation • Eliminate duplicate documentation • Improve chart availability • Improve turnaround item of order processing (order written and through dispatch)
Timing	• Order processing: 3 weeks • Documentation: 6 weeks

Analyses	• Inventory of clinical care forms: who, what, why, when
	  –excluding automation
	  –identifying duplication
	• Identifying order processing flow
	• Work flow study
	• Activities by unit by time of day

Courtesy of APM, Inc., San Francisco, California.

Exhibit 3–9 Inpatient Process Design Team's Work Plan for Personnel Flow Subteam

Outcomes	• A flexible staffing process staffing to demand • Staffing guidelines: maximize use of other team members to do the work more efficiently and effectively • Clear self-scheduling guidelines and accountabilities • Mimized premium, overtime, callback, etc.
Impact	• New staffing guidelines for reaggregated units incorporating new care model changes • Streamlined scheduling and staffing process
Analyses	• Staffing process flow • Scheduling process flow • Pay practice analyses • Staff work flow study • Skill mix analysis

Courtesy of APM, Inc., San Francisco, California.

Table 3–3 Inpatient Process Structure

Subteam	Patient Flow	Process Flow	Personnel Flow
Levers	Patient aggregation	Interdisciplinary documentation by exception	Bedside care model Skill mix
	Levels-of-care criteria	Order processing	Scheduling process
	Weighted resource staffing	Ancillary service in room	Staffing process
	Bed utilization	Direct care process and protocols	Pay practices
	Census maximization	Medication administration	Staffing guidelines
	Patient placement	Expanded telemetry	Management structure
Analyses			
Operational Processes	Patient movement and transfers	Interdisciplinary documentation study	Schedule development
	Admit and predischarge process	Order processing	Staffing procedure
Data/Analysis	Census variation by unit, shift, and day of the week	Work flow study by unit shift, and classification	Labor cost analysis Work flow study
	Length-of-stay analysis by unit		Skill mix analysis
	Number of transfers by service		Staffing variance from guidelines
Stakeholder Data			
Needs assessment	Physician interview and focus groups	Physician interview and focus groups	Physician interview and focus groups
	Nursing focus groups	Nursing focus groups	Nursing focus groups
	Patient interviews or focus groups	Patient interviews or focus groups	Patient interviews or focus groups
Issue ID	Stakeholder	Stakeholder	Stakeholder

Courtesy of APM, Inc., San Francisco, California.

charged with making decisions and design changes based on data. This charge meant that issues and hypotheses needed to be accurately evaluated with reliable and valid data. Exhibit 3–10 shows additional types of analysis conducted by the design team and subteams.

CONCLUSION

Changes in health care delivery are everywhere. However, the changes have not always been positive or successful in producing the desired outcomes. The flow framework provides insight into the care process and supporting systems. The examination of a core process using the flow framework enables one to identify and understand, through analysis, the subprocess and activities from the perspective of the customer, the process, and the performer. The framework can be effec-

---

Exhibit 3–10 Inpatient Process Design Team's Analysis

The patient care team conducted several analyses to ensure that the team's ideas/decisions were based on data.

Issues	*Analyses*
Patient Flow	• Bed utilization study • Flow charting of patient movement • Census variation study
Process Flow	• Flowcharting of key processes • Financial assessment • Staff work flow and role survey (nursing, social services, RT, OT, PT, nutrition)
Personnel Flow	• Staff work flow and role survey (nursing, social services, RT, OT, PT, nutrition) • Financial assessment • Flowcharting of scheduling and staffing process
General	• Other stakeholder input: —Physician, patient, staff, payer • Focus groups with unit staff

Courtesy of APM, Inc., San Francisco, California.

tively applied to complex core processes and activities. The three-dimensional flow process provides a foundation for further redesign work in an organization and serves as a useful mechanism to continue to provoke thoughtful change.

NOTES

1. J.P. Lathrop, *Restructuring Health Care: The Patient Focused Paradigm* (San Francisco: Jossey-Bass, Publishers, 1993).

2. K. Lewin, "Frontiers in Group Dynamics," *Human Relations* 1 (1947): 5–42; R. Lippitt et al., *The Dynamics of Planned Change* (New York: Harcourt, Brace & World, 1958).

3. J.P. Kotter, "Leading Change: Why Transformational Efforts Fail," *Harvard Business Review* 73, no. 2 (1995): 59–67.

4. T. Porter-O'Grady, "The Seven Basic Rules for Successful Redesign," *Journal of Nursing Administration* 26, no. 1 (1996): 46–53.

5. C. Caldwell, "Accelerators and Inhibitors to Organizational Change in a Hospital," *Quality Review Bulletin* 19 (1993): 42–46.

6. M. Hammer and J. Champy, *Reengineering the Corporation: A Manifesto for Business Revolution* (New York: Harper Business, 1993).

CHAPTER 4

The Redesign Process: Inpatient and Perioperative Processes

Leanne Braden Hunstock, Charles Claggett Yaney,
Martha Gunther Enriquez, and Mickey L. Parsons

Chapter Objectives

1. To describe redesign from an inpatient perspective.
2. To describe redesign of the perioperative process.

The purpose of this chapter is to describe redesign using the examples of the inpatient care process and perioperative care process. The case for action is made according to the patients served, care delivery models, utilization management practices, and community competitive forces. Therefore, in the following examples, it will be assumed that the organizations have completed their own analysis and established performance targets in terms of cost and quality for each process. The reader may find it helpful first to completely review Chapter 3 for detail on the framework, examples of planning the inpatient redesign team, and subteam function and analysis.

REDESIGN OF THE INPATIENT CARE PROCESS

The care process for inpatient services begins when the patient is received in the care or service setting. The inpatient process includes the delivery of all care directly to the patient during the course of hospitalization, terminating with the physical disposition of the patient out of the inpatient setting. Nursing care, respiratory care, clinical nutritional care, clinical pharmacy care, therapeutics, medical care, patient logistics, documentation, patient placement, social services, unit-based support services, nurse staffing and scheduling, and patient care administration are included in this process's scope. The inpatient process intersects with all other processes.

Formation of the Inpatient Redesign Team

Redesign begins with the formation of an inpatient redesign team. The vice president responsible for patient care and a recognized physician leader, as process owners in the organization, must lead the team. Team members should represent all clinical disciplines and support departments and should include nurse managers, staff nurses from each of the clinical areas, nursing supervisors, staffing office personnel, leading physicians from key clinical disciplines, and house staff. The complexity of the process and the size of the team necessitate the formation of subteams to complete most of the redesign work and supporting analysis. The team determines the initial areas of focus and the subteam concentration and approves recommendations identified in each subteam prior to sending recommendations to the steering committee for final approval.

The first task of the team is to understand its scope, mission, purpose, goals, vision, guiding principles, and work plan (see Chapter 3 for detailed descriptions). The initial activities of the design team are to identify high-cost, low-quality, and/or poor-service issues within the patient care process on the basis of analysis, interviews, and customer satisfaction surveys. Next, the team speculates about potential "drivers," or causes, of high cost, low quality, and/or poor service. A large list of issues can surface in every organization. The team members then validate the list with the stakeholders or their colleagues, coworkers, and customers. The list of issues is then expanded, refined, and revised according to feedback from the stakeholders. The issues are prioritized as high, medium, and low potential for impact on the desired outcomes of low-cost, high-quality, and excellent service. The medium- to high-priority issues are grouped into one of three dimensions of flow according to the flow framework—patient flow, process flow, and personnel flow—as shown in Table 4–1. Hypotheses are then developed that link drivers of identified issues to systems or process breakdowns. An example of poor service might be cold food. A driver of cold food might be delay in food delivery somewhere in the production and delivery process. Or it might be letting the food sit too long in the kitchen or patient care unit.

Analysis of Patient Care Operations

Patient care labor cost contributes the greatest proportion of cost to the patient care operations. Therefore, it is important to analyze the costs and activity levels in the clinical and ancillary areas to determine patterns of resource utilization and

Table 4–1 An Inpatient Process Redesign Team: Framework, Opportunities, and Impact

Framework	Opportunities	Impact
Patient Flow	Patient aggregation Levels of care	Reduced patient transfers Improved utilization Reduced cost
Process Flow	Documentation simplication Order processing	Improved order turnaround time Improved patient service Treatment begun earlier Reduced cost
Personnel Flow	Maximized role design Skill mix enhancement Flexible staffing to demand	Better utilization of skill Increased staff availability Reduced cost

Courtesy of APM, Inc., San Francisco, California.

management practices. The drivers of patient care costs offer the greatest benefit for redesign. The areas best suited for analyses are discussed in Chapter 1.

Analysis of Key Levers for Patient Care Redesign

The design team's goal is to achieve a new cost per unit target while maintaining or enhancing quality and service. The key levers within each of the subteams for the inpatient process are important in achieving the goal. Those five key levers in the patient care process are as follows:

1. *Levels of care* describes the process of admitting patients to units or patient care centers where they are most likely to receive the most appropriate intensity of nursing care. Assessment of intensity is factored with staff workload and the patient's ongoing nursing care resource needs. In some organizations, the designation of levels of care is roughly driven by physician's orders, known staffing ratios, or chance based on random bed availability.
2. *Patient aggregation* is concerned with how the demand for resources is organized, based on where patients receive care. The goal is to group patients homogeneously according to the resources they consume, including medical staff resources.
3. *Pay practices* are the components of any system or process that controls or should control the use of labor resources. The nurse staffing office may be re-

structured to decentralize staffing decisions and control to the division level. This strategy places decisions closer to the bedside and reduces overhead.

4. *Care model* includes the components of skill mix and productivity or hours per patient day. Skill mix is the outcome measurement of the role and workload shift as a result of role redesign. As more organizations have implemented various redesigned roles, it is important to update the evaluation of actual role performance to assess whether assistive personnel are being fully utilized and whether the registered nurse (RN) role has evolved more fully in professional practice. The hours per patient day (HPPD) is the productivity outcome measurement of the workload and is directly tied to the amount of efficiency and process streamlining that occurs in the redesign process.

5. *Administrative restructuring* is concerned with designing a streamlined administrative and unit support structure that decentralizes and aligns authority and accountability to the level of the organization closest to the patient.

Use of Flow Framework

The flow framework organizes the issues and analysis into three processes. It is based on the dimensions of flow that occur in the patient care process. Those dimensions are patient flow, process flow, and personnel flow. The flow framework provides the context and structure for subteam organization. It is described in detail in Chapter 3.

The actual redesigned work is facilitated by the designation of three initial subteams based upon the flow framework. Each subteam uses the initial analyses to decide more specific causes of ineffective and inefficient processes. Additionally, the subteams complete further analysis as determined by the subteam. The work of each subteam is discussed.

Patient Flow

The patient flow subteam's goal is to determine a more effective patient placement process and more efficient resource utilization. The outcome desired is to develop criteria by which patients can be configured as aggregated on the various units. The configuration is the cornerstone of the inpatient care process redesign, because it determines the care model, as well as the management structure, decentralization of nursing support services, physician organization of clinical specialties, care management, education, and the development of a center-based interdisciplinary team focused on particular disease processes.

Additional analysis is required to determine the most optimal patient aggregation as well as the demand by patient type, resources consumption, and medical service. A specific bed utilization analysis is required to assess type of beds needed versus perceived needs based upon current operational problems. For example, it may be found that the demand for beds at the intermediate care with cardiac monitoring rather than a perceived intensive care bed shortage may be the actual problem. A concurrent level-of-care analysis is conducted to determine to what extent patients in particular units met the established criteria for intensive care, intermediate care, and general unit status. It is not uncommon to find that intensive care unit patients could be treated at lower levels of care and that some percentage of intermediate care unit patients meet intensive care unit criteria. Additional bed placement issues concern cardiac monitoring. It is helpful to evaluate the frequency with which cardiac monitoring is the only indicator for patient placement at the intermediate level of care.

Redesign teams then recommend, on the basis of the specific organization's data, grouping patients into care centers that reflect similar resource needs and the organization of clinical service specialties. Figure 4–1 provides one example of a reconfiguration. In this example, each center encompassed one or more units that would now deliver at least two levels of care without transferring or moving the patient.

Once the most optimal aggregation model or unit configuration is determined, a mechanism is required to assess patient placement within determined levels of care within each clinical service. Following the development of the level-of-care assessment, a mechanism and a tool needs to be drafted and field tested for validity on all the units. The tool is used to determine staffing levels on a shift-to-shift basis according to level-of-care criteria for all patients. Two separate sets of criteria are needed for pediatric patients and for intensive care nursery patients. Each follows the same mechanism of assessment once per shift to determine prospective staffing needs for patients. With this mechanism, patients can be cared for at a variety of levels and still remain within the aggregated patient group or center. More common recommendations from the patient flow subteam include the following:

- Group patients into clinically driven clusters or patient care centers.
- Offer two to three levels of care within each center.
- Cross-train staff to work within a center specialty at two levels of care.
- Use level-of-care criteria to determine patient placement and project resource and staffing needs.
- Expand telemetry capability throughout centers to support center configuration, based upon hospital-specific data (may not apply to all hospitals), and remotely throughout high-use ancillary areas to reduce RN off-unit accompanied transport hours.

Process Flow

The process flow subteam is concerned with patient care processes that support patient flow. These processes and subprocesses include order processing, docu-

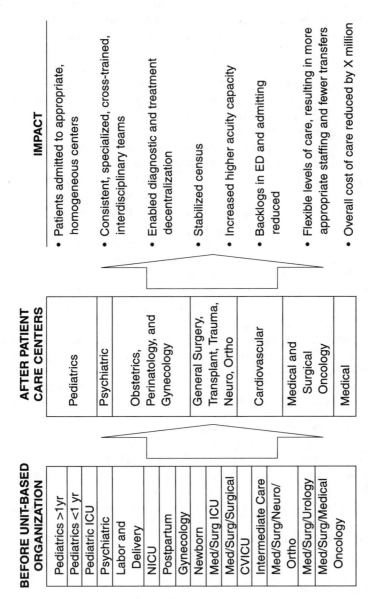

Figure 4–1 An Inpatient Care Reaggregation. Courtesy of APM, Inc., San Francisco, California.

mentation, medication administration, and patient transfer and transport. The team uses information to determine the scope of the issues associated with the subprocesses prior to designing new processes. Key data for this subteam and for personnel and patient flow teams are the results of a staff study of time spent in various direct and indirect care activities. A real-time monitored or self-report work flow study measuring major staff activities may be conducted with a random sample of staff in all categories and jobs involved in the inpatient care process, including ancillary clinical staff and environmental staff. The results provide information about registered nurse and assistive personnel time spent in all direct and indirect activities. Figure 4–2 illustrates the results of a work flow survey. In the example, a large percentage of nursing time is spent following up and coordinating the work of other departments whose systems are impaired. Considerable intervention may be required by nursing staff to get services to the patient. Support systems such as pharmacy distribution and dispensing and laboratory test turnaround should be addressed in an ancillary process team. Common recommendations from a process flow subteam may be as follows:

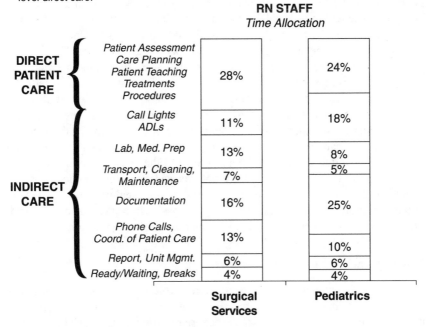

Skill mix shift was achieved through increasing the proportion of time RNs spend in high-level direct care.

RN STAFF
Time Allocation

DIRECT PATIENT CARE	Patient Assessment, Care Planning, Patient Teaching, Treatments, Procedures	28%	24%
	Call Lights, ADLs	11%	18%
INDIRECT CARE	Lab, Med. Prep	13%	8%
	Transport, Cleaning, Maintenance	7%	5%
	Documentation	16%	25%
	Phone Calls, Coord. of Patient Care	13%	10%
	Report, Unit Mgmt.	6%	6%
	Ready/Waiting, Breaks	4%	4%
		Surgical Services	**Pediatrics**

Figure 4–2 Work Flow Study Results. Courtesy of APM, Inc., San Francisco, California.

- Install pharmacy automated dispensing machines and a medication documentation system.
- Redesign the documentation process to feature an interdisciplinary charting-by-exception system.
- Redesign the documentation process and forms to make it easier to locate pertinent documentation.
- Automate clinical documentation.
- Station a unit secretary at a central location to do chart and order processing.
- Fax orders and consult requests to departments.
- Reduce transfers due to aggregation and patient scheduling efficiencies.
- Reduce patient transport by decentralizing appropriate ancillary services and expanding cardiac monitoring capability.

Personnel Flow

The personnel flow subteam's goal is to facilitate the development of a bedside care model, based on the patient aggregation plan, that will enable staff to deliver the appropriate level of care within a specific cost target. The design team relies on data collected by other teams about staff activities. In addition, data are collected to analyze pay practices, staffing and scheduling effectiveness, and other personnel costs. The team should analyze cost components of the productive direct care salary expense within each patient care division, including types and cost of premium pay, special differentials, and on-call and callback pay. Units should be identified in which the majority of the higher expenses are occurring. The redesign of premium-pay practices, particularly those that arose during the height of the most recent nursing shortage, and the decentralization of staffing and scheduling to the patient care centers will reduce costs substantially. The team needs to involve the senior patient care leadership throughout the organization. A large retreat of senior nurses, therapists, managers, educators, and involved departments should meet to learn about the overall progress of the hospital and inpatient team and subteams and to contribute to development of the bedside care model. After the planning retreat for bedside care model redesign, the final model is recommended to the hospitalwide steering committee. This final model addresses the decentralization of services to unit-based roles, assistive workers, and the overall skill mix and predicts costs savings of the proposed recommendations.

Management/Administrative Restructuring

The management/administrative restructuring typically occurs at the administrative level rather than in the process redesign team. The reaggregation of patients and the creation of patient care centers create opportunities to redesign management. Reducing the number of managers from one for every one unit or two units to larger configurations results in cost reductions. Second, decentralizing nursing support services to the patient care centers, including the resource pool, staffing and scheduling, and staff education, and creating resource coordinators to support the managers place resource decisions closer to the patient and reduce overhead expenses. Clinical and management changes provide the opportunity to develop further collaborative professional practice among the clinical disciplines. New creative approaches to interdisciplinary staff governance may develop, as well as increased nursing and physician collaborative leadership. Additionally, other services such as a center-based medical director, center-based case management, and decentralized admitting will be possible on the basis of the patient aggregation redesign. Figure 4–3 gives an example of a center interdisciplinary clinical practice model.

REDESIGN OF THE PERIOPERATIVE CARE PROCESS

The perioperative process is critical to every hospital, because perioperative services in a typical hospital can generate up to 40 percent of hospital revenue and costs. Because of the significance of perioperative services to a hospital's overall performance, clinical and process redesign should consider several dimensions. The entire surgical process encompasses numerous areas that must coordinate their efforts jointly: admitting, outpatient services, materials management, sterile processing, surgery, recovery, and nursing. This section outlines perioperative services process redesign.

The framework for the perioperative process is similar to that of the inpatient process. It is organized around three flows: personnel, products, and process.

- *Personnel:* Are the right people doing the right tasks?
- *Products:* Are products and equipment available at the right time?
- *Process:* Are the processes before, during, and after the surgical procedure organized efficiently?

This framework, shown in Figure 4–4, provides an organizational format for the redesign team and three subteams. An interdisciplinary team is convened, composed of anesthesiologists, surgeons, nurses, surgical technicians, materials management staff, radiology technicians, clinical pharmacists, and staff from the recovery room, ambulatory surgery, and the clinics. Teams normally meet weekly for two hours for at least three months. Subteam meetings may be necessary, and numerous physician briefing meetings and individual meetings with surgeons are critical.

Personnel Flow

Personnel flow encompasses all processes to ensure that the right person is available to do the right tasks. Aspects to consider include:

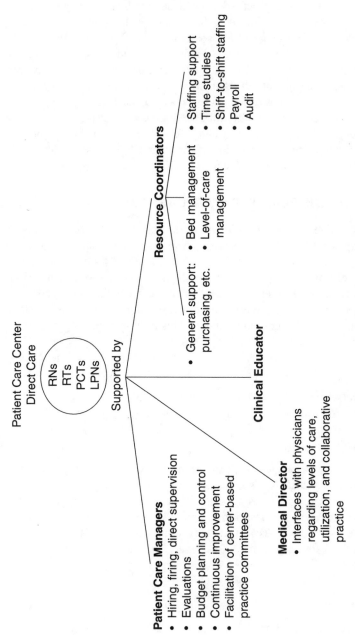

Patient Care Center
Direct Care

RNs
RTs
PCTs
LPNs

Supported by

Patient Care Managers
- Hiring, firing, direct supervision
- Evaluations
- Budget planning and control
- Continuous improvement
- Facilitation of center-based practice committees

Medical Director
- Interfaces with physicians regarding levels of care, utilization, and collaborative practice

Clinical Educator

- General support: purchasing, etc.

Resource Coordinators
- Bed management
- Level-of-care management

- Staffing support
- Time studies
- Shift-to-shift staffing
- Payroll
- Audit

Note: RNs = registered nurses; RTs = respiratory therapists; PCTs = patient care technicians; LPNs = licensed practical nurses.

Figure 4–3 A Center Interdisciplinary Clinical Practice Model

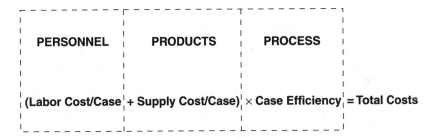

Figure 4–4 Perioperative Services Process Redesign Framework. Courtesy of APM, Inc., San Francisco, California.

- Is the most efficient mix of staff utilized?
- Are teams available when cases are scheduled?
- Is the management structure appropriate for the scale and scope of operations?

Assessment of mix, demand, and management structure enables the team to address the key personnel process levers for perioperative services.

Staff Mix

The redesign team compares actual staffing with target staffing levels. For example, one operating room nurse may team with one core technologist for any given case. Therefore, in the operating room, if this mix is maintained, a 50 percent direct care skill mix of RN hours should be achieved. This same approach is used in the postanesthesia care unit (PACU). If staffing guidelines indicate that one patient care technician (PCT) assists three PACU nurses, a 75 percent direct care skill mix of RN hours will be maintained. An example of a team's initial skill mix is shown in Figure 4–5. In this example, in the main operating room, skill mix is close to the mix expected. However, in PACU, the RN skill mix is higher than expected. Further analysis may indicate that enhanced use of PCTs will optimize the skill mix in the PACU. For example, an RN should not collect equipment, transport patients, or perform housekeeping chores. These tasks should be delegated to PCTs and patient support attendants (PSAs). Nevertheless, in many institutions, RNs frequently perform such activities in the operating room and PACU due to

- lack of appropriate staff
- convenience or necessity
- lack of responsiveness of departments who provide support

If RNs spend significant time performing tasks and activities that do not require their skill level, the redesign effort should focus on adjusting the skill mix. Time

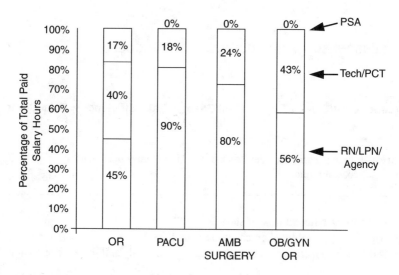

Figure 4–5 Perioperative Services Skill Mix Analysis. Courtesy of APM, Inc., San Francisco, California.

saved by utilization of support personnel can be realized in savings or can increase direct patient care time for professional staff, depending on the needs of the service area.

Matching Resources to Demand

Ensuring that the right resources are performing the right tasks addresses only one part of the personnel segment of the perioperative process. The other is that staff must be available as needed. The redesign team needs to evaluate surgical volume at different times of the day and compare the volume to the number of staff scheduled.

Commonplace findings include

- the scheduling of additional teams because of high variability of the number of cases running
- the scheduling of additional teams for case overruns and delays

Figure 4–6 demonstrates an analysis that can be performed to evaluate the number of cases in progress in the operating room and actual staffing of the teams (operating room nurse and technician). Results will enable a redesign team to propose revisions in the number of rooms to schedule cases and have a more closely matched demand readily available for emergencies and staffing assignments.

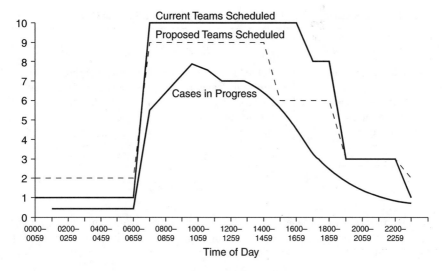

Figure 4–6 An Analysis of Surgical Volume and Staffing

Appropriate Management Structure

Ensuring that the management structure of perioperative services is consistent with the organization is another important focus of the redesign team. As with the inpatient process, a subset of the overall team may need to review the organization chart. The subset should involve the organizational leaders (vice president of patient care services and chief of anesthesiology) and the director of perioperative services with consultation of the chief of surgery. Development and implementation of processes to simplify coordinating and scheduling activities performed by management will reduce management activities.

Process Flow

The process flow subteam's objective is to improve case efficiency through the perioperative process. Specifically, the team analyzes presurgical, surgical, and postsurgical activities to streamline and/or eliminate non–value-added activities. The team should first perform a study to assess the timing of a sequence of key events during a patient's surgical case, such as that shown in Exhibit 4–1.

An example of a surgical case process flow may be seen in Figure 4–7. Inspection of the intervals between the events enables the team to develop specific solutions to streamline the process. The improvements more commonly planned are shown in Exhibit 4–2.

Exhibit 4–1 Sequence of Key Time Points during a Patient's Surgical Case

Presurgical Time	*Surgical Time*	*Postsurgical Time*
• Patient brought into room • Anesthesia induction • Surgeon arrives • Start position • Start prep	• Cut time • Attending leaves room • Last dressing • Patient out	• Housekeeping arrives • Next case cart arrives • Room ready

It is important to forecast the result of the process changes in actual average case time reduction, such as 20 minutes or 10 percent. This improvement in case timing will yield

- enhanced physician, staff, and patient satisfaction with an efficient and effective system
- increased case capacity and room availability
- fewer case delays and late starts
- reduction of excess costs associated with idle staff time, overtime, and callback

Product

The process subteam's objective is to reduce the cost per case by focusing on costly supply items such as implants and disposable supplies. A primary strategy is to analyze the 20 percent of supply items that represent 80 percent of total supply expenditures in the operating room. The subteam should review those high-dollar products and apply the following tests:

- Can we standardize to a less expensive product?
- Can we standardize and achieve an increase in vendor discounts?
- Can we reduce use of expensive disposables?
- Can we substitute less expensive products?

The initial recommendations should be reviewed with surgeons. The surgeons will either agree to the recommendations or ask for further analysis prior to approving the changes. Overall, the product subteam typically can achieve significant supply cost reductions of 15 to 20 percent.

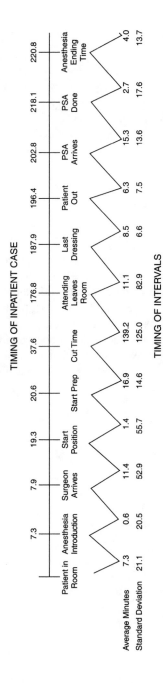

Figure 4–7 A Surgical Case Process Flow Analysis

Exhibit 4–2 Some Measures To Streamline the Surgical Case Process

Presurgical Time	*Surgical Time*	*Postsurgical Time*
• Improve anesthesia protocols • Create new prep and positioning protocols • Streamline medical record	• Improve scheduling • Modify block scheduling • Introduce initiatives to reduce surgeon late time	• Improve room turnaround procedures Create turnover teams Establish new room cleaning procedures

CONCLUSION

Approaches to inpatient redesign and perioperative process redesign offer ideas to improve quality and reduce costs dramatically. Both processes follow a similar framework. Extensive opportunities are discussed in the inpatient process in the three subteams: patient flow, process flow, and personnel flow. The perioperative service process subteam addresses patient flow in a comprehensive manner. A personnel subteam and a specially designated product subteam address cost savings in their areas. The ideas presented provide ideas and suggested actions for organizations to maintain and enhance quality while reducing costs.

Approaches to Clinical Process Redesign

Part Editors

Mickey L. Parsons and Carolyn L. Murdaugh

CHAPTER 5

From Quality Assurance to Organizational Improvements and Process Redesign at the Emory University System of Health Care

Susan L. Smith, Alice F. Vautier, and Carl Smith

Chapter Objectives

1. To describe the organizational improvement plan for process redesign for a growing system of health care.
2. To discuss the role of clinical pathways in an outcomes assessment program.

As health care reform gains momentum, the demands on health care providers are radically changing. Rising health care costs, changing patient population demographics, and increased severity of illness are factors that health care delivery systems must respond to competitively. Outcome, not process, has become the ultimate quality indicator. Successful delivery systems, therefore, must provide outcomes data to payers and clients that document efficient, effective, accessible, and timely care. No longer should outcomes data be reported solely in terms of financial indicators. We must provide evidence that care is clinically effective and that customers are satisfied and functioning at a disease- or health-appropriate level. The bottom line is that care considerations must include effectiveness, efficiency, and efficacy in both the short term and the long term, and this requires organizations to move from process improvement to process redesign.

The model of organizational improvement at the Emory Hospitals has evolved over the last decade from one that was primarily user centered to one that is progressively becoming patient centered. Patient-centered care incorporates respect for patients' values, preferences, and expressed needs and is responsive to patients' demands. In a patient-centered care model, care delivery occurs in an environment in which staff are empowered to deliver excellence. Patient care is characterized by coordination, continuity, efficiency, and effectiveness through the transitions and across the continuum of care.

The term *outcome* has been redefined conceptually, and the process of outcomes assessment is being redesigned from a retrospective utilization review process that met the needs of traditional quality assurance to continuous quality, performance, and organizational improvement processes based on concurrent identification and management of variation in operations and clinical practice. This chapter describes the evolutionary process of defining and implementing this redesign model and future plans for ensuring patient-centered care. This is an ongoing process that is continually changing in synchrony with advances in biomedical technology and the demands of consumers and payers for quality and cost-effective patient care. Our challenge is to provide innovative, high-quality, patient-centered, and service-oriented care that is affordable and has demonstrated value.

THE EMORY UNIVERSITY SYSTEM OF HEALTH CARE

The Emory University System of Health Care (EUSHC), located in Atlanta, Georgia, was incorporated in 1994 to facilitate and coordinate managed care contracting, corporate health initiatives, network development, and special initiatives related to health care delivery in the Atlanta area. EUSHC includes the Emory Clinic, Emory University Hospital and Crawford Long Hospital (Emory Hospitals), Emory-Adventist Hospital, Egleston Children's Hospital, and Wesley Woods Geriatric Center. Departments within EUSHC that support managed-care contracting and network development include managed care and primary care. The Emory Clinic and Emory Hospitals are also part of the Woodruff Health Science Center of Emory University which also includes Emory University School of Medicine, Nell Hodgson Woodruff School of Nursing, and Rollins School of Public Health. In addition to a growing number of primary care clinics in metropolitan Atlanta, EUSHC has affiliations with 45 community hospitals throughout Georgia and in North Carolina, South Carolina, and Delaware.

Emory University Hospital (EUH) is a 591-bed academic tertiary referral health center located on the campus of Emory University. Admitting privileges are limited to the more than 700 Emory Clinic physicians. Crawford Long Hospital (CLH) is a 583-bed tertiary referral center hospital located in midtown Atlanta about 10 miles from EUH. CLH has a physician staff of over 1,000, and two-thirds of admissions are from community physicians. Although CLH has been owned by Emory University since 1940, EUH and CLH were merged in 1995 to form Emory Hospitals.

MANAGED CARE AND THE ATLANTA MARKET

Health care in the United States is in a revolution. The paradigms of clinical sovereignty and medical economics are in conflict, causing a shift from a system that is physician driven and in which the financial risks are borne by the payers to a system that is driven by quality and cost that are largely determined by the payers and in which the financial risk is borne by the providers. This shifting of financial responsibility brought about by managed care is a primary driving force for changes from within the health care system. It is estimated that by 1998, over 60 million Americans will receive their health care through some form of managed-care organization.[1] Managed care results in decreases in hospital admissions, length of stay, inpatient procedures, and reimbursement per episode of care, forcing hospitals to offer discounted rates and to integrate into larger health care delivery systems. Academic health centers face a unique set of challenges in this environment.

Despite a late arrival, managed care has penetrated the Atlanta market. Approximately 1.1 million Atlantans were enrolled in health maintenance organization and preferred provider organization plans as of August 1996.[2] Atlanta is in stage 3 of the four stages of the managed-care market evolution model (Figure 5–1). In the last three years, EUSHC has increased its number of managed-care contracts from 0 to 116, accounting for 3 million covered lives or approximately one-third of the state's population.

THE QUALITY IMPROVEMENT PLAN FOR PROCESS REDESIGN AT EMORY HOSPITALS

In the majority of stage 3 market providers, the strategic focus is primarily on cost containment. Quality and outcomes management strategies are usually found only in the most advanced markets. This is where the Emory Hospitals differ from most providers in the stage 3 market. The current focus of the performance improvement plan at Emory Hospitals is based on parallel planning, monitoring, and improvement efforts designed to accelerate the transition from process improvement to process redesign and systems thinking. The primary goal is to design processes to improve performance and quality. It is believed that as quality improves, costs will decrease. The plan is dependent on five basic interrelated concepts: customer focus, data-driven decisions, systems thinking, teamwork, and empowerment. Key initiatives of the quality improvement plan include

- development of a consistent approach to performance and organizational improvement

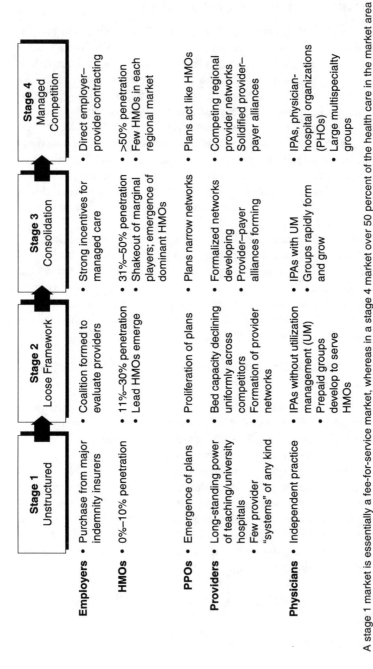

A stage 1 market is essentially a fee-for-service market, whereas in a stage 4 market over 50 percent of the health care in the market area is under a capitated payment system. In the early-stage markets, overutilization and excess capacity in the system offer potential competitive advantage to providers who reduce costs by managing resources efficiently.

Figure 5–1 The Stages of Market Evolution. *Source:* Reprinted from R.C. Browne and D.A. Burnett, The Rigors and Rewards of Clinical Evaluation in the Alliance of Academic Health Systems, *Quality Management in Health Care*, Vol. 4, No. 4, p. 4, © 1996, Aspen Publishers, Inc.

- design of a leadership development program to continuously enhance competence in managing change, systems thinking, and performance and organizational improvement
- integration of performance and organizational improvement into daily operations and practice
- use of clinical pathways and practice guidelines to improve clinical processes and outcomes
- identification of best practices through internal and external benchmarking projects and incorporation of these into clinical processes
- establishment of a strategic planning process (Emory Hospitals vision alignment matrix) to identify priorities for action

Oversight for this plan is provided by the Performance Improvement Coordinating Council (PICC). PICC, composed of members of the senior administrative staff and other key clinical and administrative leaders at Emory Hospitals, provides direction for performance improvement activities at Emory Hospitals. Its early work focused on learning, practicing, and developing the organization's quality framework. The quality framework assisted the organization in providing constancy of purpose in the quality improvement plan. The components of the quality framework outlined in the Emory Hospitals vision alignment matrix (Exhibit 5–1) are mission, vision, values, and behaviors.

Two process improvement models provide structure, methods, and tools for day-to-day operationalization of the plan. The FOCUS-PDCA model (Figure 5–2) is used for process improvement,[3] and clinical pathways are used to develop clinical practice guidelines to improve patient care. Both initiatives support the strategies "Improve patient care," "Improve patient and family satisfaction," and "Maintain a strong financial position in the Emory Hospitals vision alignment matrix."

FOCUS-PDCA is a systematic method for improvement that is an extension of the plan, do, check, act (PDCA) cycle, sometimes called the Shewart/Deming cycle for continual improvement, designed to look specifically at processes. The PDCA is a patient-centered model in which the customer is the patient. Through FOCUS-PDCA, knowledge of how a process is currently performing to meet patients' needs and expectations is used to plan and test process changes. The purpose of these process changes is to improve the patient care services from the patients' viewpoints. More than 100 leaders at all levels of the organization are receiving intensive training to facilitate teams in the use of FOCUS-PDCA for operational and clinical improvement processes.

Clinical pathways, which are discussed in more detail in a later section, are at the core of clinical process improvement at Emory Hospitals. They are used to plan, deliver, monitor, and evaluate care with the goal of balancing cost and quality through achievement of best clinical outcomes.

Exhibit 5–1 Emory Hospitals Vision Alignment Matrix

MISSION (Why we exist)

The Emory Hospitals are leaders in today's competitive health care environment committed to:

- high-quality, cost-effective patient care
- clinical and financial support for teaching and research
- the mission of the Emory University System of Health Care (EUSHC)
- partnership with the community to promote wellness

VISION (What we strive for)

The Emory Hospitals, in support of EUSHC, strive to be premier providers of patient care recognized for:

- quality
- value
- innovation
- service

VALUES (Our principles)

We place the highest value on service to others

We value our commitment to our community

We respect the contribution and worth of each individual

We are dedicated to continuous learning and innovation

We manage our resources responsibly

We are committed to the success of EUSHC

BEHAVIORS (Expectations)

We always make the care of our patients, our primary customer, our highest priority

We are customer focused in everything we do

We treat each other with dignity, respect, and courtesy

We actively listen and allow different views to be openly communicated

We work together as a team to find constructive solutions to problems

We accept responsibility for our own actions and behaviors

We act for the greater good of EUSHC rather than for our specific departments or ourselves

We make decisions that are fact based and data driven

STRATEGY: Improve Patient Care	STRATEGY: Improve Patient and Family Satisfaction	STRATEGY: Promote the Development of Employees	STRATEGY: Improve Physician Relations	STRATEGY: Integrate Systems and Services among the Hospitals and Clinic	STRATEGY: Maintain a Strong Financial Position	STRATEGY: Support the Development of EUSHC
TACTICS: • Expand development and use of clinical pathways • Identify and use best patient care practices • Measure outcomes of patient care	TACTICS: • Promote a caring attitude and professional image • Improve all communication with patients and families	TACTICS: • Implement common human resources systems, policies, procedures, and pay practices • Enhance all aspects of employee communications	TACTICS: • Make it easy for physicians to be as efficient and effective as possible • Enhance collaboration and partnership with the hospitals	TACTICS: • Integrate all information systems • Improve service delivery systems • Merge clinical and operational	TACTICS: • Support the EUSHC managed-care strategic plan • Continue cost reduction efforts • Standardize financial policies and reporting between hospitals	TACTICS: • Support continuum-of-care components • Improve communication systems • Seek new business opportunities

continues

Exhibit 5–1 continued

• Enhance patient and family education • Promote well-being and healing through everything we do • Respond promptly to patient and family concerns and needs • Set clear expectations, standards, and individual responsibilities for serving our patients, visitors, and each other • Help people find their way to, and within, our hospitals	• Recognize employee contributions • Continuously educate and train all employees • Provide customer service training for all staff • Improve how we assess competency • Enhance computer skills • Provide a safe, secure environment	• Enhance communication	services where appropriate • Streamline administrative processes • Improve admission and discharge systems	• Consolidate materials contracts to obtain best price and value • Manage costs through education and participation • Maximize reimbursement for hospital services • Work closer with payers • Identify and coordinate acute care alternatives	• Support community programs

Courtesy of Emory University Hospital, Atlanta, Georgia.

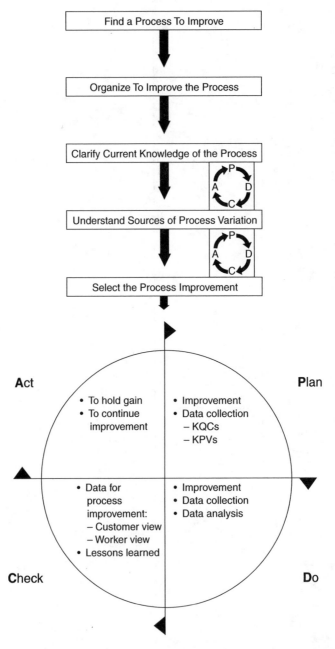

Figure 5–2 FOCUS-PDCA. Courtesy of Columbia/HCA Health Care Corporation, Nashville, Tennessee.

Monitoring activities are conducted on a hospitalwide and department-specific basis at Emory Hospitals. Macro indicators are reviewed regularly by PICC. Patient satisfaction is monitored through participation in the University Health-system Consortium patient satisfaction monitoring process. A network-based monitoring system for use at the department level is currently under development. That system will serve as the data repository and communication vehicle for all departmental monitoring activities. To support the use of the system by administrative and clinical staff, hands-on training in the methods and tools of quality monitoring and statistical process control is provided on a regular basis.

THE COLLABORATIVE CASE MANAGEMENT PROGRAM AT CRAWFORD LONG HOSPITAL

In 1991, the Quality Initiative, based on Deming's 14 points,[4] was launched at CLH. It was at this time that collaborative case management, an interdisciplinary approach to coordination, integration, and continuity of patient care services, was selected as the clinical practice model at CLH to facilitate the delivery of quality patient care and maintain a sound financial base. Case management was chosen as a method of linking the appropriate use of resources with specific patient populations that were high volume, high cost, high risk, or high interest. The process was decentralized through the medical departments with the accountability for coordinating clinical services across the full continuum of care vested in the case manager. The goals of collaborative case management at CLH were coordination of care, achievement of desired clinical and economic outcomes, effective and efficient use of resources, collaborative interdisciplinary practice, and job satisfaction among caregivers.

Implementation of this model required careful planning. A steering committee consisting of members of the medical practice committee and administrators from patient services, the division of nursing, and the nursing quality management division of the hospital quality department was formed. Clinical case managers were hired and initially appointed to coordinate the case management of designated high-volume and/or high-cost diagnosis-related patient groups (DRGs). A population-based approach was chosen to allow case managers to focus on how the system could better serve specific groups of patients. Key responsibilities of the case manager were

- identification and referral of complex and high-risk patients in need of intense intervention and/or specific resources and planning for effective delivery of intervention/resources
- coordination of the many diverse elements of a treatment and discharge plan
- monitoring patient progress to ensure that appropriate services were provided in a timely and cost-efficient manner
- continuous reevaluation of the process

The Care Map was conceptualized as the critical process instrument of this model. A Care Map is a cause-and-effect grid that identifies expected patient/ family and staff behaviors against a timeline for a case-type or otherwise defined population.[5] The four essential components of a Care Map are a timeline, an index of problems with intermediate and ultimate outcome criteria, a clinical pathway, and a variance record. Interdisciplinary teams were formed to develop each Care Map and an outcomes monitoring tool (variance report) for each specified case type. Case types were determined by meeting any of the following criteria: high volume, high cost, high risk, or high interest. In fact, the first Care Map was developed for the patient with community-acquired pneumonia, which was of high interest to a particular physician champion of case management but was neither high volume, high cost, nor high risk.

Thirty-two Care Maps have been implemented at CLH. When CLH and EUH merged, the term *clinical pathway* replaced the term *Care Map*. Approximately 30 percent of patients at CLH are managed via a clinical pathway. In this model, case managers are accountable for monitoring the use of and collecting process variance data from the clinical pathways, which are combined with financial indicators to evaluate and improve outcomes. Use of the Care Map was formally evaluated in 1993 by consultants from National Cash Register, Inc. Results of this evaluation revealed that the Care Map was perceived by the nursing staff as a valuable training tool for new staff and a potentially valuable documentation tool but validated the need for standardization and computerization of the process. Improved patient teaching was also attributed to Care Maps. An especially innovative spin-off of the Care Maps was "picture maps," which are pictorial versions of the Care Maps developed at a sixth-grade reading level to assist patients in understanding their plan of care outlined in the Care Map. Another outgrowth was the development of a community-based smoking cessation curriculum. Criticisms by the staff were that the Care Maps were not specific enough in terms of age and severity of illness and that some of the key indicators chosen for variance tracking provided "nice-to-know," but not necessarily meaningful, data and therefore were a waste of time to collect.

THE CLINICAL PATHWAYS PROGRAM AT EMORY UNIVERSITY HOSPITAL

In 1993, the clinical pathways program was established at Emory University Hospital as the core initiative for the redesign of the patient care delivery system. The clinical pathway is a "best-practice/best-treatment" clinical practice guideline designed for all patients within a given disease or treatment category, with the exception of those in the upper quartile (25 percent) of acuity and complexity. The clinical pathway outlines multidisciplinary care processes that achieve desired outcomes within an appropriate length of stay while using resources efficiently. Overriding goals of the clinical pathways program were to standardize care, decrease practice variation, monitor quality, evaluate outcomes, and develop a high level of interdependence within the institution. *Interdependence* was defined as the ability of health care providers from multiple disciplines to form alliances to achieve outcomes that could not be achieved independently. Initially, the goals were set that 100 percent of services at EUH would implement at least one clinical pathway within 24 months and that 80 percent of patients cared for would be managed according to a clinical pathway within 30 months.

An advisory steering committee consisting of administrators, nurse leaders, and physicians was formed to support the development of and provide oversight to the Clinical Pathways Program. The process was centralized through a department for clinical pathways with a department manager. The clinical pathways operations team, a multidisciplinary group that makes recommendations regarding the general operations and ongoing development of the program and that is accountable for implementation of program initiatives, was formed. Multidisciplinary clinical pathway teams were formed to develop, monitor, evaluate, and revise each clinical pathway with technical support from the clinical pathways, clinical resource management, and operations engineering departments. Performance measures for each clinical pathway included

- concurrent monitoring of variance data
- linking of financial data (cost, length of stay) to clinical data
- external benchmarking when feasible
- development of patient-friendly versions

The role of the case manager was not a component of the EUH clinical pathways program. The responsibility for monitoring the clinical pathways was assigned to the multidisciplinary "team." The nursing staff at the points of care, however, were responsible for collection of data from the variance reports. Clinical nurse specialists and nurse clinicians were responsible for coordinating the development, implementation, and revision of the pathways and were most consistently the team leaders. Thirty-six clinical pathways have been implemented at EUH. Approximately 30 percent of patients are managed via a clinical pathway.

CLINICAL OUTCOMES ASSESSMENT AT EMORY HOSPITALS: AN AGENDA FOR CHANGE

Although not all of the previous programs' goals were met, significant progress has been made in changing from a traditional quality assurance to an outcomes management model. The Emory Hospitals have been the clinical benchmark for the following pathways: Congestive Heart Failure (EUH), Cardiac Surgery (both hospitals), Cardiac Catheterization and/or Percutaneous Transluminal Coronary Angioplasty (EUH), Carotid Endarterectomy (EUH), and Total Hip Arthroplasty (EUH).

Data management has been the greatest challenge to both programs; the weak link is the lack of an information technology infrastructure capable of standardizing the production of clinical pathways and storing, managing, analyzing, interpreting, and reporting data. Both programs were initiated without the benefit of a software program specifically designed to computerize this process, and neither hospital had a point-of-care computer network system. Furthermore, there was no mechanism for making the important quality connection of directly linking key indicators of the clinical pathways with financial indicators.

Until 1996, outcomes indicators at Emory Hospitals were derived primarily from financial data (charge or cost and length of stay). These data were measured and retrospectively reported by the department of clinical resource management (formerly *utilization review*) with technical support from the department of operational performance improvement (formerly *management systems*). These data were linked to clinical pathways, but not concurrently. Parallel with these efforts, the "process" component of the clinical pathways has been well developed and is considered useful in terms of decreasing variation in practice and educating providers from multiple disciplines about how to manage care for specific patient groups. The outcomes component, however, has not kept pace with the process component, primarily because of the lack of systems to monitor variances from the pathways. Several attempts have been made to incorporate outcomes measurement and analysis into the programs, but without adequate technical support, these attempts have been unsuccessful.

The next objective was to establish an outcomes assessment program as an interim step toward preparation for a disease management program. In July 1996, significant changes were made in the organizational structure and goals of the collaborative case management and clinical pathways programs. Although the programs were structurally and theoretically different (CLH's program was theory based in case management, and EUH's program was not), the goals were fairly consistent. In addition, CLH and EUH had merged to form Emory Hospitals. Therefore, a hybrid program—one program in two locations, combining the best of both programs, but with one purpose and set of goals—was established under the leadership of one program director. The name of the program was changed to *clinical outcomes assessment* to reflect expansion of the scope of the former programs and to add the focus of outcomes assessment to the clinical pathways program. The program recognized the strengths of both former programs and endeavored to build on those. What resulted was a strengthening of the clinical pathways programs and new opportunities for identifying and managing outcomes.

Outcomes assessment incorporates measurement, monitoring, and management of outcomes associated with specific care processes.[6] The three core activities of outcomes assessment are (1) *outcomes measurement,* or the observation of outcomes indicators; (2) *outcomes monitoring,* or the systematic measurement of key indicators over time; and (3) *outcomes management,* or the use of information to manage core processes that bring about outcomes.

The clinical outcomes assessment program is designed to use outcomes assessment information from clinical pathways and other sources of clinical, financial, and quality improvement data at Emory Hospitals. The overriding goals are to develop a comprehensive measurement model for evaluating disease and treatment outcomes, to develop and implement an outcomes-based practice model at both hospitals, and to establish priorities for outcomes research. Traditional clinical measures of disease status (e.g., biologic indicators, mortality, unexpected readmission, or return to surgery) are being incorporated in parallel with generic and population-specific concepts that are patient centered, such as patient-expressed perceptions and experiences of disease and treatment (e.g., satisfaction, functional status, quality of life). In this new model, clinical pathways are the primary driving force for defining best practice and monitoring clinical outcomes. While only approximately 30 percent of patients cared for at the Emory Hospitals are managed according to a clinical pathway, the foundation has been laid to expand the scope of this process within the acute care environments to reach the goal of 80 percent and ultimately to develop the program across the entire continuum of care with the addition of longitudinal and ambulatory care pathways.

The clinical outcomes assessment program is an integral component of the EUSHC-wide strategies to enhance patient care and to compete effectively in the managed-care market. The Joint Commission on Accreditation of Healthcare Organizations identifies four ways that an outcomes assessment program can define itself in the context of the larger organization or system: as an operating division, a service bureau, an internal consulting firm, or a leadership group.[7] The clinical outcomes assessment program, while a separate business unit, will concentrate on the service, consulting, and leadership functions. The program will provide staff support and technical expertise to other operating divisions of the organization and will advocate the mission in the vision alignment matrix to promote change throughout the organization.

Keeping in mind that clinical pathways and outcomes assessment are only as effective as the people involved, the role of the outcomes manager, a new role, was carefully defined in terms of key responsibilities and accountabilities. There was a conscious effort to differentiate this role clearly from the previous accountable roles of the case manager and the clinical nurse specialist. The job description for the outcomes manager is given in Exhibit 5–2.

Planning for, establishing, and building an outcomes assessment program occurs in three phases (Exhibit 5–3), beginning on a small scale with one or two projects and expanding over time to a large-scale operation that becomes an invisible part of the practice model and care delivery process. Phase 1 is the start-up

Exhibit 5–2 Clinical Outcomes Manager Job Description

Emory University Hospitals
Job Description

Title: Clinical Outcomes Manager
Department: Nursing

Job Class Code: EEO Code:
FLSA Status: EEO Sub Code:
Last Revised: Pay Grade:

Summary:

Facilitates development and implementation of a variety of structured care method-ologies including clinical practice guidelines, protocols, and clinical pathways for designated patient populations; assesses and evaluates outcomes to enhance health care delivery practice patterns; collaborates in the management of designated patient populations across the continuum of care in the EUSHC; conducts outcomes re-search; ensures outcomes research utilization and implementation of clinical prac-tice improvement based on outcomes analysis and evidence-based literature.

Minimum Qualifications:

Current licensure as a Registered Nurse in the state of Georgia. A master's degree in nursing, public health, health administration, or business. Four years of clinical nurs-ing experience that includes two years' recent (within the last five years) experience in the practice specialty area. Experience in quality improvement and research pre-ferred. Computer literate.

Key Responsibilities:

1. QUALITY IMPROVEMENT: Participates and may serve as project coordina-tor for the development, implementation, and evaluation of quality improve-ment projects to improve patient outcomes. Serves as a trained facilitator for quality improvement and clinical pathway projects.

2. CLINICAL PATHWAYS: In collaboration with the interdisciplinary health care team, facilitates and directs the development and ongoing evaluation of clinical pathways for designated patient populations. Identifies variances in per-formance standards and reviews them with the appropriate interdisciplinary team members. Determines and facilitates implementation of actions to correct variances. Uses variance data and other information generated by the EUSHC resources to evaluate and refine clinical pathways and improve patient out-comes.

3. BENCHMARKING: Participates in internal and external clinical bench-marking projects.

continues

Exhibit 5–2 continued

4. DATA ANALYSIS AND MANAGEMENT: In collaboration with the Department Directors, is accountable for accurate and timely data collection for quality improvement projects, clinical pathways, and outcomes research projects. Assists in the maintenance of databases. Analyzes data from EUSHC quality improvement and outcomes research projects, current literature, and benchmark reports. Consults with statistician and/or Director as needed for data analysis and interpretation.

5. OUTCOMES RESEARCH: In collaboration with the interdisciplinary team and researchers from the Center for Clinical Evaluation Sciences, determines important outcomes to monitor and conducts outcomes research at the patient, institution, system, and community level. Consults with the biostatistician, the Director, and researchers from the Center for Clinical Evaluation Sciences to analyze and interpret outcomes data. Stays abreast of research findings in specialty practice area that have implications for outcomes improvement.

6. OUTCOMES ASSESSMENT: Accountable for the development, implementation, and evaluation of outcome assessment projects for defined populations. Uses outcomes data to revise clinical practice and improve patient outcomes. Assists in the development of a clinical practice model based on outcomes assessment.

7. COMMITTEES: Actively participates on ongoing or ad hoc committees or teams to identify and/or resolve clinical practice/patient care issues. Serves in a leadership role for clinical pathway teams.

8. RESOURCE: Serves as an expert consultant to interdisciplinary team in data collection, analysis and interpretation, and research utilization. Facilitates the translation of research findings into clinical practice. Provides expert consultation to assist other institutions in the development of outcomes management programs.

9. PROFESSIONAL DEVELOPMENT: Maintains professional accountability for clinical expertise and continuing education. Maintains skills in use of current information technologies and research methods.

10. PUBLIC RELATIONS: Promotes the organization through involvement in professional and community services.

11. Performs related responsibilities as required.

Courtesy of Emory University Hospital, Atlanta, Georgia.

phase. During this phase, planning for the program occurs. Phase 2 is the phase of technical development. Identification and building of an information services infrastructure (a systemwide support structure for outcomes management) is the focus of this phase. Phase 3 is the phase of ongoing operations. Outcomes assessment is the focus of this phase.

Exhibit 5–3 Establishing the Clinical Outcomes Assessment Program at Emory Hospitals

Phase 1 (3–6 Months)
- Clarify how purpose and goals support the vision alignment matrix
- Clarify administrative commitment to necessary resources for a successful program
- Inventory existing structure, capabilities, and related activities
- Assess needs from various constituents
- Establish key collaborative relationships with other internal and external departments
- Use consultants to assist with program design and education
- Establish an operations base
- Identify and hire necessary core staff
- Educate core staff for a shared understanding of outcomes assessment and to develop technical skills required to carry out projects
- Market program
- Begin pilot projects

↓

Phase 2 (6–9 Months)
- Enlist technical support from information services department
- Purchase a clinical pathways/outcomes database management system
- Identify key outcome indicators and appropriate measurement instruments
- Develop plan for data analysis; anticipate types of necessary analytic expertise and technology
- Develop standardized data-reporting formats
- Expand projects beyond pilot work
- Market program

↓

Phase 3 (Ongoing)
- Design, coordinate, and facilitate outcomes assessment projects
- Report outcomes data
- Establish priorities for outcomes research
- Conduct outcomes research

Courtesy of Emory University Hospital, Atlanta, Georgia.

Critical to the success of this program is administrative commitment of the necessary resources to establish, develop, and maintain the program. Sufficient financial and technical resources are necessary for a successful program. Many independent departments within an organization and organizations within a system are involved in patient care that can either positively or negatively affect outcomes. Therefore, such a program requires recognition of important customer (patients, staff, physicians, payers) relations and collaborative efforts among them over time. Because up to 80 percent of medical care expenditures are for services and procedures prescribed by physicians,[8] physician involvement is especially important. By participating in all phases of the clinical pathways and outcomes assessment programs, physicians have become more aware of the relationship between practice variation, cost, and quality. Special consideration is also being given to finding the appropriate balance between the scientific interests (outcomes research) of physicians and other researchers and the economic and quality interests (organizational improvement) of the organization as a whole.

The work of the clinical outcomes assessment department must occur comfortably within the context of the larger system. Therefore, the director of clinical outcomes assessment is a member of the clinical integration steering committee, made up of members from both hospitals, the Emory Clinic, Managed Care, Primary Care, and the Center for Clinical Evaluation Sciences. The charge of this committee is to integrate clinical pathways, practice guidelines, and strategies for improving patient satisfaction across the system and the continuum of care; to develop collaborative strategies for disease management; and to foster physician leadership in all of these endeavors.

Perhaps the most important resource allocation will come in the form of a systemwide mechanism for automating the process. Automation will allow staff from all disciplines concurrent access to clinical patient information and information on compliance with and variance from established standards. This will facilitate not only continuous quality and performance improvement but the full scope of outcomes assessment.

Rather than trying to make significant widespread changes all at once, we decided to test the redesigned clinical outcomes assessment process with several pilot projects that will demonstrate assessment of clinical, financial, and social outcomes across the multiple transitions of the continuum from home, to acute care, to outpatient care, and back home. These pilot projects will center on the following service lines with high-volume, high-cost, and/or high-risk DRG case types that span our entire continuum of care: cardiac services (cardiology and cardiovascular surgery), orthopedic services, and neurologic and neurosurgical services. Significant practice variation, established clinical pathways, and probability of success are also factors to be taken into consideration when choosing which service lines will be targeted. Each pilot project will address the seven strategies in the vision alignment matrix. A clinical outcomes manager will be appointed to coordinate each of these pilot projects.

For instance, stroke is the third leading cause of death in the United States today and is the most common cause of adult disability. Ischemic stroke is the most common type of stroke. As a strategy to address our risk associated with caring for patients with ischemic stroke, we will look at improving care and decreasing costs across the entire continuum—from asymptomatic people in the community all the way through the Primary Care Clinics, the Emory Clinic, the Emory Hospitals, the Center for Rehabilitation Medicine, Wesley Woods, and the Visiting Nurse Health Service (VNHS) encounters, and back to the community. We will evaluate appropriateness and cost-effectiveness of movement of a patient with ischemic stroke through the system to different levels of care to determine if patients are in the right setting/appropriate level for their unique needs. Because this patient population has multiple encounters for different levels of care, we need to know the total cost of care for patients with ischemic stroke. At present, our focus is on distinct episodes of care. In addition, we will add indicators related to functional status, quality of life, and sickness impact to those that we now assess to measure quality of care and outcomes, especially longitudinally.

The neuroscience service line was also chosen because there is significant practice variation in care of patients with ischemic stroke. There are two independent pathways at the two hospitals that address only the acute episode of care. Although many of these patients from both hospitals are transferred to the Center for Rehabilitation Medicine (CRM) at Emory University or the VNHS for home health care at discharge, neither the CRM nor the VNHS has a clinical pathway that dovetails with or continues the care processes established at either of the Emory Hospitals. In addition, there is no continuity between discharge from the VNHS and return to the Emory Clinic for follow-up appointments. Therefore, one clinical pathway will be developed to guide the care of the patient with ischemic stroke throughout the EUSHC, and ultimately an emphasis on prevention will be added.

CONCLUSION

The journey from quality assurance to organizational improvement at Emory Hospitals has been described. The two key initiatives are the quality improvement plan and the clinical outcomes assessment program, which complement each other in the quest for improved patient care and customer satisfaction. The motivation for change has been multifactorial. Certainly health care reform is at the forefront, but other important factors are also responsible, not the least of which is the desire by an entire organization to be truly patient centered. This is well explicated in the Emory Hospitals vision alignment matrix, in which quality, value, innovation, and service are the primary commitments to our customers.

As we roll out a comprehensive program of clinical outcomes assessment, we are also laying the groundwork for disease management. To be successful in this endeavor, we must bring together the acute and primary care constituents within our system, which have heretofore been operating almost independently. We must redefine many things, including roles, boundaries, customers, and once again outcomes. This is perhaps the greatest test of whether we can truly construct a seamless system of health care that is not episodic and disease based but is all-encompassing of the health and illness needs of the patients we care for. What we have going for us that will take us far in this quest is a shared commitment to our mission, vision, values, and behaviors. We are aiming to do it "right" this time, linking our outcomes with our processes, learning from the experiences of others, and keeping at the forefront of our thinking that this is itself a process that, like all else, is continually changing.

NOTES

1. R.C. Browne and D.A. Burnett, "The Rigors and Rewards of Clinical Evaluation in an Alliance of Academic Health Systems," *Quality Management in Health Care* 4 (1996): 1–10.

2. Harkey & Associates, Inc., *Georgia Managed Care: The Harkey Report* (Nashville, TN: 1996).

3. Executive Learning, Inc., *Focus-PDCA* (Atlanta, GA: 1996).

4. W.E. Deming, *Out of the Crisis* (Cambridge, MA: Massachusetts Institute of Technology Press, 1986).

5. Center for Case Management, Inc. (South Natick, MA: 1996).

6. Ibid.

7. Joint Commission on Accreditation of Healthcare Organizations, *A Guide To Establishing Programs for Assessing Outcomes in Clinical Settings* (Oakbrook Terrace, IL: 1994).

8. R.M. Gibson et al., "National Health Expenditures," *Health Care Financing Review* 5, no. 1 (1982): 1–31.

CHAPTER 6

Management of the Adult Patient with Acute Hepatic Failure: From Referral to Liver Transplant

Susan L. Smith and Robert D. Gordon

Chapter Objectives

1. To describe a collaborative interdisciplinary process for defining best practice and measuring outcomes in an extremely high-risk patient population.
2. To discuss the role of clinical pathways in decreasing practice variation.

As described in Chapter 5, clinical pathways at Emory Hospitals are a key component of the plan for organizational improvement. One of the first three clinical pathways developed at Emory University Hospital was the Clinical Pathway for Liver Transplantation. This case type was chosen because it is high cost and there was extremely high interest by the liver transplant team members. Subsequently, the Clinical Pathway for Liver Transplant Evaluation and the Clinical Pathway for Acute Hepatic Failure were developed. This chapter describes the project for describing best practice in the care of the adult patient with acute hepatic failure (AHF).

Acute hepatic failure is a clinical syndrome characterized by sudden and severe impairment of liver function due to fulminant and massive hepatocellular necrosis in someone with recently normal liver function. The most common causes of AHF in adults in the United States are acute viral hepatitis and drug toxicity, most notably acetaminophen toxicity. Patients with acetaminophen toxicity who are given the antidote acetylcysteine (Mucosil) have a much better prognosis than patients with other etiologies for AHF. The prognosis in the latter group is poor; the outcome was until recently almost always fatal. The advances made in liver transplantation, however, have drastically improved the outcomes for patients with

AHF.[1] At present, liver transplantation is the only life-saving therapy for this infrequent but important clinical syndrome. With proper preoperative management in the intensive care unit, survival rates as high as 92 percent after liver transplantation have been achieved.[2]

The patient with AHF is uniquely challenging to the critical care team in terms of the urgency of the clinical situation, the difficulty of the decision making required, and the need for innovative management approaches. Rapid deterioration of liver function is associated with severe multisystemic alterations: respiratory alkalosis, coagulopathy and bleeding, hypoglycemia, peripheral edema, ascites, hepatorenal syndrome, sepsis, metabolic acidosis, cardiovascular collapse, and intracranial hypertension. Progression from a fully alert and functional state to deep encephalopathic coma may occur in a period of only a few days. Neurologic demise (beginning with cerebral edema and intracranial hypertension that systematically and predictably progresses to cerebral herniation) accounts for the majority of deaths. Once interventions to maintain an acceptable cerebral perfusion pressure (CPP) become necessary, a narrow window of time (48–72 hours) exists in which the patient must receive a liver transplant to survive. Within this window of time, a coordinated treatment plan is critical.

The goal of management is to select, in a timely manner, patients who will not survive without liver transplantation and treat them to effectively prevent and minimize complications to reasonably ensure survival after transplantation. A well-organized, collaborative, multidisciplinary approach is necessary for favorable outcomes. The severity of the situation and the potential for rapid deterioration must be recognized early to avoid unnecessary delays in diagnosis and treatment. Survival of the patient depends on preservation of vital organs, particularly the brain, until liver transplantation can be performed.

CURRENT CLINICAL PRACTICE

Liver transplantation is one of several treatment options offered at Emory University Hospital (EUH) to patients with end-stage liver disease. Liver transplantation is undoubtedly, however, the most costly of these options. EUH, the only medical center in the state with a liver transplant program, is a 592-bed academic health center located in Atlanta, Georgia. Since January 1986, over 400 adult liver transplants have been performed at EUH. The major indication for transplant has been cirrhosis from a variety of diseases, but 73 patients with AHF have been referred for evaluation for emergent liver transplantation to date. All patients referred to EUH with a diagnosis of AHF are admitted to the hepatology service and cared for in a 20-bed surgical intensive care unit (ICU).

The approach to clinical management of the patient with AHF was always multidisciplinary. However, it was not well organized and lacked a scientific basis for diagnostic or treatment decisions. There was significant variation in practice among the physicians caring for these patients. Specifically, there were major differences in the approach of physicians on the medical and surgical services. Although we knew that preservation of whole-brain integrity is necessary for survival and good quality of life, controversy existed among the members of the transplant and critical care teams as to what measures are most effective in this patient population to decrease cerebral metabolism and maintain CPP in the patient with loss of cerebral autoregulation. All patients who were determined to be candidates for liver transplantation received a fiber-optic subarachnoid catheter for continuous monitoring of intracranial pressure (ICP). However, timing of catheter placement was inconsistent. In some patients the catheter was placed early, and in others it was placed late in the clinical course. Some, but not all, patients were administered a continuous infusion of pentobarbital to induce complete coma for the purpose of decreasing cerebral metabolism. Other areas of clinical practice that were inconsistent were the timing of endotracheal intubation, which is critical for airway protection in the patient progressing to a deeper level of encephalopathy, and the use of nursing and medical interventions to lower ICP and maintain CPP.

A PROPOSAL FOR CHANGE

In 1995, a data-based approach to management of the patient with AHF was developed. This project, which is consistent with the strategy "Improve patient care" described in Emory Hospitals' vision alignment matrix (refer to Chapter 5), supports the following tactics under "Improve patient care": (1) expand development and use of clinical pathways, (2) identify and use best patient care practices, and (3) measure outcomes of patient care.

A multidisciplinary protocol in the form of a clinical pathway for management of the patient with AHF was developed based on data entered into the AHF database from 1987 to 1995 and relevant research findings. The AHF database was designed to collect clinical information about patients with AHF referred to EUH. Demographic, clinical, and outcomes data were collected on each patient. The clinical nurse specialist for the liver transplant service conducted an extensive review of the literature using Medline for reports of clinical experience with and experimental studies involving management of the patient with AHF. This review of 21 centers' experiences from 1985 to 1990 was subsequently published.[3]

On the basis of what was learned from this review, a group of physicians and critical care nurses met informally to discuss the development of a clinical protocol for management of the patient with AHF. When EUH adopted clinical pathways as a core continuous quality improvement strategy, however, resources to address this problem were allocated and a formal team was appointed to develop the Clinical

Pathway for AHF. The rationale for development of this pathway included the following factors. The AHF patient population is a very high-cost and very high-risk population, and it is a subset of a larger population (liver transplantation) for which two other pathways had been developed: the Clinical Pathway for Liver Transplant Evaluation and the Clinical Pathway for Liver Transplantation.

Because outcomes reflect the interventions and actions of numerous health care providers from multiple disciplines, this project was undertaken within the context of multidisciplinary collaborative practice. The clinical pathway team consisted of over 30 members, including physicians and nurses from multiple subspecialties, respiratory therapists, pharmacists, laboratory technicians, dietitians, social workers, analysts, and administrators. The clinical nurse specialist for the liver transplant service was the team leader, and the manager of the clinical pathways department was the team facilitator. The focus of the team's work was to define precisely best practice for the care of the patient with AHF and the desired outcomes and then to describe the process that would lead to achievement of both.

The Clinical Pathway for AHF was completed on February 1, 1996. The pathway is a multidisciplinary tool that outlines in detail the clinical process of patient care and desired outcomes for the first 96 hours after admission. The first 96 hours was chosen as the time frame for this pathway because it is within this narrow window of time that assessment and treatment decisions are the most critical, and rarely does a patient with AHF survive more than 96 hours without a liver transplant. Therefore, getting the patient to transplant (given that a donor organ is available) within this time frame is the primary goal. The pathway also includes a standing physician's order set for initiation and ongoing implementation of the pathway; two supporting protocols, the Cerebral Edema Protocol and the Acetaminophen Toxicity Protocol; and a variance reporting tool (see Appendix 6–A).

PATIENT-FOCUSED DATA AND RELEVANT RESEARCH USED IN PROJECT DEVELOPMENT

Data from the AHF database and published research findings were used to develop the Clinical Pathway for AHF. Data were sought from the literature to validate continuation of or changes in existing practice as it related to care of the patient with AHF. The AHF database is an Access 2.0 database. Since January 1, 1987, 73 patients have been entered into the database, including 11 in 1995 and 9 in 1996 thus far. Of these patients, 25 have been transplanted, 20 survived without transplant (all with acetaminophen toxicity as the etiology of AHF), and 28 died before transplant could be performed (none with acetaminophen toxicity). Five of the 25 patients transplanted died during the operative admission. Therefore, the actual operative survival rate is 80 percent. However, 38 percent died before transplant could be performed. If patients with acetaminophen toxicity (the lowest risk patients in this group) are excluded, then the mortality rate in this subgroup increases to 54 percent. From these findings, we identified the need for a more effective treatment protocol. Although organ donation is a critical factor in survival, we suspected that we could improve outcomes in this group by using a better management approach. Therefore, we asked the question, "Can we design our process of care to improve outcomes not only in the subgroup that is transplanted but in the subgroup that is not?"

RELEVANT RESEARCH FINDINGS

In addition to the literature review already mentioned,[4] recent reports of center-specific experiences[5] and summary reports of management protocols[6] were reviewed. These reports validated that good outcomes are achievable and that a well-defined management protocol that focuses on interventions for whole-brain preservation is critical to survival. Because many body systems are affected and multisystem failure is common in AHF,[7] the literature describing best practice for several areas of critical care nursing and medicine was scrutinized in the development of the Clinical Pathway for AHF. Clinical evidence was specifically sought to support the use of ICP monitoring and drug-induced coma and to determine how best to manage the patient in AHF with intracranial hypertension. The literature on management of acetaminophen toxicity was also reviewed to develop the Acetaminophen Toxicity Protocol for patients with acetaminophen toxicity as the etiology of AHF.

Because patients with AHF have a global brain lesion similar to patients with severe head injuries, the literature on severe head trauma served as a starting point for the development of the Cerebral Edema Protocol. In addition, we reviewed the literature that specifically addressed care of the patient with AHF. We looked especially at recommendations regarding general management of cerebral edema,[8] intracranial hypertension,[9] and the use of barbiturate anesthesia.[10]

Nursing interventions for general management of the patient with cerebral edema and intracranial hypertension were well known to the critical care nurses caring for patients with AHF at EUH. However, two nursing interventions were clarified using research findings. The Cerebral Edema Protocol directs the team to consider elective endotracheal (ET) intubation for the patient who is in grade III or IV hepatic encephalopathy for the purpose of airway protection. Often there are minimal or no pulmonary secretions, but the ICU standard is for the patient with an ET tube to receive endotracheal suctioning every two hours. Rudy et al. recommended preoxygenation with 100 percent oxygen, limiting suctioning to only when necessary, and limiting the number of suction passes to two per procedure to minimize compromise of the cerebrovascular status in the patient with intracranial hypertension.[11] These recommendations were incorporated into the protocol. The second issue relates to patient positioning. It is common practice in cases of head-injured patients to elevate the head of the bed 30° above supine. The findings of Davenport et al. did not support this recommendation but instead advocated positioning the patient at 10° above supine.[12] However, we chose not to follow these recommendations for the following reasons. The sample size in this study was small ($N = 8$), all were in AHF from acetaminophen toxicity, and all were in grade IV hepatic encephalopathy at the time of the study. In addition, patients were studied at head-of-bed elevations of 20° and 40° but not at 30°, even though 20° was found to be therapeutic. Our clinical observations supported caring for the patient with the head of the bed elevated at 30° above supine.

Two medical issues were also in need of clarification. Mannitol (Osmitrol) has traditionally been used as a temporary measure to decrease ICP in the head injured and the patient in AHF.[13] The dose used at EUH was arbitrary and varied among physicians' preferences from a 25- to a 50-g bolus. On the basis of the recommendations of Hoofnagle et al.,[14] the dose has been changed to 0.5 to 1.0 g/kg of body weight. The second medical issue related to the use of computed tomography (CT) for diagnosis of cerebral edema and determination of the need for ICP monitoring. On the basis of the findings of Munoz et al. that the CT scan is of little value in detecting cerebral edema in the patient with AHF,[15] the CT scan is no longer used for this purpose. It is used only to rule out intracerebral hemorrhage prior to insertion of the subarachnoid catheter. The decision to institute ICP monitoring is now more appropriately based on the grade (I–IV) of hepatic encephalopathy. In addition, a costly procedure that was routinely done without evidence to support its use was deleted from the standard management protocol.

The aim of sedation for critically ill patients in general is to provide relief from anxiety and pain; the patient should be asleep but easily arousable. In the patient with AHF, the aim and the desired clinical effects are different. The major aim is to sedate the patient to the level of deep coma to protect the brain. Barbiturate coma with pentobarbital and thiopental have been used with variable success since the 1970s in an attempt to improve neurologic outcomes in head-injured patients. At EUH, this practice was extrapolated to the patient with AHF, and pentobarbital was arbitrarily chosen as the drug of use. On the basis of clinical observations, however, pentobarbital coma was found to be suboptimal, primarily because the patients took prolonged periods of time (up to four weeks) to regain consciousness after an otherwise successful transplant and discontinuation of the drug. This was presumably due to two factors: (1) the fat solubility and relatively long-acting nature of pentobarbital,[16] and (2) severely decreased liver metabolism, allowing for rapid accumulation of very high drug levels before transplant that persisted after transplant. We therefore sought an alternative drug that would not cause prolonged sedation after discontinuation. This eventually led us to the inclusion of sedation of the patient with propofol (Diprivan)[17] in the Cerebral Edema Protocol.

Propofol, an alkyphenol hypnotic, was chosen because it is short-acting, its effects are rapidly reversed after discontinuation, it is primarily metabolized in extrahepatic sites, and there are no significant alterations associated with its use in patients with liver or kidney disease.[18] The use of propofol was already described in the ICU Sedation Protocol familiar to critical care nurses and physicians at EUH, and therefore this protocol is referenced in the Cerebral Edema Protocol in the Clinical Pathway for AHF. However, because the patient is sedated to the point of deep coma, clear guidelines for critical care nursing assessment and interventions were necessary. In particular, the Glascow Coma Scale (GCS), which is the normal basis for documentation of neurologic status on the ICU flowsheet at EUH, is not suitable for monitoring sedation.[19] Therefore, the assessment parameters for determining whether the desired clinical effect of deep coma that mimics brain death is attained needed to be clarified. Guidelines for nursing assessment and interventions for the patient in deep drug-induced coma were developed from the critical care nursing literature[20] and incorporated into the Cerebral Edema Protocol.

A common language for use in documenting assessment of hepatic encephalopathy is necessary because critical treatment decisions in the Cerebral Edema Protocol are based on the grade of encephalopathy. We ruled out the use of the GCS for describing neurologic status in favor of the use of descriptive levels of hepatic encephalopathy because the GCS does not provide clear definition of levels of consciousness and is not predictive of outcome,[21] whereas the grade of encephalopathy is. We therefore developed a standardized nomenclature for describing grades of hepatic encephalopathy. This grading system is incorporated into the Clinical Pathway for AHF.

EVALUATION OF THE PROJECT

The Clinical Pathway for AHF was implemented on March 1, 1996. The desired outcomes of the clinical pathway are to determine in a timely manner the potential for survival in the patient who is a viable candidate for liver transplantation and to maintain integrity of the entire brain in the patient who is a candidate for transplant. A most important aim of this project is to understand the results of our actions and to determine if the care we provide has both immediate and long-term effectiveness. Although cost reduction was not a primary goal, it was predicted that by implementing a best clinical practice guideline, that cost would subsequently decrease.

Data collection is ongoing. Although data have been collected on the prepathway group since 1987, sufficient data from the postimplementation comparison group are not yet accumulated. The project is being evaluated in the following ways: analysis of data from the AHF database, analysis of data from the variance reports, and comparison of clinical and financial outcomes in the pathway-managed patients versus patients who were entered into the database before the clinical pathway was implemented. In addition, we are attempting to determine if there are significant relationships between the use of ICP monitoring and drug-induced coma and outcomes. The use of propofol (Diprivan) in this patient population has not been previously described. Therefore, descriptive data are being collected related to responses of patients with AHF to continuous propofol (Diprivan) infusion.

The AHF database includes information on demographics, etiology of disease, clinical status parameters that characterize an admission profile, information on whether the patient was transplanted, and ultimate outcome (survival without transplant, death without transplant, transplanted and alive, transplanted and deceased). The variance report provides information on clinical status during the 96 hours after admission and information about whether the prescribed temporal sequence of care was followed. From the variance reports, we will be able to determine if the pathway was followed, any factors that interfered with using the pathway, and the relationship of the use or nonuse of the pathway to outcomes. Financial data (cost, length of stay in the ICU and hospital) will be used to compare patients (survivors and nonsurvivors) who are managed versus those who are not according to the Clinical Pathway for Acute Hepatic Failure. AHF is not a common event. Therefore, it will be some time before there will be a large enough group of patients managed according to this pathway to make the comparisons already mentioned. However, observed benefits thus far are a heightened awareness by all members of the team of the importance of comprehensive assessment and early interventions to maintain cerebral stability and integrity in this patient population. Along these lines, variation in the temporal sequence of this process, assumed so critical to good outcomes, has decreased.

NOTES

1. S.L. Smith and M. Ciferni, "Liver Transplantation for Acute Hepatic Failure: A Review of Clinical Experience and Management," *American Journal of Critical Care* 2 (1993): 137–144.

2. W.J. Wall and P.C. Adams, "Liver Transplantation for Fulminant Hepatic Failure: North American Experience," *Liver Transplantation and Surgery* 1 (1995): 178–181.

3. Smith and Ciferni, "Liver Transplantation."

4. Ibid.

5. Wall and Adams, "Liver Transplantation"; D.F. Mirza et al., "Timing and Candidacy for Transplantation in Acute Liver Failure: The European Experience," *Liver Transplantation and Surgery* 1 (1995): 182–186.

6. J.H. Hoofnagle et al., "Fulminant Hepatic Failure: Summary of a Workshop," *Hepatology* 21 (1995): 240–252; J. Cordoba and A.T. Blei, "Cerebral Edema and Intracranial Pressure Monitoring," *Liver Transplantation and Surgery* 1 (1995): 187–193.

7. J. Pitre et al., "How Valid Is Emergency Liver Transplantation for Acute Liver Necrosis with Multi-Organ Failure?" *Liver Transplantation and Surgery* 2 (1996): 1–7.

8. Hoofnagle et al., "Fulminant Hepatic Failure"; S. Aggarwal et al., "Relationship of Cerebral Blood Flow and Cerebral Swelling to Outcome in Patients with Acute Fulminant Hepatic Failure," *Transplantation Proceedings* 23 (1991): 1978–1979; J. Canalese et al., "Controlled Trial of Dexamethasone and Mannitol for the Cerebral Oedema of Fulminant Heptic Failure," *Gut* 23 (1982): 625–629; A. Davenport et al., "Effect of Posture on Intracranial Pressure and Cerebral Perfusion Pressure in Patients with Fulminant Hepatic and Renal Failure after Acetaminophen Self-Poisoning," *Critical Care Medicine* 18 (1990): 286–289.

9. E.B. Rudy et al., "Endotracheal Suctioning in Adults with Head Injury," *Heart and Lung* 20 (1991): 667–674.

10. M.P. Mirr et al., "Nursing Management for Barbiturate Therapy in Acute Head Injuries," *Heart and Lung* 12 (1983): 52–59; M.D. Malkoff et al., "Barbiturate Coma as Salvage Therapy in Aneurysmal Subarachnoid Hemorrhage," *Journal of Neurosurgery* 80 (1994): 367; A Forbes et al., "Thiopental Infusion in the Treatment of Intracranial Hypertension Complicating Fulminant Hepatic Failure," *Hepatology* 10 (1989): 306–310.

11. Rudy et al., "Endotracheal Suctioning."

12. Davenport et al., "Effect of Posture."

13. Hoofnagle et al., "Fulminant Hepatic Failure."

14. Canalese et al., "Controlled Trial."

15. S.J. Munoz et al., "Elevation of Intracranial Pressure and Computerized Tomography of the Brain in Fulminant Hepatocellular Failure," *Hepatology* 13 (1991): 209–213.

16. Mirr et al., "Nursing Management."

17. A.M. Burns et al., "The Use of Sedative Agents in Critically Ill Patients," *Drugs* 43 (1992): 507–515; J.J. Lunn and J.S. Larson, "How Best To Provide Sedation and Analgesia for Critically Ill Patients," *Journal of Critical Illness* 7 (1992): 1090–1104; J. Mirenda and G. Broyles, "Propofol as Used for Sedation in the ICU," *Chest* 108 (1995): 539–548.

18. Lunn and Larson, "How Best."

19. Ibid.

20. Mirr et al., "Nursing Management"; M. Zellinger, "Paralytics and Sedatives in the ICU," *Current Issues in Critical Care Nursing* (1995, suppl.): 17–20.

21. M. Segatore and C. Way, "The Glasgow Coma Scale: Time for Change," *Heart and Lung* 21 (1992): 548–557.

Appendix 6–A

Clinical Pathway: Acute Hepatic Failure

	Immediate Stabilization	
	Admission: Admit to 5EICU Date: ___ / ___ / ___ Hours 0–4	**Date: ___ / ___ / ___ Hours 4–8**
Desired Outcomes	Stabilize patient's condition Determine if patient is a potential candidate for liver transplant	Continuous stabilization of patient Determine probable cause of hepatic failure Determine if patient is candidate for liver transplant
Teaching and Discharge Plans	Initial meeting with family if available	Begin evaluation for liver transplantation Continue discussions with family
Consults	Liver Transplant Service Transplant/Surgery Service for line placement Infectious Disease Service Liver Transplant Coordinator	Neurosurgery for grade III & IV encephalopathy for ICP monitoring device placement Social Services, extension 2–4185 Transplant Psychiatry
Diagnostics	CHEM 18 q 6 h; gamma GT; lacate; ceruloplasmin; ammonia; CBC with differential and platelet count, then q day; PT, PTT, then q day fibrinogen; DD dimers; factor V, VII, VIII; HIV; VDRL; anti-CMV hepatitis serology panel; HBsAg; HBeAg; anti-HBsAg; anti-HBc (IgM); HCV RNA; anti-HCV Serum osmolality Surveillance (pan) cultures; acetaminophen level; blood type and screen; liver research specimen (red-top tube) UA; urine electrolytes; urine culture; urine toxicology screen, urine screen for methadone ABGs, then PRN CXR, 12-lead EKG	CT scan of head prior to ICP monitoring device placement Bedside blood glucose monitoring q 2 h CP18 q 6 h PT, PTT, q day

121

Courtesy of Emory University Hospital, Atlanta, Georgia.

Assessments	Complete medical history and physical exam Assess Grade of encephalopathy (I–IV) Hemodynamic status Respiratory status Renal status GI status Infectious disease status Psychosocial status	Assess for potential contraindications to transplant: Psychosocial condition(s) HIV+ Malignancy Septicemia Severe systemic disease Massive intracranial hemorrhage Brain death Monitor BP (MAP), ICP, CPP (CPP = MAP – ICP) Monitor response to Cerebral Edema Protocol
Treatments	IV fluids: Line placement Arterial catheter Triple lumen catheter Indwelling urinary catheter Initiate pulse oximetry monitoring For grade III encephalopathy: Consider elective endotracheal intubation—Consult Anesthesia CCM 0700–1700, Anesthesiology 1700–0700 Consider ICP placement and monitoring Implement Cereral Edema Protocol For grade IV encephalopathy: Endotracheal intubation ICP placement and monitoring Implement Cerebral Edema Protocol	Interventions as necessary to: Decrease elevated ICP Maintain CPP > 50 mm Hg Maintain systolic BP > 100 mm Hg Maintain normothermia Maintain SpO_2 > 92% Maintain blood glucose > 70 mg/dl < 150 mg/dl Treat seizures
Nutrition	NPO	NPO
Medications NEVER GIVE NARCOTICS, HYPNOTICS, OR SEDATIVES TO PATIENT UNLESS ORDERED BY ATTENDING MD	If acetaminophen toxicity, initiate Acetaminophen Toxicity Protocol within 48 h of ingestion H_2 blocker Vit K 10 mg SC (one dose) D_{10} W infusion if blood glucose < 70 mg/dl Insulin infusion PRN blood/glucose > 150 mg/dl: 125 units reg insulin/250 1/2 NS: # ml/h = (BS – 60) × (0.03) × (2)	D_{10} W infusion if blood glucose < 70 mg/dl Insulin infusion PRN blood/glucose > 150 mg/dl: 125 units reg insulin/250 1/2 NS: # ml/h = (BS – 60) × (0.03) × (2) Propofol (Diprivan) prn per Cerebral Edema Protocol Mannitol (Osmitrol) and furosemide (Lasix) prn per Cerebral Edema Protocol Atracurium bresylate (tracrium) prn per Cerebral Edema Protocol
Documentation	Answer questions 1–7 on Variance Report	

	Continuous Stabilization Hours 8–24 Date: __/__/__	Pretransplant Hours 24–96 Date: __/__/__	Perioperative Care To OR	DESIRED OUTCOMES
Desired Outcomes	Continuous stabilization of patient Maintain CPP > 50 mm Hg	Continuous stabilization of patient Maintain CPP > 50 mm Hg		1. Determine if patient is in need of and is an acceptable candidate for liver transplant. 2. If patient is a candidate for liver transplant: a) maintain viability of brain b) transplant before irreversible brain injury occurs 3. Maintain renal function. If CPP < 40 mmHg > 2 h, patient is not a candidate for liver transplant on the basis of very poor prognosis for neurologic recovery **Begin Liver Transplant Pathway postoperatively**
Teaching and Discharge Plans	Family teaching	Family teaching		
Consults		Liver Transplant Dietitian		
Diagnostics	Bedside blood glucose monitoring q 2 h Hepatic Doppler Ultrasound	If CPP has been < 55 mm Hg for > 1 h, rule out brain death via cerebral perfusion scan before transplant CP18 CBC with platelet count PT, PTT Bedside blood glucose monitoring q 2 h		

			Intraoperative ICP monitoring
Assessments	Monitor BP (MAP), ICP, CPP (CPP = MAP − ICP) Monitor response to Cerebral Edema Protocol	Monitor BP (MAP), ICP, CPP (CPP = MAP − ICP) Monitor response to Cerebral Edema Protocol	
Treatments	Interventions as necessary to: Maintain ICP Maintain CPP > 50 mm Hg Maintain systolic BP > 100 mm Hg Maintain normothermia Maintain SpO$_2$ > 92% Maintain blood glucose > 70 mg/dl < 150 mg/dl Maintain MAP adequate to maintain CPP > 50 mm Hg Treat seizures	Interventions as necessary to: Decrease elevated ICP Maintain CPP > 50 mm Hg Maintain systolic BP > 100 mm Hg Maintain normothermia Maintain SpO$_2$ > 92% Maintain blood glucose > 70 mg/dl < 150 mg/dl Treat seizures To OR with ICP monitoring for liver transplant	
Nutrition	NPO	NPO	
Medications NEVER GIVE NARCOTICS, HYPNOTICS, OR SEDATIVES TO PATIENT UNLESS ORDERED BY ATTENDING MD	D$_{10}$ W infusion if blood glucose < 70 mg/dl Insulin infusion PRN blood/glucose > 150 mg/dl: 125 units reg insulin/250 1/2 NS: # ml/h = (BS − 60) × (0.03) × (2) Propofol (Diprivan) prn per Cerebral Edema Protocol Mannitol (Osmitrol) and furosemide (Lasix) prn per Cerebral Edema Protocol Atracurium bresylate (tracrium) prn per Cerebral Edema Protocol	D$_{10}$ W infusion if blood glucose < 70 mg/dl Insulin infusion PRN blood/glucose > 150 mg/dl: 125 units reg insulin/250 1/2 NS: # ml/h = (BS − 60) × (0.03) × (2) Propofol (Diprivan) prn per Cerebral Edema Protocol Mannitol (Osmitrol) and furosemide (Lasix) prn per Cerebral Edema Protocol Atracurium bresylate (tracrium) prn per Cerebral Edema Protocol	
Documentation	Answer question #8 on Variance Report	Consent for surgery	Answer questions 9–12 on Variance Report

CEREBRAL EDEMA PROTOCOL

The Cerebral Edema Protocol is for use in all unstable patients in an advanced hepatic coma (grade III and IV) who are candidates for liver transplantation.

1. Prior to initiation of this protocol, all patients must have an intracranial pressure (ICP) monitoring device to facilitate prompt detection and guide treatment of intracranial hypertension.
   A. ICP is monitored using a subarachnoid fiber-optic cable.

2. Prior to initiation of this protocol, all patients must be orally intubated.

3. Monitor ICP and cerebral perfusion pressure (CPP) q hour and prn. Maintain CPP > 50 mm Hg. In case of refractory intracranial hypertension, maintenance of CPP > 50 mm Hg is more important than normalization of ICP.
   A. If systolic BP < 100 mm Hg, administer dopamine HC1 (Intropin) to increase BP and CPP; if HR > 120/min or dose > 14 mcg/kg/min, begin administration of phenylephrine HCL (Neo-Synephrine) or norepinephrine bitartrate (Levophed), and wean dopamine HC1 (Intropin) as tolerated.

4. Monitor ICP intraoperatively *and* for at least 48 hours after transplant; discontinue when no longer needed to guide treatment.

5. For an ICP greater than 20 mm Hg or CPP less than 50 mm Hg that is sustained for at least 5 minutes, initiate the following measures:
   A. Position HOB at 30°.
   B. Hyperventilate prn to keep $paCO_2$ 25–30 mm Hg.
      a. Use end-tidal CO_2 monitoring for measurement of $ETCO_2$.
      b. If patient has high airway pressures and cannot be hyperventilated, adminster atracurium besylate (Tracrium) prn. The loading dose is 0.3–0.5 mg/kg over 15 min; the maintenance infusion rate is 5–15 mg/kg/min.
      c. Titrate atracurium bresylate (Tracrium) dose according to patient's response to the "Train of Four."
   C. Administer mannitol (Osmitrol) 0.5–1.0 g/kg IV over 30 minutes every 4–6 hours and repeat as needed to maintain serum osmolality < 310 mcg/dl.
      a. Draw serum osmolality 6 hours after every dose of mannitol (Osmitrol).
      b. Do not administer mannitol (Osmitrol) if serum osmolality > 310 mg/dl or patient is in oliguric renal failure.
      c. Administer furosemide (Lasix) 20 mg prn q 4 h for increased ICP when serum osmolality > 310 mg/dl *if* CVP ≥ 8 mm Hg.

    D. Avoid the following situations that will increase ICP: Valsalva maneu-
ver, neck vein compression, turning of head or neck, vasodilating agents,
fever, seizures.
      a. Consider discontinuing PEEP if CPP < 50 mg Hg.
    E. Limit endotracheal suctioning to only when absolutely necessary.
    F. Keep patient normothermic.
      a. Treat fever.
      b. Administer atracurium besylate (Tracrium) prn to prevent/stop shiv-
ering. The loading dose is 0.3–0.5 mg/kg over 15 min; the maintenance infusion rate is 5–15 mcg/kg/min. Refer to Department of
Nursing Drug Administration Guideline for atracurium besylate
(Tracrium).
    G. Treat seizures.

6. Monitor ICP during surgery and for at least 48 hours after liver transplant.

7. If the patient is unresponsive to the above measures to decrease ICP and increase CPP, consider sedation with continuous propofol (Diprivan) infusion*
unless patient is hemodynamically unstable or severe coagulopathy precludes
insertion of a subarachnoid fiber-optic catheter for monitoring ICP.
    A. Patient must have an indwelling pulmonary artery catheter.
    B. Begin a propofol (Diprivan) infusion [1,000 mcg/ml] (5–50 mcg/kg/
min).
      a. Increase propofol infusion rate by 5–10 mcg/kg/min until there is loss
of all spontaneous movement. If > 150 mcg/kg/min is required, call
the Hepatology Fellow of Attending on call.
      b. Be prepared to support BP with dopamine HC1 (Intropin), phenyl-
ephrine HCL (Neo-Synephrine), and/or norepinephrine bitartrate
(Levophed).
      c. Titrate propofol infusion to keep ICP < 20 mm Hg and CPP > 50 mm
Hg.
      d. Decrease the rate or discontinue the infusion if CPP < 50 mm Hg.

---

*Refer to protocol for "Sedation in the ICU for the Mechanically Ventilated Patient" and
the Department of Nursing Drug Administration Guideline for propofol (Diprivan).

Grading for Hepatic Encephalopathy

	Grade 1	Grade 2	Grade 3	Grade 4
Level of consciousness	Awake	Level of consciousness decreased, but opens eyes spontaneously	Patient goes to sleep but is arousable to verbal and painful stimuli; does not open eyes spontaneously	Comatose; no response to pain
Orientation	Total orientation with progression to confusion, then disorientation to time and place	Disoriented to time events; severe confusion	Complete disorientation when aroused	Comatose
Intellectual functions	Mental clouding; slowness in answering questions; impaired handwriting; subtle changes in intellectual function; psychometric test scores decrease	Amnesia for past events; psychometric test scores decrease	Inability to make computations	Comatose
Behavior	Forgetful, restless, irritable, untidy, apathetic, disobedient	Decreased inhibition, lethargic	Bizarre behavior (rage)	Comatose
Mood	Euphoria, depression, crying	Apathetic, paranoid	Apathy increased	Comatose
Neuromuscular	Muscular incoordination, tremors, yawning; insomnia	Hypoactive reflexes, asterixis, ataxia, slurred speech	Cannot cooperate, nystagmus and Babinski, clonus, decortication, decerebration, ridigity, seizures	Seizures; rigidity decreases to flaccidity; dilated pupils
EEG	Mild to moderate abnormalities	Moderate to severe abnormalities	Severe abnormalities	Severe abnormalities

ACETAMINOPHEN TOXICITY PROTOCOL

A toxic acetaminophen ingestion for an adult is defined as an acute ingestion of greater than or equal to 10 g of acetaminophen, or a chronic (daily) ingestion of greater than or equal to 3 g of acetaminophen. Acetylcysteine (Mucosil) is the antidote for toxic acetaminophen ingestion. If a toxic ingestion of acetaminophen has occurred within 24 hours, initiate this protocol.

Prior to Administration

- If possible, empty patient's stomach by lavage or inducing emesis with syrup of ipecac 30 ml.
- Obtain acetaminophen plasma level. The acetaminophen plasma level is considered toxic if it is > 10–20 mg/l at 4 hours after ingestion. An acetaminophen level $\geq$ 200 mg/l at 4 hours post ingestion is associated with hepatotoxicity. A nomogram is used to estimate the probability that plasma levels in relation to intervals post ingestion will result in hepatotoxicity.

Dosage/Administration

- Acetylcysteine (Mucosil) is available from the pharmacy in 10-ml vials. Each ml of 20% Mucosil contains 200 mg of acetylcysteine. Three ml of diluent are added to each ml of Mucosil.
- Acetylcysteine (Mucosil) is administered either orally or via an NG tube. Oral doses may be administered with soft drinks. Doses administered via an NG tube may be diluted with water. Acetylcysteine (Mucosil) CANNOT be administered intravenously.
- The dose is determined by the patient's body weight. The exact loading and maintenance doses can be determined by using the attached table.
- Administer a loading dose of 140 mg/kg.
- Four hours after administration of the loading dose, begin the maintenance dose of 70 mg/kg q 4 hours.
- Continue the maintenance dose for a total of 17 doses if the first acetaminophen level is on or above the level indicated on the nomogram.
- If the patient vomits a dose (loading or maintenance) within one hour of administration, repeat that dose and continue as above.
- If a patient is persistently unable to retain doses that are administered orally or via an NG tube, duodenal intubation is indicated.

DETERMINATION OF LOADING AND MAINTENANCE DOSES OF ACETYLCYSTEINE (MUCOSIL) 20% ACCORDING TO BODY WEIGHT

Loading Dose

Body Weight (kg)	(lb)	g of Acetylcysteine	ml of 20% Mucosil	ml of Diluent	Total ml of 5% Solution
100–109	220–240	15	75	225	300
90–99	198–219	14	70	210	280
80–89	176–196	13	65	195	260
70–79	154–174	11	55	165	220
60–69	132–152	10	50	150	200
50–59	110–130	8	40	120	160
40–49	88–108	7	35	105	140
30–39	66–86	6	30	90	120
20–29	44–64	4	20	60	80

Maintenance Dose

Body Weight (kg)	(lb)	g of Acetylcysteine	ml of 20% Mucosil	ml of Diluent	Total ml of 5% Solution
100–109	220–240	7.5	37	113	150
90–99	198–219	7.0	35	105	140
80–89	176–196	6.5	33	97	130
70–79	154–174	5.5	28	82	110
60–69	132–152	5.0	25	75	100
50–59	110–130	4.0	20	60	80
40–49	88–108	3.5	18	52	70
30–39	66–86	3.0	15	45	60
20–29	44–64	2.0	10	30	40

Thrombosed Bovine Graft Clinical Pathway: An Interdisciplinary, Community-Focused Approach to the Care of the Patient

Rebecca McKee-Waddle

Chapter Objectives

1. To describe the development of the collaborative clinical pathway process at Emory University System of Health Care.
2. To identify factors that influence the success of the clinical pathway program.

In the managed-care climate of today, hospital systems are forced to look at innovative methods of coordinating patient care. The focus on care has shifted from the hospital setting to the community setting. This can be especially challenging when dealing with high-volume patients and disease management. An example of this is the hemodialysis patient with a permanent venous access such as a bovine graft. Thrombosed bovine graft is the primary reason for hospital admission for the renal patient population at Crawford Long Hospital (CLH). It has been estimated that the average national hospitalization rate for this patient population is 1.8 per patient per year.[1] Most of their care is provided in the community dialysis clinic setting, and there are many challenges to coordinating the continuum of care.

Recently, CLH addressed the issues related to care of the patient with a bovine graft. Several system procedures were identified that impeded the flow of the patient's care. Transportation of the patient from the dialysis clinic, where thrombosed graft is identified, to the hospital for surgery for thrombectomy was often delayed. Frequently, this caused surgery to be canceled and increased the patient's length of stay. In addition, the vascular surgeons often had to wait to get the history and physical completed by the nephrologist, and this also delayed surgery. The interdisciplinary clinical pathway process was chosen as the method to address these problems.[2]

THE PLANNING PHASE

The physicians from the department of nephrology meet quarterly to discuss clinical issues. Nurses from administration, staff nurses, and dialysis nurses are part of this group. The nursing staff and physicians work well together in an environment of mutual respect. Communication is valued, and problems are usually identified and addressed in a timely manner.

In the fall of 1995, the renal unit at CLH began to look at implementation of clinical pathways. This 22-bed unit also includes a 9-bed dialysis unit. Thrombosed graft was identified as a beginning point for this process because of the very high volume (>450 cases/year) for this diagnosis-related group (DRG) case type. In addition, patients with a thrombosed graft were frequently admitted to other patient care units. Therefore, it was hoped that standardizing the care of the thrombosed graft patient via development of a clinical pathway would address this issue.[3]

The renal unit department manager appointed a planning group with representatives from both the nursing and dialysis units. Two key physicians became a part of this group, one from the Emory Clinic and one from the community setting. These physicians were very supportive of this process. They were both well respected by their colleagues, and they represented the two highest admitting physician groups for this DRG. At the initial meetings, the process and goals for this project were agreed upon. The primary goals were to identify the best practice and for all practitioners to use the new clinical pathway. The expected outcome was to define a streamlined interdisciplinary care process that began in the community setting and flowed through the system and then back to the community.

During this initial phase, necessary background information was collected, including baseline data to determine current practice and provide a picture of the average patient with a thrombosed graft at CLH. Subsequently, this profile was compared with those at other hospitals. Data regarding length of hospital stay, average charges, and number of cases were collected and benchmarked with comparable hospitals within the region and nationally. Individual physician practice was also identified. The results of this data reflected that the length of stay and charges were very competitive. However, there was significant variation in how the patient presented to the hospital system from the community dialysis center. In addition, there was no follow-up from the hospital with the patient at discharge or with the community dialysis clinic. These two factors were identified as opportunities for improvement. The data were presented to the nephrologists, who were supportive of standardizing care with a community focus. This was the "green light" to proceed with the development of a comprehensive task force to develop the pathway.

THE DEVELOPMENTAL PHASE

The initial planning group first looked at expanding its size to form the task force.[4] Although general recommendations for optimal task force size were not followed, the planners believed it was necessary to include all services to ensure a total picture of the process. Nursing representation included members from the renal, dialysis, general surgery, and ambulatory surgical units; physicians from the specialties of nephrology, vascular surgery, and anesthesia were represented; additional disciplines represented were social services, food and nutrition services, clinical resource management, and a private insurance case manager. The task force felt very strongly that community representation was necessary. The renal and dialysis units at CLH work very closely with the community dialysis clinics. Therefore, representatives from four community dialysis clinics were invited. Their insight proved to be very helpful in meeting the needs of the patient from the community perspective. The final task force consisted of 20 members.

The task force was chaired by the medical case manager. Initially, the physicians stated that their goal was to complete the planning phase in three meetings. This seemed unrealistic, considering the task. However, the physicians were very committed to the process and participated fully. Education occurred between meetings in the form of meeting minutes and the initial planning group's work with the staff and physicians on a one-to-one basis. Organization was a high priority. Meetings were very focused, always addressing specific goals and keeping to a specified time frame. Subgroups were appointed to complete tasks as needed.

It was decided early in the process to begin by developing the standing admission and postoperative order sets and to complete the process in the form of a clinical pathway. In the initial meeting, the task force flowcharted the process as it was currently in practice. Opportunities for improvement were readily identified to move the patient seamlessly through the continuum of care. The new process was flowcharted (Figure 7–1).[5]

The renal unit used a template of admission orders from a community physician group. Beginning with the template facilitated the completion of the admission and postoperative order sets within the first two meetings. The group discovered how important the physician history and discharge record is to the process. Each of the lead physicians took responsibility for these pieces—admission history and discharge record—and brought a completed version to the group. Basically, the standard forms are customized to the patient with a thrombosed graft. To decrease the amount of paperwork, documentation of discharge education was included in the physician's discharge record. The form was designed with an attached carbon

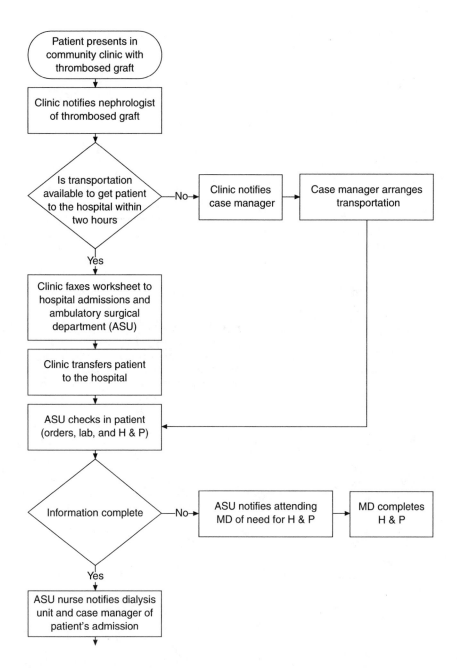

continues

Figure 7–1 continued

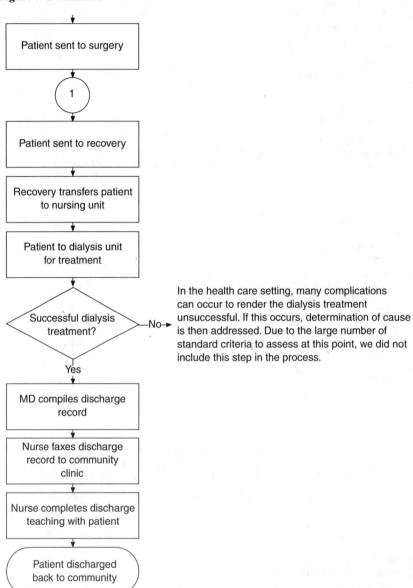

In the health care setting, many complications can occur to render the dialysis treatment unsuccessful. If this occurs, determination of cause is then addressed. Due to the large number of standard criteria to assess at this point, we did not include this step in the process.

Figure 7–1 Flowchart of Desired Thrombosed Graft Process. Courtesy of Columbia/HCA Health Care Corporation, Nashville, Tennessee.

copy that was given to the patient at discharge. A subgroup developed a draft of the pathway and brought it back to the task force for input. To complete the process, four desired clinical outcomes were selected: (1) surgery completed on admission day, (2) two-day length of hospital stay, (3) patient satisfaction measured one week postdischarge, and (4) patency of the graft one week postoperatively.

It was decided that the clinical pathway and attachments would be assembled together as a package and that the pathway would serve as an interdisciplinary documentation tool. To accomplish this, the clinical pathway documentation section was integrated into the physician progress notes. To facilitate communication and patient flow, information about when the patient is made NPO (nothing by mouth) for surgery and other pertinent medical history is faxed from the dialysis clinic to the admissions department and ambulatory surgery unit for each patient admission. This information then follows the patient to the nursing units for continuity of care. The hospital in turn faxes a copy of the discharge record to the community dialysis clinic where the patient originated to complete the circle.

The design phase took six months and included three major task force meetings and several subgroup meetings. The subgroup meetings were very helpful to accomplish problem resolution and work on nonphysician aspects of care. This approach allowed the members maximum use of meeting time, especially because several of the group members were community based. It did place a great deal of pressure on the case manager to coordinate the process and communicate progress to the rest of the task force. Written evaluations of the meetings showed that all members felt the process was organized and focused. Task force members expressed appreciation for renewal of written material before meetings so that they were prepared to make decisions at the meetings.

IMPLEMENTATION PHASE

June 1996 was chosen as the target month for implementation of the pathway (see Appendix 7–A). Because the Olympics were held in Atlanta during that time, the printers were delayed in delivering the completed documents to the hospital until August. However, this gave the case manager ample time to educate the staff and coordinate the process with the community physicians and dialysis clinics. Because patients with a thrombosed bovine graft are placed throughout the hospital, education for the staff was twofold. Initially, all nursing and clerical staff attended an inservice on the clinical pathway. During the first week of implementation, the case manager monitored these patients very carefully. She was available on all shifts to answer the staff's questions and clarify confusion regarding the process. The case manager visited each community dialysis clinic and nephrologist's office to provide them with copies of the clinical pathway and other necessary documents needed for the process and to educate them.

Initially, our major concerns were how the staff and physicians would respond to interdisciplinary documentation, which meant changing from the use of individual progress notes to one integrated tool. The physicians have responded very favorably. Placing the pathway documentation under the physician progress notes was the key.[6] This made access to documentation easy. There are no separate physician progress notes or nursing notes because they are built into the pathway. Hospital staff have had a more difficult transition with this change. Reeducation of the clerical staff was necessary. The pilot will last for three months, and then revisions will begin based upon an evaluation of clinical outcomes, and physician, staff, and patient satisfaction. The task force will meet quarterly to evaluate the process and outcomes.

CONCLUSION

We have begun our first-quarter postimplementation data collection. Follow-up phone calls regarding patient satisfaction and graft patency have yielded favorable preliminary results. Clinical pathways are a powerful method to organize and evaluate patient care with an interdisciplinary focus. Several factors, however, must be in place to ensure success. There must be support from administration, nursing, physicians, and all hospital departments involved in the care of the patient. Preparation, or "doing your homework," is the key to laying the foundation. It is important to obtain data to provide a picture of current physician practice patterns and analyze hospital processes. This helps the task force to benchmark with other facilities and identify relevant goals. Leaders must be identified early and educated to build support for the changes necessary to put best practice into place. Nurse and physician leaders who are well respected, are verbally positive, and believe in the process must be recruited. They are the champions. The role of case manager varies among different institutions. The use of an advanced-practice nurse (master's prepared) in this position can be an effective means to accomplish accountability and communication for the process. The evaluation of outcomes is research oriented. The combination of advanced clinical and research expertise is key. This person is responsible for education, communication, organization, and keeping the task force focused. In addition, an adequate, user-friendly data management system is critical.

Interdisciplinary, patient-focused care across the continuum is possible with much planning, dedication, and commitment. Although the system benefits greatly from the process, it is the patient who is the biggest winner.

NOTES

1. "Developing Clinical Pathways for Vascular Access Is a Crucial Part of Dialysis Patient Care Management, Say ANNA Nurses," *Contemporary Dialysis and Nephrology* 17, no. 6 (1996): 24, 32.

2. Center for Case Management, Inc., "The Continuum: The Walls Come Tumbling Down," *Issues and Outcomes* 1, no. 6 (1995): 11–13.

3. Center for Case Management, Inc., "Mapping Care: Pathways as a Complete Documentation System," *Issues and Outcomes* 1, no. 6 (1995): 4–5.

4. M.L. Etheredge, *Collaborative Care Nursing Case Management* (Chicago: American Hospital Association, 1989).

5. Executive Learning, Inc., *FOCUS-PDCA* (Atlanta: 1996).

6. Center for Case Management, Inc., "The Thrills and Chills of Collaboration: Interdisciplinary Teamwork," *Issues and Outcomes* 2, no. 3 (1996): 1–3.

Appendix 7–A

The Thrombosed Graft Clinical Pathway, Including Admission Orders and Record and Discharge Record

THROMBOSED GRAFT CLINICAL PATHWAY GUIDELINES

General Information

1. Physicians, RNs, LPNs, SNs, and related disciplines will document on this form.
2. The Clinical Pathway replaces the physician's progress note, the nursing care plan/standard of care, and the patient assessment for those patients who are in the Clinical Pathway Program.
3. The Clinical Pathway serves as a guide for patient care and does not replace physician's orders. Specific items on the Pathway are covered by the routine orders.
4. The Pathway will be initiated upon admission.
5. The Pathway serves as a basis for shift-to-shift/unit-to-unit report, patient care rounds, and communication with all departments involved in the care of the patient.
6. Health care disciplines caring for the patient must initial the interventions implemented. Initialing in one of the three (N, D, E) columns next to the listed activity indicates completion of the activity.
7. All initials must have signature verification.
8. Gray shaded areas indicate not applicable, or non-nursing responsibilities. Other items not applicable to the shift should be recorded by the nurse as "N/A."
9. The nurse responsible for the care of the patient will (1) complete a patient assessment at least every 8 hours, (2) write an evaluative note at the end of the shift, and (3) review and record progress toward expected patient outcomes at the directed time(s). Documentation for patients whose length of stay exceeds the Pathway shall be recorded on the Medical Pathway-Continuation form. A new continuation form should be used daily until the patient is discharged.
10. Additional documentation of patient's progress will be recorded on the Clinical Pathway Interdisciplinary Progress Notes Continuation Page.
11. The Pathway will be kept under the Case Management section of the chart.

Courtesy of Emory University Hospital, Atlanta, Georgia.

Clinical Pathway Outcomes (To be completed by the Nurse)

12. Stamp the form with the patient's identification plate.
13. Complete the first line (initiated by, date, and time).
14. Check "yes" for the completion of the outcome, and sign your name. If the patient did not complete the outcome, check "No," and give the explanation in the space provided. Date entry.

Patient Assessment

15. Indicate the date and time of assessment.
16. Complete an assessment for each shift. Check the box to indicate that the patient meets the standard. If the standard is not met, describe the variation in the space provided or in the Interdisciplinary Progress Notes.
17. Verify all signatures.

Interdisciplinary Action Plan

18. Initial completed interventions in the appropriate column.
19. Place an asterisk (*) next to interventions not completed, and explain in the Interdisciplinary Progress Notes. Variances not resolved within 12 hours must be documented on the Clinical Progress Report.
20. ◆If Risk Management protocol implemented during shift, write in time of implementation and follow protocol. Protocol includes visual check q 1 h, bed in low and locked position, call light in reach, side rails up × 4 at all times, and ID armband on patient.

Interdisciplinary Progress Notes

21. Enter date and time of note.
22. Enter notes that further detail assessments or interventions, evaluate the patient's response to interventions, or explain variations for that shift. Do not restate that which is already addressed in the Patient Assessment.

Clinical Pathway Report

23. Stamp the form with the patients' identification plate.
24. Complete that portion of the Clinical Pathway Report according to the direction for day 1 and day 2.
25. Check type of surgery in question 1.
26. If there is a variance that is not included, write it in the appropriate day.
27. Initial entry when made.
28. Check appropriate comments if needed. If "No" answer circled, please explain reason.

THROMBOSED GRAFT CLINICAL PATHWAY

Initiated by: _____   Date: ___/___/___   Time: _____   Expected LOS: 2 Days

Patient Problem	Desired Outcome at Discharge	Date Achieved/Signatures Explain all "No" Responses
1. Knowledge deficit related to revision/insertion of bovine graft	Patient/family voices understanding of surgical procedure	☐ Yes ☐ No Date achieved: ___/___/___ _____ Signature
2. Thrombosed graft	Functioning graft	☐ Yes ☐ No Date achieved: ___/___/___ _____ Signature
3. Knowledge deficit related to home care of bovine graft	Patient/family voices understanding of home care of graft	☐ Yes ☐ No Date achieved: ___/___/___ _____ Signature
Other _____	_____	☐ Yes ☐ No Date achieved: _____ _____ Signature

Interdisciplinary Action Plan — Date: ___/___/___ — Day 1

Patient Assessment

Action Plan	Initials N D E	Patient Assessment — Time: ___	Time: ___	Time: ___
Consults/Other Therapies				
Case manager				
Social services				
Clinical nutritionist				
Tests				
Check routine orders:				
STAT BCP I Notify Anesthesia STAT if K > 5.5				
STAT Hematology profile Notify physician if HCT < 20				
Differential (if ordered), PT, PTT EKG, CXR (per anesthesia guidelines)				
Treatments				
VS q 4 h				
Fluid restriction ___ cc's				
No BP/venipuncture to affected extremity and post sign over bed				
Admission weight				
Hemodialysis as ordered: adequate dialysis ☐ Yes ☐ No (if no, see Dialysis Record)				
Medications				
Per routine orders				
Insert INT				
Nutrition				
Diet: Preop NPO Postop per diet order				
Circle amount consumed:				
Breakfast: All 3/4 1/2 1/4 0 NPO				
Lunch: All 3/4 1/2 1/4 0 NPO				
Dinner: All 3/4 1/2 1/4 0 NPO				
Activity/Safety				
Ad lib				
Other				

Patient Assessment (each Time column):

Neurological—Standard: Alert, oriented to person, place, and time.
☐ Meets standard

Respiratory—Standard: Respirations regular and unlabored. Lungs clear.
☐ Meets standard

Cardiovascular—Standard: Regular rate.
☐ Meets standard   Edema (describe)___

Functioning Graft   ☐ Yes ☐ No

Gastrointestinal—Standard: Abdomen soft, flat with positive BS.
☐ Meets standard   BM ☐ Yes ☐ No

Genitourinary
☐ Voiding
☐ Anuric

Activity/ Safety *(continued)*	♦ *Risk Management protocol* ☐ Yes ☐ No Implemented @ ___ Visually checked q 2 h ♦ Bed in low position and locked Call light in reach Side rails up × 2 ♦ ID armband on patient	**Skin**—Standard: Warm, dry, intact. ☐ Meets standard **Level of Comfort** 0 = no pain, 10 = worst pain Level ___ Controlled with analgesics? ☐ Yes ☐ No (circle route) PO/IM/IV—Comment ___	**Skin**—Standard: Warm, dry, intact. ☐ Meets standard **Level of Comfort** 0 = no pain, 10 = worst pain Level ___ Controlled with analgesics? ☐ Yes ☐ No (circle route) PO/IM/IV—Comment ___	**Skin**—Standard: Warm, dry, intact. ☐ Meets standard **Level of Comfort** 0 = no pain, 10 = worst pain Level ___ Controlled with analgesics? ☐ Yes ☐ No (circle route) PO/IM/IV—Comment ___
Teaching/ Discharge Planning	Admitting nurse to assess DC needs and order social services consult on computer if necessary Social services consult ☐ Yes ☐ No Admitting nurse to assess need for preop videos and teaching materials Videos ☐ Yes ☐ No Teaching material ☐ Yes ☐ No			
Documentation of Outcome(s)	Complete Preoperative documentation and Day of Surgery documentation on Clinical Pathway Report	**IV Therapy**—Standard: No redness, swelling, or tenderness ☐ Meets standard Site ___ Comment/IV changes ___	**IV Therapy**—Standard: No redness, swelling, or tenderness ☐ Meets standard Site ___ Comment/IV changes ___	**IV Therapy**—Standard: No redness, swelling, or tenderness ☐ Meets standard Site ___ Comment/IV changes ___

● Document any variation from Standard in Interdisciplinary Progress Notes.
♦ Reflects changes if Risk Management protocol implemented.

Nurses—do not document in gray shaded areas

Initials/Signature ___ Initials/Signature ___ Initials/Signature ___ Initials/Signature ___

Day 1

Date/Time	Interdisciplinary Progress Notes

Date																			
Time		0001	0400	0800	1200	1600	2000	0001	0400	0800	1200	1600	2000	0001	0400	0800	1200	1600	2000
F	C																		
104°	40°																		
102.2°	39°																		
100.4°	38°																		
Temp. 98.6°	37°																		
96.8°	36°																		
Pulse																			
Respiration																			
Blood Pressure																			
Weight (kg)																			

Date									
Shifts	11–7	7–3	3–11	11–7	7–3	3–11	11–7	7–3	3–11
I Parenteral									
N Blood									
T									
A									
K **8-Hr. Total**									
E **24-Hr. Total**									

Date									
Shifts	11–7	7–3	3–11	11–7	7–3	3–11	11–7	7–3	3–11
O GI Suction									
U Emesis									
T									
P Stool									
U **8-Hr. Total**									
T **24-Hr. Total**									

THROMBOSED GRAFT CLINICAL PATHWAY REPORT

Answer the questions in the left column by circling "Yes" or "No" in the center column or filling in the blank. If you answer "No" to any question, check the number of the reason(s) in the right column or fill in the blank as indicated. If the goal is accomplished before the respective day, your answer is still "No," and the reason will be "Other: accomplished early." N/A = not applicable.

	Initials	Comments
Day of Surgery 1. Indicate type of surgery: ❑ Thrombectomy ❑ Patch ❑ Interposition ❑ New graft ❑ Other: _____		
2. Was the surgery completed on admission day?	Yes/No	If No, please check reason: ❑ Patient required dialysis, reason _____ ❑ Patient hyperkalemic ❑ Patient in fluid overload ❑ Patient ate prior to surgery ❑ Transportation problem in getting from clinic/home to hospital ❑ Other _____
Upon Discharge 3. Did the patient stay on the pathway throughout the hospitalization?	Yes/No	If no, please describe reason: _____ _____ _____
4. Was the patient's length of stay 2 days or less?	Yes/No	If no, please describe reason: _____ _____ _____

Initials/Signature   Initials/Signature   Initials/Signature

_____/_____   _____/_____   _____/_____

_____/_____   _____/_____   _____/_____

THROMBOSED GRAFT ADMISSION ORDERS

Date:____/____/____ Time:_____ Allergies: ❑ NKA _____

1. Initiate Thrombosed Graft Clinical Pathway.

2. Obtain the following:
   - **Stat BCP I and hematology profile.**
     Notify Anesthesia STAT if K > 5.5
     If surgery cancelled, notify attending physician for order modification.
   - PTT
   - PT
   - CXR and EKG (As per Anesthesiology guidelines)
   - Other Lab(s) _____

3. Notify of patient's arrival:
   - Attending physician (if H&P needed)
   - Dialysis unit
   - Case manager

4. Request old chart to the floor ASAP.

5. Vital signs q 4 h.
   Notify attending physician if systolic BP > 160 or diastolic BP > 95

6. Glucose monitoring: ❑ No ❑ Yes (frequency) _____

7. Diet: Preop NPO
           Postop _____ g protein   _____ g Na   _____ g K
           _____ mg PO$_4$ _____ Cal ADA

8. Dialysis order: Date next treatment ____/____/____ Dialyzer type _____
                    Time treatment_____ Dialysate solution_____ UF volume ___

9. Fax copy of Thrombosed Graft Discharge Record to patient's community dialysis
   clinic upon discharge from hospital.

10. PRN medications:
    - ❑ Benadryl 25 mg po or IM q 4 h prn itching
    - ❑ Phenergan 25 mg po or IM q 4–6 h prn nausea/vomiting
    - ❑ Tylenol 650 mg po q 4 h prn headache
    - ❑ Sorbitol 70% 30 ml po q 12 h prn constipation
    - ❑ Imodium 1–2 tabs po q 4–6 h prn diarrhea

11. Scheduled medications:

_____

_____

_____

_____

_____

Physician Signature

A-V GRAFT THROMBOSIS ADMISSION RECORD

Date: _____ / _____ / _____   Time: _____

Reason for admission: _____

Outpatient dialysis clinic: _____

Dialysis schedule: MWF   TTS   Last dialysis: _____ / _____ / _____

Dialysis prescription: Type of dialyzer _____   Blood flow _____   Time _____

Dialysate solution _____   Target weight _____ kg

Etiology of renal disease: _____

Past history (including social, family, and psychosocial): _____

_____

_____

_____

_____

Review of Systems:

GI _____   Cardiovascular _____

GU _____   Pulmonary _____

GYN _____   Neurological _____

ENT _____   Musculoskeletal _____

CURRENT MEDS:

_____

_____

_____

_____

_____

_____

_____

_____

ALLERGIES:

_____

_____

_____

_____

Physical Examination: Wt _____ kg BP _____/_____ T _____ P _____ R _____ Blood Glucose _____

HEENT _____ Extremities _____

Heart _____ Skin _____

Lungs _____ Breasts _____

Abdomen _____ Graft _____

Neuro _____

EKG: _____ X-ray: _____

Lab: *Please check one* ☐ Admission ☐ Clinic/office Date _____/_____/_____

BUN/Creat. _____/_____ Na _____ K _____ Cl _____ HCO$_2$ _____ HCT _____

WBC _____ Glucose _____ Platelets _____ PT _____ PTT _____

Problems:　1 _____ 3 _____

　　　　　2 _____ 4 _____

Plans: _____ Physician's Signature _____

THROMBOSED GRAFT ROUTINE POSTOP ORDERS

Date:____/____/____ Time:_____

1. Procedure ❑ Thrombectomy ❑ Patch ❑ Interposition ❑ New Graft
   ❑ Other _____

2. ❑ May use graft
   ❑ Other access_____
   ❑ Stat X-ray to confirm placement as indicated
      ❑ Placement verified by _____
      ❑ Radiology needs to read X-ray

3. Heparin to be given in dialysis (refer to Hemodialysis Implementation Record)
      ❑ none
      ❑ minimal
      ❑ routine

4. Postop VS (q 1 h $\times$ 2, then q 4 h)

5. Resume admission orders and diet

6. Medication

   • Resume admission medication orders

   • Discontinue IV fluids

      ❑ Convert to INT

      ❑ Discontinue INT

   • Pain medication

      ❑ Darvocet N 100 mg po q 3 h prn pain

      ❑ Percocet 1 tab po q 3 h prn pain

      ❑ Other _____

7. Other

_____

_____

_____

_____

_____

_____
Physician Signature

THROMBOSED GRAFT DISCHARGE RECORD

Date: ___/___/___ Time: ___

Additional preprinted instructions given—copy attached ❑

Diet ❑ No restrictions

___ g protein ___ g Na ___ g K

___ Cal ADA ___ mg PO₄

Activity ❑ Progress as tolerated

❑ Other ___

Communication

Follow-up appointment:

❑ Call physician office

Dialysis Center ___

Next treatment date ___/___/___

Call in emergency: ❑ Physician @ ___

❑ Other ___

Discharge to: ❑ Home self-care

❑ Skilled nursing facility (SNF)

❑ Another type of institution

❑ Another acute care hospital

❑ Intermediate care facility (ICF)

❑ Home health care

Medications ❑ Unchanged ❑ May Go

___

___

___

___

___

___

Other Care Staples removed date ___/___/___

• Notify physician immediately:

If incision becomes reddened, swollen, or any drainage.

If thrill is absent from graft.

___

___

❑ Left against medical advice

❑ Expired

Medical Treatment/Operative Technique/Procedure/Findings ___

___

___

___

Please check one:

☐ **Thrombectomy**   Date ____/____/____ Location _____ Surgeon _____

    Cannulation Date ____/____/____

☐ **New graft**   Date ____/____/____ Location _____ Surgeon _____

    Cannulation Date ____/____/____

☐ **Temporary catheter**   Date ____/____/____ Location _____ Surgeon _____

Hospital course/complications: _____

_____

_____

_____

Discharge Diagnosis: _____

Patient condition on discharge: _____

Physician signature: _____

Transcribed by: _____   Date ____/____/____   Time _____

CHAPTER 8

Clinical Resource Management at the University of Texas Medical Branch at Galveston

Jana S. Stonestreet, Mary D. Naehring, Robin S. O'Toole, and C. Joan Richardson

---

Chapter Objectives

1. To describe the evolution of clinical resource management (CRM) at the University of Texas Medical Branch at Galveston (UTMB).
2. To highlight departmental and institutionwide examples of clinical resource management at UTMB.
3. To describe the implementation of an institutional CRM umbrella, including the establishment of the department of clinical resource management.
4. To discuss the future of clinical resource management at UTMB.

The purpose of this chapter is to describe the development and evolution of clinical resource management (CRM) at the University of Texas Medical Branch at Galveston (UTMB). Early CRM efforts at UTMB, as in many other health care organizations, were often initiated within individual departments. Several of these departmental initiatives are presented in this chapter, including initiatives from the departments of internal medicine, social work, and nursing case management. Additionally, one of the earlier institutionwide efforts, the cost reduction task force, is presented. The evolution of CRM to an institutionwide umbrella was primarily facilitated by the creation and establishment of the clinical resource management department. This evolution and the future direction of CRM at UTMB are also addressed.

THE SETTING

UTMB has grown from its beginnings in 1891 as Texas's first medical school to an academic health science center. The 91-acre core campus includes four schools, two institutes for advanced study, numerous research facilities, a network of hospitals totaling 906 beds that provide a full range of primary and specialized medical care, 39 campus-based outpatient clinics, and a network of 105 outreach clinics located from the Lower Rio Grande Valley to far east Texas.

UTMB is a historical provider of care to unsponsored patients, providing $270 million of charity care annually. Traditionally, the cost of unsponsored care has been largely subsidized by margins generated by insured patients. The demands of the evolving marketplace have hindered the ability of hospitals to generate significant margins on insured patients to cover the cost of the growing unsponsored population. At UTMB, capitated contracts now account for 25 percent of total admissions annually.

CLINICAL RESOURCE MANAGEMENT

The decreasing margins related to changes in reimbursement and increasing competition for managed-care contracts helped focus the institution's leadership on establishing the strategic imperative of decreasing costs while improving service and quality. The management of clinical resources was understood to be essential to the achievement of this goal. Initially at UTMB, CRM was simply defined as reducing cycle times and eliminating unnecessary or ineffectual steps or resources.

Later, the definition of CRM adopted institutionally was that given by Berwick in 1995: the elimination of waste, defined to include processing and routing time, overproduction, labor, space, energy, scrap and materials, waiting, complexity, failures, and simply overlooking opportunities.[1] Integration of this broadened concept into all of our CRM efforts has helped this organization find additional opportunities for management of clinical resources and has provided us with many more opportunities to achieve success in meeting our goals.

EARLY DEPARTMENTAL CRM INITIATIVES

Internal Medicine Department: Quality-of-Stay Initiative

Early CRM initiatives occurred without the support of an institutional infrastructure and were most often driven by the vision of one consistent sponsor. The chair of the department of internal medicine provided the impetus and sustained leadership for one of the earliest initiatives that began in 1992. With continuous high demand for inpatient services and bed occupancies consistently exceeding 95 percent, the pressure was on to increase capacity and improve service while decreasing costs.

Presentations by outside quality management experts were provided as a foundation for this initiative, and a steering committee was formed. The broad membership of this committee (Exhibit 8–1) reflected the committee's strategic purpose: a forum for clinical, administrative, and support services to solve common problems and achieve common goals for internal medicine patients.

Length of stay was targeted by the steering committee as the initial focus of this committee. This focus included decreasing the total number of hospital days and earlier discharge on the last day of hospitalization. Reducing length of stay decreased total costs per admission and, just as important in this case, increased bed availability or capacity. Earlier discharge of the patient on the last day of hospitalization also resulted in improved service by preventing delays for the admitted and discharged patient and eliminated the stockpiling of admissions for simultaneous deployment to a patient care unit.

As a first step, problem statements were developed by the committee (Exhibit 8–2). Data were collected as identified in Exhibit 8–3 and then analyzed. Plans were then developed and implemented. Some of the plans initiated were

- Preformatting the admission notes to prompt the physician to document and communicate a more comprehensive plan to the entire team at the time of admission. This included documenting expected length of stay and anticipated ancillary service needs
- Clarifying and communicating the roles and responsibilities of all of the team members for achieving early discharge and decreasing length of stay

---

Exhibit 8–1 Quality-of-Stay Initiative: Membership of Steering Committee

• Physicians (faculty and residents)	• Social Work
• Nurses	• Pharmacy
• Admitting	• Management Engineering
• Nursing Case Management	• Environmental Services
• Food and Nutrition	• Patient Financial Services
• Radiology	• Utilization Review
• Pulmonary Care	• Quality Management
• Transportation	• Hospital Information Services
• Rehabilitation Services	• Clinic Administration
• Medical Records	• Clinical Laboratory

Courtesy of University of Texas Medical Branch at Galveston, Galveston, Texas.

Exhibit 8–2 Quality-of-Stay Initiative: Problem Statements

Discharge Planning

Internal Medicine's inpatient discharge planning system currently lacks the structure to consistently discharge patients in an effective manner. The lack of structure within the Medicine Service discharge planning system allows discharge planning to go unnoticed or to be addressed too close to discharge. Postdischarge planning needs are also not consistently met.

Ward Operations

Work rounds are not structured to provide

- timely patient care decisions and communication of care plans
- consistent methods of making patient care decisions, communicating plans of care, and following up on patient care issues
- goals and objectives that are clearly understood by all patient care providers
- the right people and resources at the right time to develop and execute a patient care plan

Courtesy of University of Texas Medical Branch at Galveston, Galveston, Texas.

- Standardizing rounding practices to improve efficiency and to permit the team's achievement of individual role responsibilities
- Providing feedback to individuals and the patient care teams. Weekly team feedback was perceived to be a major factor in compliance with consistently achieving earlier discharge times. Figure 8–1 provides an example of the feedback graphs used to document outcomes related to discharges before 1 PM. These

---

Exhibit 8–3 Quality-of-Stay Initiative: Data Collection

- Patient care team survey regarding goals, objectives, teamwork, roles, and responsibilities
- Chart reviews (100) of the nursing admissions assessment, resident admission note, consults, and plan of care
- Observation of work rounds (1 month), including participation, starting time, and interdisciplinary involvement
- Readmissions within 30 days
- Emergency department visits within 72 hours of discharge
- Patient compliance with discharge order

Courtesy of University of Texas Medical Branch at Galveston, Galveston, Texas.

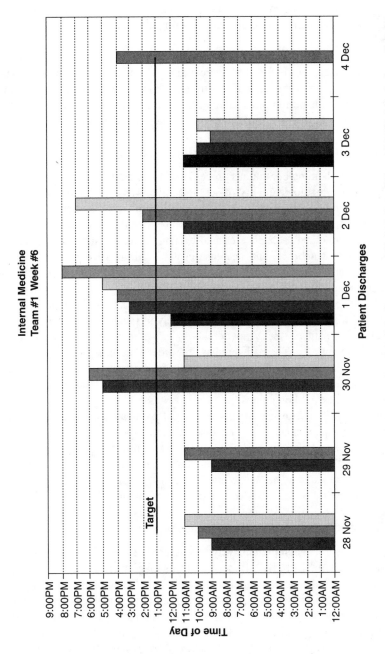

Figure 8–1 Quality-of-Stay Initiative: Discharges by Time of Day. Courtesy of University of Texas Medical Branch at Galveston, Galveston, Texas.

graphs, shared weekly with each medicine team, display the discharge time for each patient on their service discharged during the previous week

The outcomes achieved through this initiative were substantial and sustained. For example, discharges before 1 PM increased by 31 percent over two years to 66 percent. Total length of stay cannot be attributed to any one factor or intervention. However, during the period of this initiative, the internal medicine length of stay decreased from a high average of 9.8 days in 1992 to 6.6 days in 1996.

Social Work Department: Functional Critical Pathways

A discharge-planning continuous process improvement (CPI) team, emanating from the internal medicine quality-of-stay initiative, was concerned with the limited direction and coordination provided to health care team members for the discharge-planning process. Critical pathways were identified as one tool used to communicate timelines, sequence critical events, decrease variation in practice, improve patient outcomes, and decrease costs. Traditionally, these pathways, sometimes referred to as *clinical pathways* or *practice guidelines,* are focused on a particular diagnosis or diagnosis-related group (DRG).

The discharge-planning CPI team, through the leadership of the department of social work, worked to develop a critical pathway to focus on the discharge process itself.[2] This pathway (see Appendix 8–A) uses a timeline from preadmission through outpatient care. The pathway has eight identified critical dimensions for assessment, intervention, and evaluation: functional status, social status, financial status, education and cultural factors, health education status, transportation status, follow-up care, and outcomes.

Outcomes attributed to use of this functional pathway include a heightened awareness by the patient care team that discharge is a process rather than an event, improved patient satisfaction at time of discharge, improved documentation, and decreased lengths of stay. The use of a functional pathway such as the Discharge Planning Critical Pathway has been found to be very helpful in focusing attention on critical processes or functions common to many patients.

Nursing Service: Redesign for Case Management

The nursing service comprehensively restructured its support and management positions in the winter of 1992. Redesign of this magnitude was a response to a complex set of immediate and anticipated challenges. Comprehensive changes in the health care environment with rapid movement toward managed care figured most prominently. Increased coordination of services was anticipated to be required by the more complex, chronically ill, and aging population. Demand for shorter hospital stays requires a coordinated, efficient plan of care, executed by the entire health care team in a timely manner. It was clear that the changing health care environment would require new and different support structures within nursing and the entire health care team.

Case management was designed to help patients achieve their optimum wellness and autonomy through advocacy, communication, collaboration, education, facilitation, and identification of service resources. Nurse case manager positions were dedicated. A geographical or unit-based structure was initially established. This evolved to a population-based program in which the goal was to provide comprehensive management of specific high-risk patient populations. This included following patients throughout the entire episode of illness to enhance continuity of care and ensure follow-up after discharge with available community resources.

The nursing case management program contributed significantly to improved outcomes. Two case studies are presented in Chapters 9 and 10 detailing specific outcomes with capitated-contract case management and pediatric asthma. These include significantly improved quality, service, and cost outcomes.

From a more global perspective, the value of this early nursing service departmental initiative was in preparing the foundation needed for the comprehensive, institutional CRM initiative. The presence of certain foundational pieces, such as the early critical pathways, as well as the case managers themselves, was important from the perspective that the organization was not starting its initiative at the beginning.

EARLY INSTITUTIONAL CRM INITIATIVES

Supply Cost Reduction Task Forces

The need for institutionwide CRM was at last beginning to be endorsed by the hospital and medical staff leadership. In late 1994, the hospital, in collaboration with the practice plan and the medical staff executive committee, undertook a collaborative venture focused on supply cost reduction within the hospital. Following detailed review of the high-cost supplies used within the hospital, 12 different task forces were convened to study opportunities for reduction in a number of supply costs. The task forces are listed in Exhibit 8–4.

Each task force was composed of physicians, nurses, department managers, and administrators who worked in that particular area and was cochaired by a physician and a hospital administrator. Each task force was provided detailed information concerning all supplies, volumes consumed, and costs. It was responsible for analyzing the data related to its particular area and then developing and implementing an action plan that would result in either cost reduction or cost avoidance. A system for tracking projected and actual cost savings was developed with monthly reporting. Cost savings over a prespecified amount would be shared equally by the hospital and the practice plan.

Exhibit 8–4 Supply Cost Reduction: Cost Reduction Task Forces

• Endoscopic Surgery	• Orthopedic Supplies and Implants
• Catheters and Guidewires	• Pharmaco-Anesthesia
• Labor and Delivery	• Pharmacy
• Laboratory Reagents and Maintenance Contracts	• Respiratory Therapy
	• Unit Stock Supplies
• Intensive Care Units	• X-Ray Contrast Media, Film, and
• OR/Sutures, Instruments, Drapes, and Gowns	Maintenance Contracts

Courtesy of University of Texas Medical Branch at Galveston, Galveston, Texas.

In the first two years of operation, the supply cost reduction initiative has had remarkable success, with annual savings of about $4 million. The teams realizing the greatest cost reductions were the pharmacy and the operating room cost reduction task forces.

After several years of dedicated focus on managing our clinical resources, it became apparent that greater efficiency and cost-effectiveness were needed. The institutional leadership then sought to achieve the next level in CRM through the implementation of an institutional infrastructure of support.

INTRODUCTION OF THE DEPARTMENT OF CLINICAL RESOURCE MANAGEMENT

Movement to the next level provided the first coordinated opportunity for medical staff leadership to participate fully with the hospital's senior administrative leadership. In partnership, a renewed commitment was made to improve cost, service, and quality outcomes. This step required the development of a department of CRM as a base for this initiative and acquisition of an institutionwide database for internal and external benchmarking of resource consumption and patient outcomes data.

Determine Departmental Objectives

To have the opportunity to be successful, the new department's mission, goals, and objectives had to be clearly delineated within the context of the larger organization. The initial objectives of this department included providing accurate, timely, and routinely generated reports and analysis that would enable the institutional administrative and physician leadership to

- identify variations in practice patterns and outcomes through review of severity-indexed and disease-staged patient charges and outcomes data
- prioritize and develop or amend existing multidisciplinary clinical pathway guidelines
- provide performance feedback to physician groups and individuals, including comparative data for physician credentialing
- facilitate identification of opportunities to improve services
- facilitate collaboration among all disciplines and departments involved in moving a patient along the continuum of care
- review comparison data from other hospitals, managed-care markets, and state data banks prior to possible release in a public forum
- provide data as an initial step toward disease management across the continuum of care

Organizational Structure and Resource Commitment

Appropriate organizational placement is important to the success of any department or initiative. The leadership's commitment is communicated through the reporting and placement decisions made. For UTMB, this meant that medical leadership was critical. A direct reporting relationship was established with the medical director for clinical affairs. This physician position, reporting to the vice president for clinical affairs, is the most senior hospital position held by a physician.

A strong relationship with the institutional continuous process improvement/ quality management (CPI/QM) department was also believed to be critical. CPI tools and methods are most often used in achieving CRM outcomes. Also, CRM and CPI/QM require many of the same dedicated institutional resources. CRM was therefore positioned within the department of CPI/QM.

Dedication of human resources is also essential to the success of any project. In this era of dwindling total resources, these positions are most likely to be redirected from other parts of the organization. At UTMB, two senior nurses were hired to direct the initiatives within the inpatient and outpatient settings. A third nurse was hired as a data analyst to initially identify and evaluate the data for significant clinical variance opportunities. A secretary and data entry operator completed the personnel resources needed. The need for a larger staff was reduced through the shared resources within CPI/QM.

In addition to personnel, the acquisition of comprehensive, severity-adjusted data systems was key to the successful operation of the CRM department. At present, there are three systems in use. They provide inpatient information, are severity adjusted, and permit physician-specific analysis down to detailed usage of ancillary resources. The data systems provide DRG-based data on charges, length of stay, complications, mortality, and expected values from other state or regions that can be used as a basis of comparison.

Clinical Pathway Guidelines

The early data obtained from these systems helped to identify opportunities and drive the initial direction of the department. Initial CRM data analysis helped prioritize the focus of clinical pathway guideline (CPG) development. The priorities were first identified by objective volume and total dollar opportunity data. Equally important, however, was perceived physician interest in changing practice patterns of selected diagnoses or DRGs and a subjective assessment of the opportunity for success. These factors helped drive the prioritization of CPG development.

Using the above criteria, CPGs have been and will continue to be developed collaboratively by physicians, nurses, and other health professionals who share responsibility for the care of patients with certain diagnoses. Each CPG is ultimately reviewed and approved by the hospital quality of care committee. So that the CPGs are readily accessible, they have been placed on the UTMB website, and this is easily accessed via computer from every patient care area in the institution. There was general agreement concerning the need for a disclaimer statement for each CPG that conveyed the intent of the CPG to serve as a guideline for care and stated that whenever the condition of the patient warranted, treatment decisions had to be dictated by the skill and judgment of the health care professional.

CRM GRAND ROUNDS

CRM grand rounds were established to review the CPGs produced by the physician-led teams after they were approved by the executive committee of the practice plan. Grand rounds were facilitated by the CRM director with data provided by the clinical analyst. Key players represented included physicians, senior hospital administration, nursing case management, nursing service, social work, laboratory services, rehabilitation, home health, clinics, admitting, emergency services, health care financial management, day surgery, CRM, and CPI/QM.

Interdisciplinary communication and a common focus are prerequisites to success. Even with appropriate organizational placement and leadership, interest and participation must be continuously cultivated and nurtured. Scheduling when key participants are available is imperative. CRM grand rounds provided an excellent forum for interdisciplinary communication and were also a wonderful place to celebrate progress and achievements. This kind of forum is essential to sustain the interest, enthusiasm, and a high profile for this strategic objective.

THE FUTURE OF CRM AT UTMB

The process of optimally managing clinical resources remains a moving target. This is probably a phenomenon of increased awareness and knowledge. The more that is learned about eliminating waste in the delivery of health care, the more waste is found.

Efforts to streamline our internal CRM processes will continue. The integration of our currently loosely affiliated departments will be a logical progression of the structure of CRM. For example, recently most of the utilization review function was integrated into the role responsibilities of the case managers. This permitted the elimination of a separate department and at least one intradepartmental barrier. The elimination of redundancy and improved communication will be the major improved process outcomes. These organizational changes are just beginning.

The ongoing challenge will be to awaken and mobilize the entire organization to the imperative that every provider must become cost-effective in delivering high-quality, highly service-oriented health care. Physician and administrative leaders will need to improve their ability to focus the organization effectively on the target to achieve the desired outcomes. Continuous measurement of outcomes, collaboration, and coordination will be essential to success. The major key to success, however, will be in the leadership's sustained, visible focus on clinical resource management.

NOTES

1. D.M. Berwick, "Run to Space: Change Concepts for Health Care Systems," *Plenary Address to the Institute for Healthcare Improvement's Seventh Annual National Forum on Quality Improvement in Health Care,* Orlando, FL, 6 December 1995.
2. M. Huff, "Critical Paths for Critical Functions? An Evolving Discharge Planning Pathway," *Continuum: An Interdisciplinary Journal on Continuity of Care* 15, no. 6 (1995): 1–2, 8.

Appendix 8–A

Discharge Planning Generic Critical Pathway

Resident: _____

Case Manager: _____ (signature) _____ (initials)

Estimate LOS: _____

DRG: _____

Attending: _____

Admitting Nurse: _____ (signature) _____ (initials)

Social Worker: _____ (signature) _____ (initials)

	Preadmission (any assessments scheduled for day 1 should be done at preadmission visit)	**Day 1**—at admission. Determine tentative discharge date	**Day 2**
Functional Status 1) ADL status 2) Equipment needs 3) Cognitive status, esp. capacity for consent/ability to understand and participate in care planning		**Admitting Nurse** Assess 1—if not ADL independent, then PT and OT consults; if oxygen dependent, then PCS consult Assess 3—if not able to participate in care planning and no family available, then SW consult; consider psych consult	**Nurse Case Manager or Social Worker** Review consultations Assess 2—if equipment needed, then SW consult

Social Status
1) Living site
  a) accessibility
  b) utilities/phone
2) Living situation
  a) caregiver availability
  b) caregiver functional/educational status
  c) caregiver capacity to meet patient's care needs
3) Availability of resources in local community to meet patient's anticipated care needs
	Clinic Nurse
	Assess 2—if day surgery, then is companion available
		Admitting Nurse
		Assess 1—if homeless, no utilities, or admitted from a nursing home, then SW consult; if access issues, OT consult
		
		Assess 2—if admitted due to caregiver's inability to provide adequate or continuing care, then SW consult, consider family conference
		
		Assess 3—if needs add. community resources, then SW consult
			Nurse Case Manager or Social Worker
			Review consultations
			
			Identify discharge site if subacute/SNF/nursing home or rehab SW consult
			
			If managed care and placement, contact insurance case manager re: potential discharge site and contractual requirements/providers.

Courtesy of University of Texas Medical Branch at Galveston, Galveston, Texas.

	Preadmission (any assessments scheduled for day 1 should be done at preadmission visit)	Day 1—at admission Determine tentative discharge date	Day 2

Financial Status
1) Ability to meet basic needs (housing, food, etc.)
2) Ability to meet medical needs
  a) equipment
  b) medications
  c) supplies
  d) daily care
		Admitting Nurse
		Assess 1—if unable to meet basic needs, SW consult
			Nurse Case Manager or Social Worker
			Assess 2—if services needed and no funding sources, SW consult for equipment, medications, and supplies; if assistance with daily care needed, SW consult for community referrals

Educational/Cultural Factors 1) Literacy 2) Language factors 3) Cultural factors 4) Spiritual issues		**Admitting Nurse** Assess all—if translator needed, call patient services; if cultural factors impacting care and TX, then SW consult; if spiritual issues, then pastoral care consult; if literacy or language issues, then adjust educational plan and locate culturally focused educational materials	**Nurse Case Manager or Social Worker** Review consultations
Health Education Status 1) Nutrition 2) Daily care 3) Medications 4) Equipment 5) Compliance 6) Health promotion 7) Disease process 8) Adjustment to illness 9) Advanced directives	**Clinic Nurse** Assess need for education re: admission or procedure Identify advanced directives. If none, then provide education and materials	**Primary Nurse** Routine health assessment. If risk factors, then provide education and materials If compliance or adjustment issues, then SW consult **Admitting Nurse** Identify advanced directives. If none, then provide materials and education	**Primary Nurse** Assess all—if educational needs, then prepare education plan; consider dietary, pharmacy, PT consults
Transportation Status 1) Home on day of discharge 2) To follow-up 3) Special needs (ambulance, oxygen, etc.)	**Clinic Nurse** Assess availability of transportation for medical care, esp. to hospital for admission	**Admitting Nurse** Assess availability of transportation home at discharge	

	Preadmission (any assessments scheduled for day 1 should be done at preadmission visit)	Day 1—at admission Determine tentative discharge date	Day 2
Follow-up Care 1) Medical 2) Psychosocial 3) Financial support 4) Home care support			
Outcomes	If day surgery, patient verbalizes understanding of procedure, outcomes, and postprocedure care needs	Meets admission criteria Patient verbalizes understanding of plan of care for admission	
Variance Reporting and Care Adjustment			

	Day 4 (or more than 48 hours before planned discharge date)	Day of Discharge	Postdischarge Follow-up	Outpatient
Functional Status 1) ADL status 2) Equipment needs 3) Cognitive status, esp. capacity for consent/ability to understand and participate in care planning	**Nurse Case Manager** Reassess 1—if still not ADL independent, then SW consult for community services and/or home care consult for home health **Social Worker** Reassess 2—order equipment for delivery on proposed discharge date *Precert equipment if managed care*	**Nurse Case Manager or Social Worker** Finalize home health referral Check status of equipment delivery; obtain scripts for equipment prn Finalize PT/OT home program or outpatient appts	**Nurse Case Manager or Social Worker** Check: 1) Equipment received 2) Home care started 3) Continuing PT/OT program	**Clinic Nurse or Social Worker** Reassess all for progress vs. deterioration

Social Status
1) Living site
  a) accessibility
  b) utilities/phone
2) Living situation
  a) caregiver availability
  b) caregiver functional/educational status
  c) caregiver capacity to meet patient's care needs
3) Availability of resources in local community to meet patient's anticipated care needs
	Nurse Case Manager or Social Worker
	Reassess 2—if caregiver unable to provide necessary care, then (1) home care consult for home health or hospice, and/or (2) SW consult for community services
	Reassess 3—if community/home care/family resources insufficient, then discuss with physician
		Social Worker
		If discharge to another facility, then have medical info copied, have case manager call report to facility
				Clinic Nurse or Social Worker
				Reassess 2—for caregiver ability to meet patient's care needs
				Reassess 3—for denial of services by referrals

Financial Status
1) Ability to meet basic needs (housing, food, etc.)
2) Ability to meet medical needs
  a) equipment
  b) medications
  c) supplies
  d) daily care
	Social Worker
	Review consultations
		Social Worker
		Provide patient/family with referral documentation
			Social Worker
			Check:
			1) Referral status
				Clinic Nurse or Social Worker
				Check:
				Do referrals continue to meet patient's needs?

	Day 4 (or more than 48 hours before planned discharge date)	Day of Discharge	Postdischarge Follow-up	Outpatient
Educational/Cultural Factors 1) Literacy 2) Language factors 3) Cultural factors 4) Spiritual issues				
Health Education Status 1) Nutrition 2) Daily care 3) Medications 4) Equipment 5) Compliance 6) Health promotion 7) Disease process 8) Adjustment to illness 9) Advanced directives	**Nurse Case Manager** Review consultations Reassess needs—continue education, consider family meeting if caregiver education; consider home care consult for education consolidation postdischarge	**Primary Nurse** Finalize education and/or home care Have filled scripts available for medication education	**Nurse Case Manager** Check: 1) Medication side effects 2) Questions re: medications or equipment	**Clinic Nurse** Reassess all for patient understanding and compliance
Transportation Status 1) Home on day of discharge 2) To follow-up 3) Special needs (ambulance, oxygen, etc.)	**Primary Nurse** Assess all—if patient to arrange transportation, then advise of proposed discharge date. If special needs or no transportation, then SW consult	**Primary Nurse or Social Worker** Finalize transportation *If managed care, then prior authorize and use approved provider*		
Follow-up Care 1) Medical 2) Psychosocial 3) Financial support 4) Home care support	**Nurse Case Manager or Social Worker** Consult with physician re: Advise all involved services of proposed discharge date Assess 2 and 3—if community referrals needed, SW consult If follow-up labs or home health required, then obtain prior authorization and provider for managed care, arrange and have reports sent to PCP for managed care Precert all medical follow-ups for managed care patients with PCP	**Nurse Case Manager or Social Worker** Determine if follow-up call necessary, who will do it and when	**Nurse Case Manager or Social Worker** Make follow-up call. Change plan as necessary	

	Day 4 (or more than 48 hours before planned discharge date)	Day of Discharge	Postdischarge Follow-up	Outpatient
Outcomes	Any required patient/family education initiated Patient education plan documented	Meets discharge criteria: 1) Pain controlled for 24 hrs 2) Afebrile 3) Nutrition and hydration adequate 4) Vital signs stable Patient verbalizes understanding of posthospital care needs, outpatient follow-up, and community referrals	All services documented in discharge care plan have been initiated in the home or community	Patient using available community resources Patient compliant with medical plan of care
Variance Reporting and Care Adjustment				

CHAPTER 9

Case Management for Capitated Contracts

Beverly A. Massey, Suzanne S. Prevost, and Michael M. Warren

Chapter Objectives

1. To discuss issues to consider in planning for capitation and managed care.
2. To give an overview of case management at an academic medical center.
3. To discuss case management of patients in capitated populations, with emphasis on a capitated contract with the Texas Department of Criminal Justice.

Managed care, especially capitated managed care, requires modifications to the procedures that hospitals and providers use to care for enrolled patients. This chapter will discuss issues related to planning and implementation of programs to manage capitated contracts, drawing examples from one academic medical center, the University of Texas Medical Branch (UTMB) at Galveston. Because nurse case managers were actively involved in the care of these patients at UTMB, the evolution and development of the case management program will also be addressed.

CAPITATION

The incentives to manage patients in a capped reimbursement arena differ from traditional fee-for-service incentives (Exhibit 9–1). In capitated contracts, hospitals and providers receive a fixed amount of money per enrolled person per year. For this fixed sum, hospitals and providers agree to provide comprehensive services to the members with no additional cost to the members. If care is efficiently managed, the money left over at the end of the year can be kept by the hospital and providers as profit; if not, often the hospital and provider must pay money back to the plan.[1]

Exhibit 9–1 Differing Incentives: Fee-for-Service versus Capitated Plans

Fee for Service	*Capitation*
• More admissions/full beds	• Fewer admissions/empty beds
• Longer lengths of stay	• Shorter lengths of stay
• Catastrophic emphasis	• Prevention emphasis
• Retrospective billing	• Prospective payment
• Reactive "planning"	• Proactive planning
• Low financial risk	• High financial risk

Courtesy of University of Texas Medical Branch at Galveston, Galveston, Texas.

With this in mind, it behooves the hospital and providers to improve existing resource utilization procedures. No longer can the hospital allow inefficient utilization management to continue. Financial risks to the hospital increase with capitation. Patients must be managed aggressively and efficiently. At the same time, quality of care must remain high. Quality of care must be managed first because poor quality is expensive.[2] Quality of care is defined as the degree to which care and service influence the *probability* of optimal patient outcomes.[3]

Important criteria for quality of care include the best outcomes related to the patient's physiological and emotional status, physical functioning, cognitive functioning, and comfort achieved at the earliest possible time. Other quality criteria include health and disease prevention and wellness promotion, participative interaction between the physician, the health care facility, and the patient with informed consent, and care delivered in an efficient and timely manner with specific awareness of the patient's individual situation related to his or her anxiety, stress, and overall welfare. Finally, quality care is well documented in the patient's record to ensure continuity of care.[4] Quality of care and strict concurrent management of resource utilization are integral to the success of providers and their positions within the competitive managed-care market.

Academic medical centers, forced to expand their focus beyond providing learning experiences and research opportunities, must compete for patients with private hospital corporations. UTMB is no exception. UTMB is a 906-bed academic medical center in southeast Texas. The hospital and clinics provide tertiary care for 35 Texas counties and primary care for many residents in surrounding Galveston County. UTMB offers multiple specialized services to patients. Southeast Texas and the Galveston area are in the second stage (limited) of managed-care market penetration (Exhibit 9–2). Galveston will soon be entering into stage 3 (consolidated), because UTMB recently became the sole medical center in the area.[5] Because UTMB is in an early stage of evolution in the managed-care mar-

Exhibit 9–2 Managed-Care Market Evolution

Stage 1
Unstructured

Stage 2
Loose framework

Stage 3
Consolidation with horizontal and vertical integration

Stage 4
Managed competition

Courtesy of University of Texas Medical Branch at Galveston, Galveston, Texas.

---

ket, methods of patient management are not as advanced or as complete as in hospitals working within a higher stage of managed-care evolution.

PLANNING FOR CAPITATION: ISSUES TO CONSIDER

Planning for different methods of patient management is vital for the success of a new venture into managed care. Planning includes considering all the issues relevant to the new venture. The following are some of the issues to consider before beginning a capitated managed-care program.

Population

The population of enrollees should be considered in terms of size and age range. What health problems are common to similar populations? What degree of service utilization should be anticipated? A risk assessment survey of all new enrollees can be used to determine who might need case management services. Once a member has enrolled, he or she can be sent a risk assessment to identify potential high-risk patients, and case managers can help high-risk members connect with primary care physicians.

Interdepartmental Relationships

How will departments such as case management, social work, finance, utilization management, quality management, risk management, and the medical staff integrate and collaborate to manage the population? Communication must flow freely and frequently between departments. To whom, what, and when will various individuals and departments report? Should any departments be collapsed or combined into one department to serve the population better? Are there territorial concerns between departments? Clearly delineating functions and accountability between departments is essential to reduce territorial concerns and confusion among all staff members and internal and external customers.

Vertical Integration

Is the institution vertically integrated to provide continuity of care? That is, does the institution have all levels of care available, from outpatient services to all inpatient services, including a skilled nursing facility, rehabilitation, and subacute care? If not vertically integrated, the institution may need to develop subcontracts with existing facilities in the community to provide services such as outpatient dialysis, hospice, home health, and skilled nursing care. If all services are not available within the institution, it is essential to develop networks with community facilities to expedite smooth patient transitions between hospitals and other facilities.

Horizontal Integration

Is the institution horizontally integrated? That is, are comprehensive services provided in outlying regions of the community? If not horizontally integrated, the institution may need to plan for transportation and housing requirements for patients coming from a distance. Proactive planning and budgeting for transportation and housing needs will ease patients' return to their home community.

Information Systems

Sophisticated information systems (ISs) are required to provide comprehensive monitoring of members in a capitated plan. Consider the accessibility of ISs. Are there integrated financial, clinical, and registration systems? Consider the ability of different systems to communicate with each other. Are the systems user friendly? Who will develop, use, and provide maintenance for databases? Who will design workable, functional systems for outcomes measurement? Are there adequate experienced IS personnel to support the needs of users? Shared ISs are integral to efficient case management. Before engaging in capitated managed-care contracts, case managers will need access to patient registration and financial information. When persons in various departments are collaborating to manage and care for these patients, the ability to integrate computer communication systems between all collaborating departments is vital.

Data Management and Reporting

Program managers must decide how clinical and financial outcomes will be monitored. Relevant clinical outcomes vary by population but often include in-hospital mortality, readmissions within 30 days, nosocomial infections, adverse medication events, falls, and pressure ulcers. Common financial and resource utilization outcomes in the industry include tracking admissions, length of stay, hospital days per thousand members per year, avoidable hospital days, charges and costs per case, primary care visits, and referrals to specialists. If many departments are involved with tracking information, it is important to determine what data are needed and the mechanisms for collecting, recording, and reporting the information needed by each department.

Education and Training

Educational needs for all principal players, including physicians, nurses, case managers, social workers, and patients, must be considered. Do they understand the goals of capitated managed care? Are they able to modify their practice accordingly? Education and training include timely updates regarding pending and negotiated contracts and regular reporting of tracked outcomes from current contracts.

Physician Considerations

Common issues of concern for physicians include scope of authority, liability, confidentiality, and utilization review roles and responsibilities. All involved must know the expectations related to patient management. Specific processes should exist for resolving disparities between physicians, administrators, and other members of the patient management team. Expert managed-care physician consultants can be effectively used to assist with physician education and respond to physicians' concerns.

Case Management

If case management is the intended strategy for coordinating care, additional questions and issues must be addressed. These issues include the model of case management to be used; assignment of case managers by clinical specialty, geography (e.g., per nursing unit), or medical team; and the focus of the case managers on patients in the acute care setting only or across the care continuum. It must be determined if case management should begin with proactive screening for high-risk patients prior to hospital admission or if case managers will identify their patients in the primary or tertiary care setting.

Another important issue is: Who will function as case managers? Will they be nurses, social workers, physicians, or a combination of various types of professionals? Collaborative plans with other providers, such as social workers, can help to identify patients in the primary care/clinic setting, with a referral relay system for when patients are admitted.

What are the chain-of-command procedures when resistance and/or misunderstandings occur with physicians or other providers? Is there a physician advisor? If so, what is his or her role in relation to the case managers? What is the acceptable time frame for responses from physicians and physician advisors for resolution of clinical problems and case management recommendations? A physician advisor program can help circumvent stalemates between case managers and physicians. Many institutions hire an impartial physician not involved with the physicians providing patient care to allow for peer-to-peer consultation about difficult cases and utilization controversies between case managers and physicians. In other situations, the physician advisor is a member of the staff who has volunteered to provide this service for the case managers and the physicians.

Another issue to be addressed is the definition and tracking of avoidable days. How and to whom are avoidable days reported? How will catastrophic cases be monitored and managed? What information about catastrophic cases will be reported and how and to whom will it be reported? Is there a provision for stop-loss or reinsurance for catastrophic cases? How will the payer and institution interface, and what are the payers' information needs? Collaboration with payers is essential to determine which information will be needed by them and included in case management data collection.

Outcome variables that the case managers monitor, track, and report must be determined. Examples of financial outcomes include length of stay (LOS) compared to benchmark LOS per diagnosis-related group (DRG), total charges (or costs) versus expected reimbursement per DRG, and readmissions (unplanned, unscheduled) within 30 days. Quality outcomes monitored frequently include nosocomial infections, falls, adverse medication reactions, pressure ulcers, functional and cognitive declines, discharge disposition, and mortality. The number of consults and time taken to answer consults per patient and number of procedures costing greater than $500 may be tracked and monitored also. A standard, simple tool can be formatted to classify avoidable hospital days. Outcomes will vary depending on the goals of the institution and may or may not include the above criteria.

Accreditation

Even though a capitated plan means risk for the institution, there is risk for the payer also. Payers will need information about utilization of resources and quality assurance requirements to achieve National Committee for Quality Assurance (NCQA) accreditation. This accreditation raises additional issues. Who will be responsible for ensuring that standards are met for accreditation? What is the hospital's role in NCQA accreditation? What role do physicians and payers play with regard to NCQA accreditation? Both the hospital and the payer need to be involved with ensuring that NCQA guidelines are followed and fulfilled.

This extensive list of issues and questions begins to illustrate the complexity of making the transition from managing patients in a fee-for-service environment to managing within a capitated plan. Careful, proactive examination of these matters will ensure a preliminary plan to handle potential problems when they occur.

Management of Patients in a Capitated Plan: UTMB's Experience

Our institution invested heavily in preliminary planning that enabled the institution to begin to streamline procedures. Interdepartmental meetings were held weekly for approximately nine months to design methods for efficiently managing our capitated patient populations. Departments involved included nursing case management, health care finance, resource utilization, admitting, social work, pharmacy, quality management, home health, emergency services, psychiatry, and managed care. Various managed-care issues were discussed. Flowcharts were developed to outline relevant procedures, such as the process of admitting contract patients to our hospitals. Policies for precertification, authorization for services, consults, and delivery of expensive procedures (costing greater than $500) were developed. Information about managed-care contract development was shared and discussed on a regular basis.

At our institution, admitting, nursing case management, resource utilization, social work, quality management, risk management, and managed care were all separate departments. If procedures between the departments were not managed proficiently, there were multiple opportunities for system failure; thus the reason for weekly, and now monthly, operations meetings.

The department of managed care was established to provide an internal control mechanism for our prison contract. The department precertifies and authorizes procedures, services, and transportation for our incarcerated patients. With the advent of commercial capitated contracts at UTMB, the department's role expanded. It now authorizes and precertifies outpatient procedures and visits to specialists within these contracts. It collaborates with nursing case managers. Its role includes a gatekeeping function and an interface between the payer and the hospital. Managed care negotiates for new managed-care contracts and carve-out plans. It also responds to members' requests for out-of-network services and second opinions.

Most managed-care plans require the primary care provider to perform the gatekeeper role. Some institutions and networks contract for this type of service on a private basis. Another method of internal control uses hospital-based physicians; primary care physicians (PCPs) turn over the responsibility for their admitted patients to these "hospitalists," who aggressively manage inpatient cases. The model used for internal control depends on the type of network and the resources and priorities within the institution.

THE ROLE OF NURSING CASE MANAGEMENT

Case management's evolution at UTMB was well underway before capitated managed care arrived. Case management was initiated with a unit-based model, with the case manager reporting to the unit nurse manager. The case manager's role often blurred with the staff nurse role and included staffing the units. After two years, case management was restructured to a population-based model. The majority of our nurse case managers were assigned to specific clinical populations (e.g., cardiac surgery or pediatric asthma). Additionally, we assigned some of our case managers to focus specifically on our capitated managed-care patients. Most of our case managers focus their interventions on the inpatient phase of care. However, our long-term vision is that most will make a transition from the inpatient to the outpatient, full continuum-of-care focus.

Because resource utilization (RU), admitting, nursing case management (CM), and social work are all separate departments at UTMB, maximum collaboration is imperative. Cooperation between admitting, RU, and CM began early, with the admitting department agreeing to e-mail CM anytime a capitated member was admitted. Case management's goal is to begin active case management within 24 hours of admission to the hospital. To that end, case managers must provide coverage seven days per week. In many institutions, avoidable days tend to occur over the weekend, especially if the hospital has not adopted a 24-hour, seven-day-per-week operational philosophy.[6]

Case management begins with an assessment of the patient and situation. Factors assessed include psychosocial history, clinical facts, functional and cognitive status prior to admission, potential barriers to discharge, and a brief financial screening. Case managers formulate the patient plan, considering the medical treatment plan and the individual patient and family needs. Plans include prompt nurse-to-nurse referrals to specialists, such as the enterostomal nurse, skin and wound care nurse, pain management team, nutrition support team, social workers, or dietitians as needed. Suggestions to physicians are made regarding appropriate and timely referrals to physical, occupational, and/or speech therapy. Case manager plans are monitored concurrently and modified as needed during the hospital stay. Case managers follow the patient through the continuum of care in the hospital regardless of the nursing care unit or floor where the patient is located. Because ours is an academic medical center, resident and faculty physicians change frequently, as do other personnel. Case managers often serve as one of the few providers of continuity for the patient during his or her hospital stay.

The case manager collaborates with many other team members during the course of a patient's hospital stay. Utilization issues, such as appropriate status of admission (observation status versus full admission), are negotiated with other departments, such as the admitting department. The CM collaborates closely with managed care to verify patient benefits and eligibility and to discuss plans of treatment and expected length of stay. The CM works closely with the physician(s) to enhance the treatment plan and discharge plan, which are initiated as soon as possible after admission.

The patient and/or family is consulted early in the hospital stay to explore expectations about the hospitalization and to begin discharge planning. Case managers provide education about diseases or conditions to patients and families on an ongoing basis. Social workers and CMs often facilitate discharge plans together, especially when nursing home placement, ambulance transfers, and/or subcontracted services are necessary. Case managers review clinical patterns and ensure that patients are discharged appropriately, neither too soon nor too late. They ensure that patients are discharged when they are medically stable and safe to be discharged. CMs then monitor patients for unplanned clinic visits or readmissions. Follow-up phone calls are made to patients and/or families if the patient is considered to be at risk for problems post discharge.

Data collection and reporting responsibilities of UTMB case managers include DRGs (number of admissions for each), LOS, anticipated versus actual charges per case, negative outcomes (including nosocomial infections, falls, adverse medication reactions, pressure ulcers, cognitive or functional decline, and readmissions), patient satisfaction, living arrangements before and after hospitalization, and number and type of case management interventions provided to each patient. Reports of admissions and bed days per thousand members per year (PTMPY) are also generated and reported monthly to provide timely feedback on institutional performance with each of our contracts.

Case managers also distribute a weekly outlier patient report that describes patients who remain as inpatients longer than five days and those that suffer a major catastrophic condition or illness or for whom an unfavorable outcome of hospitalization is anticipated. This report is distributed to the payer and various physicians and administrators, including our internal physician advisor.

Program Evolution

Fine-tuning of our CM process has occurred over time and will continue. For example, we are currently revising our "avoidable day" definition and monitoring process. All CMs are being educated on the correct assignment and standardized tracking of avoidable days. Reporting has evolved to meet customer and user requirements and wishes. Case management has developed new processes for collaborating with our risk management and quality management departments to monitor and address quality concerns.

Our program is progressively moving to a "beyond the walls" concept as exemplified by programs like Carondolet in Tucson, Arizona, and the Friendly Hills

System in California.[7] Our case managers now follow patients who are transferred (under subcontracts) to other facilities in the community to monitor resource utilization and patient progress. Also, a plan is in progress to survey new enrollees to the capitated plans to assess their risk status for problems related to major chronic illnesses or conditions. High-risk members will be targeted to implement proactive plans with the PCP and social worker.

Additionally, a plan was implemented to facilitate the transfer of out-of-network patients back to their home networks. A major metropolitan sister network exists 50 miles north of our facility. Frequently people travel to Galveston to vacation or visit, become ill or injured, and are admitted to our facility. We have created a plan to ease these patients' transitions back to their PCPs and network hospitals.

Our case managers receive ongoing education and training as we gain experience in working within a managed-care environment. We also continuously look for opportunities to join our clinical case management processes with outcomes research studies.

TEXAS DEPARTMENT OF CRIMINAL JUSTICE CONTRACT

UTMB's first and largest capitated contract was established with the Texas Department of Criminal Justice (TDCJ) to provide health care for inmates in the Texas prison system. UTMB opened one of the nation's first university-affiliated correctional hospitals in 1983. Since 1994, UTMB assumed responsibility for providing 80 percent of the primary care and 100 percent of the tertiary care to Texas inmates. In 1994, the correctional hospital at UTMB admitted approximately 3,750 patients and provided 30,000 hospital clinic visits. UTMB also provides telemedicine services to the correctional sites in Texas and has one of the largest telemedicine programs in the United States. In 1995, 5,079 patients were admitted to the hospital, and in 1996, the population and services continue to grow. Texas has one of the largest inmate populations in the United States. This is the first contract of its kind and has demonstrated significant clinical and financial success in the first three years of operation.

Historically, there has been little continuity of care for incarcerated persons in the Texas prison system and inadequate communication between jails and health care providers. Texas legislators enacted into the Health and Safety Codes provisions to improve continuity of care and communication to improve the care provided to the inmates. Inmates are screened and identified as elderly, physically disabled, mentally impaired, or terminally and significantly ill. Transfer procedures are streamlined, and patients are tracked and monitored when they enter the health care system. Case management was instituted in the correctional hospital to promote continuity of care for inmates. An incentive structure was established to encourage medical teams to use hospital resources more efficiently.

Collaboration between case managers and physicians has resulted in favorable outcomes, as detailed in Table 9–1. For example, with DRG 410, Chemotherapy, LOS decreased from 10.61 days in 1995 to 6.35 days in 1996. Simultaneously, actual charges decreased from $8,264 per patient admission in 1995 to $5,651 in 1996, a decrease of $2,613 in actual charges per patient admission. At the same time, the expected charges in 1996 were $7,063, $1,412 more than the actual charges. While this experience of decreased LOS and decreased actual versus expected and prior-year charges has not been completely consistent across all DRGs (e.g., DRG 202), the favorable results have been the most frequent outcome of our program implementation.

After initial success with the prison contract, UTMB began its first capitated commercial contract in May 1995 with a Medicare plan. Two additional commercial plans and a military plan followed within the same year. With the TDCJ contract, approximately 25 percent of total admissions are fully capitated. While each contract is unique, there are similarities between UTMB's prison contract and commercial contracts, specifically in regard to the internal control procedures.

Table 9–1 Texas Department of Criminal Justice Program Outcomes

DRG	Year	No. of pts.	Actual charges	Expected charges	Average LOS
56	1995	160	$3,639	$4,310	4.21
Rhinoplasty	1996	73	$4,265	$4,853	2.79
63	1995	94	$7,427	$7,628	6.64
Other ENT Procedures	1996	74	$6,610	$7,391	3.97
162 Inguinal/Femoral	1995	161	$3,910	$3,836	3.07
Hernia Prodedure	1996	157	$3,991	$3,858	2.24
202	1995	76	$10,836	$10,239	6.27
Cirrhosis and Alcoholic Hepatitis	1996	86	$10,865	$10,775	7.76
222	1995	150	$5,650	$7,057	3.74
Knee Procedures Age <70 w/o CC	1996	106	$5,419	$6,814	2.93
410	1995	179	$8,264	$6,735	10.61
Chemotherapy	1996	137	$5,651	$7,063	6.35

Courtesy of University of Texas Medical Branch at Galveston, Galveston, Texas.

Table 9–2 Capitated Contract Management Actual versus Expected Outcomes

Contract	Year	No. of Patients	LOS/ Exp. LOS	Readmits/ Exp. Readmits
Defense contract	1995	88	7.7/8.1	0/3.8
	1996	177	5.0/5.8	3.0/5.8
Medicare replacement contract	1995	39	4.8/5.2	2.0/1.7
	1996	298	6.0/6.8	18/11
Commercial contract	1995	3	3.0/4.2	0/0.1
	1996	135	4.2/4.5	0/3.1

Courtesy of University of Texas Medical Branch at Galveston, Galveston, Texas.

COMMERCIAL CASE MANAGEMENT PROGRAM OUTCOMES

Patient outcomes related to our case-managed commercial contracts have also been favorable. Patient satisfaction as measured by the Press, Ganey, Inc., Survey revealed that our capitated-contract patients reported the highest overall hospital rating of all payer groups. Both length of stay and unplanned readmissions were lower than expected (Table 9–2). For example, with our defense contract, the expected LOS in 1996 was 5.8, with an actual LOS of 5.0 days. Unplanned readmissions for the same population occurred at a rate of 3 of the 177 total patients, which was lower than the expected rate of 5.8.

CONCLUSION

Designing and implementing programs to manage patients in a capitated managed-care environment is challenging. Forethought, advance planning, and collaboration are essential. Support and collaboration among the various providers are imperative to success with capitated managed-care plans. Streamlined, efficient processes that promote efficient resource management and quality of care will lead to patient and payer satisfaction and will facilitate the maintenance and acquisition of current and future managed-care contracts.

NOTES

1. J. Dunham-Taylor et al., "Surviving Capitation," *American Journal of Nursing* 96, no. 3 (1996): 26–30.
2. E. Kennedy, *Assertive Utilization Management* (San Mateo, CA: MAGE Corp., 1990).

3. American Medical Association, ed., *Proceedings from the AMA Annual Meeting of the House of Delegates* (Washington, DC: 1991).

4. E. Kennedy, "The Assertive Utilization Management Workshop" (presented to United Health Care, Minneapolis, MN, September 1994); based on E. Kennedy, *Assertive Utilization Management* (San Mateo, CA: MAGE Corp., 1990).

5. K. Ackerman, "The Movement toward Vertically Integrated Regional Health Systems," *Health Care Management Review* 17, no. 3 (1992): 81–88.

6. S. Posar and P. Katz, "A Managed Care Survival Guide for Hospitals," *Healthcare Financial Management* 46, no. 9 (1992): 100, 102.

7. V.A. Mahn, "Clinical Nurse Case Management: A Service Approach," *Nursing Management* 24, no. 9 (1993): 48–50; N. Brown et al., "The Case Management Network at Friendly Hills Healthcare Network," in *An Executive Guide to Case Management Strategies,* ed. M. Satinsky (Chicago, IL: American Hospital Publishers, 1995).

SUGGESTED READINGS

Barrett, M.J. 1993. Case management a must to survive managed care. *Computers in Healthcare* 14, no. 6, 22–25.

Coile, R.C. 1994. Transformation of American healthcare in the post-reform era. *Healthcare Executive* 9, no. 4, 8–12.

Firshein, J. 1995. The state of health care in America 1995. *Business and Health* 13, no. 3: 36–40.

Shoor, R. 1993. Looking to manage care more closely. *Business and Health* 11, no. 10, 46–53.

Weston, C.M, and R.G. Reese. 1996. Looking towards the next managed care milestone. *National Underwriter (Life/Health/Financial Services)* 100, no. 19: 26–28.

Williams, F.G., et al. 1993. Critical factors for successful hospital-based case management. *Health Care Management Review* 18, no. 1: 63–70.

CHAPTER 10

Management of Pediatric Asthma

Nanette E. Martorell and Edward G. Brooks

Chapter Objectives

1. To describe the management of pediatric asthma, including the evolution of the asthma case management program at the University of Texas Medical Branch at Galveston.
2. To describe program implementation, evolution, evaluation, and outcomes.
3. To discuss future directions for the program.

Due to changes in health care reimbursement, university-based academic hospitals have increasingly had to reexamine how they do business. Models of care in these institutions, traditionally focused on quality and the academic mission of research and education, are being redesigned to optimize economics as well as quality. The dilemma of delivering cost-effective care without compromising quality or the educational and research missions is a major shift in focus. At the University of Texas Medical Branch at Galveston (UTMB), efficiency measures initiated within the inpatient hospital areas have evolved to a more comprehensive focus and include disease management. This chapter outlines that evolution within the pediatric asthma population.

In the pediatric asthma case management program, the central philosophy that has emerged is that to be competitive in a capitated market, the health care delivery system must strive to reduce not only the cost of delivering high-quality care but also the need for high-cost care. This goal is accomplished through disease prevention and shifting responsibility or the locus of control from the health care enterprise to the patient.

A corollary to this philosophy is that only the highest quality of care will satisfy newly savvy health care consumers to accept responsibility for their own care, for ultimately the health care product purchased is the skill to manage one's own illness. Confidence in the quality of that care is paramount for accepting responsibility for and gaining confidence in self-management. Poor quality care and education will result in poor care by patients and a failure of the system. Upon failure to manage their disease, patients will return to consume more resources. As an academic institution, our institution is well suited to capitalize on this concept. As expert educators, we can quickly and efficiently apply our skills to educate the patient populations we serve.

A CHANGING SYSTEM OF REIMBURSEMENT

University hospitals historically utilize greater resources in patient management. Longer lengths of stay and increased test consumption have been attributed to the teaching environment. This practice has been supported by government- and state-funded health care plans that pay a slightly higher rate of reimbursement to university hospitals to manage supplemented populations. A guaranteed patient base of traditionally indigent care has meant guaranteed revenues and state funding. This reimbursement mode has not fostered cost consciousness or efficacy of treatment. The advent of managed care has changed delivery of health care at all levels and necessitated radical measures to correct the old inefficiencies.

Managed care organizations—health maintenance organizations (HMOs) and preferred provider organizations (PPOs)—set strict guidelines for reimbursement. Precertification for routine admissions, costly procedures, laboratory tests, and referrals to specialists are now routinely scrutinized by payers. Insurance companies and other payers are increasingly directing how health care professionals should care for patients.

PEDIATRIC ASTHMA POPULATION

Review of the UTMB pediatric asthma population statistics revealed a high hospital readmission rate. In 1995 and 1996, at least 5 percent of patients were readmitted at least once in a 12-month period. This readmission rate to the acute hospital setting is considered high due to the potential manageability of this disease in the outpatient or home environment. In a "fee-for-service" reimbursement system, revenue is generated with each admission. In a capitated environment, the payer contracts with the institution to manage a group of patients for a specified dollar amount. If the institution's costs exceed the capitation, no adjustments are generally made.

In 1994, capitated Medicaid contracts were being formulated to be tested in Texas. By 1995, three counties were testing a Medicaid capitated program. It was projected that approximately 60 percent of UTMB's Children's Hospital Medicaid admissions could become part of a capitated contract. With that scenario, significant financial losses were projected for asthma patients on the basis of the high readmission rate for that population.

In addition, these patients now had a choice of where they would receive their care. Patient satisfaction surveys revealed low patient confidence in hospital staff. In some instances, it was perceived that nurses often did not know lab results or were unaware of impending patient discharges. Strategies had to be formulated to improve patient satisfaction and quality.

Hospitals that once turned away Medicaid patients now gladly accepted them, especially because Medicaid reimbursement in some ways was superior to that of many other third-party payers. Patient care delivery models to improve patient satisfaction, care coordination, and patient outcomes were reviewed, and one solution proposed was nursing case management.

NURSING CASE MANAGEMENT

Nursing case management (NCM) was viewed as a method by which to reduce not only expenditures on asthma admissions but also readmission rates by educating those patients admitted for asthma. This program was expected to improve the quality of care and also to enhance patient confidence. However, there were significant barriers to overcome.

Patient care at the UTMB Children's Hospital often involved excessive waiting periods for evaluation, admission, and discharge. Physician-directed teaching rounds implemented and evaluated patient care. Nursing infrequently participated in these rounds due to increasing demands on their time in direct patient care. Some services such as cardiology, gastroenterology, infectious diseases, and nephrology hired nurses to care for their individual populations in order to fill this void. Surgery, orthopedics, endocrinology, ear/nose and throat, and allergy-immunology either did not have the budget for these positions or did not perceive a need for supplemental nursing coordination of care.

Thus, the existing model of patient care operations was physician driven. In this teaching institution, the primary focus was education of young health care professionals. Thus, little attention was given to efficient delivery of care, and in fact, quality of medical intervention was a higher priority than quality of care. In addition, because UTMB was a teaching institution, the traditional administrators and designers of the academic health care delivery system were physicians who had advanced professionally through excellence in academic endeavors. Those areas involved primarily research and scholarly teaching. The cost-effective and high-quality delivery of health care was an area in which most academicians had little to no training, expertise, or interest. Thus, a radical intervention was needed in this traditional structure.

A Unit-Based Model of NCM

Clinically proficient nurses were hired from selected areas of the hospital to case-manage patients on their hospital units. The original goal was to facilitate patient transition from admission to discharge. Decreased lengths of stay (LOSs) and decreased costs would be optimized by having one person facilitate and monitor delivery of care.

Advantages of a unit-based model were that the clinician would be familiar with the environment, the staff, and the type of care delivered to the unit's particular patient population. Disadvantages of the model were revealed when patients transferred from one unit to another. Patients and their families who had already established a therapeutic relationship with one case manager were transferred to another provider. A logical evolution of the program was to progress toward a population-based model.

A Population-Based Model of NCM

Population Identification

Changing the model meant identifying populations that would benefit most from this service. High-risk and/or high-volume populations were to be targeted. Methods to identify these patients came from various hospital databases. The reports detailed admissions by diagnosis-related groups (DRGs). DRGs were developed to group in cohorts like diagnoses with similar length of stay and resource consumption. An example of this would be DRG 98, the grouping for asthma and bronchitis in patients aged 0 to 17 without comorbidities. Reimbursement is identified by DRG and is a constant amount. It is important to note that this fee remains constant regardless of the costs incurred by the provider.

Figure 10–1 shows a comparison of costs for two groups of patients with the same DRG managed in two different settings. The relatively higher costs of an intensive care setting are shown in comparison to those of a general care unit setting. This figure also demonstrates that in year 2, even with significant case and resource management, a large cost difference still remains. It also shows that regardless of costs incurred, reimbursement is fixed at a predetermined amount ($4,427).

The projected LOS is the number of days a patient is expected to remain in the hospital for a specific diagnosis. Day 1 is the date of admission, and the discharge date is not included. The average LOS is a value calculated from 4 million hospital discharge records from participants in the Professional Activity Study (PAS) of the Commission of Professional and Hospital Activities.[1] This calculation is a mean of the nation's hospitals' longest and shortest LOS for those DRGs.

The 1996 national average LOS for DRG 98 is 3.5 days.[2] For DRG 98, UTMB LOS data demonstrated a decreasing number of patient days from the years of 1992 to 1996 (Figure 10–2). The arithmetic mean LOS (AMLOS) calculated by

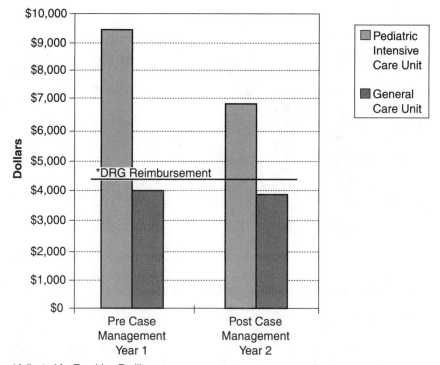

Figure 10–1 Cost Comparison by Unit Type. Courtesy of University of Texas Medical Branch at Galveston, Galveston, Texas.

the Health Care Finance Administration (HCFA) decreased during this same time period nationwide as hospitals strove to obtain lower LOSs. Since program implementation, UTMB has been significantly under the national LOS. The greatest favorable difference occurred most recently with the 1996 national LOS at 3.5 days and the UTMB LOS of 1.9 days.

To identify more completely all patients with a specific diagnosis, ICD-9 codes must be used to cross DRGs. Also, DRG 98 is not the only DRG to include asthma. DRG 475, respiratory system diagnosis with ventilator support, has an LOS of 9.8 days and a reimbursement of $11,524.25. Approximately three asthmatics per year at UTMB Children's Hospital fall into this category. In addition, not all patients in DRG 98 have a diagnosis of asthma. A substantial proportion have a diagnosis of viral bronchiolitis. This reflects the difficulty in tracking the diagnosis of asthma in hospitalized patients.

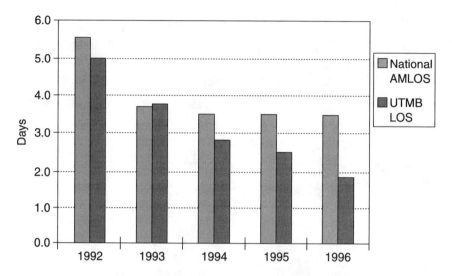

Figure 10–2 Length-of-Stay Comparison, Bronchitis and Asthma, DRG 98, 0–17 Years. Courtesy of University of Texas Medical Branch at Galveston, Galveston, Texas.

Prior to hospitalization, case identification can be even more elusive. Unlike some chronic illnesses, asthma can be an elusive diagnosis in which exacerbations are random and unpredictable, and patients may "adapt" to chronically poor pulmonary function by limiting activity. These factors thus contribute to a poor perception of illness not only on the part of the patient but also on the part of the health care provider.

Focus on Patient/Parent Education

A reduced LOS is one measure of successful case management. Thus, attention was given to identifying interventions that could enhance early discharge. The medical decision to discharge patients after treatment for an acute exacerbation involves several factors.

Treatment for acute exacerbations of asthma often requires prolonged use of medications on a nonstatic schedule. Thus, the ability of the patients and/or their parents to administer treatments and medications is critical. In addition, avoidance of certain precipitating factors for the patient's asthma and the ability of patients and/or their parents to identify worsening of symptoms after discharge are issues important to the continued health of patients. Most important, the abilities of families to understand this information and their level of dedication to ensure proper care at home become a critical part of the equation for the final discharge.

The difficulty in ensuring the above factors has prompted many physicians to maintain the hospital admission for the duration of the exacerbation. Many health care providers have had anecdotal experience that certain patients and parents were much more astute and faithful in carrying out instructions in the home environment. Thus, to facilitate earlier patient discharge, education of families and patients in a more intensive fashion than had previously been performed appeared to be necessary. An inpatient education program was therefore devised and implemented.

Inpatient Education

To identify educational issues that might promote positive outcomes in asthma, a group of nurse educators, the pediatric health education committee, met to develop the inpatient pediatric asthma educational plan. This committee consisted of pediatric faculty from the School of Nursing, pediatric inpatient nurse managers, outpatient nurses, the pediatric asthma case manager, a pediatric clinical specialist for pulmonary care, and a technical writer.

A program was designed that would be administered to each patient admitted with asthma to the Children's Hospital. These children and their families would receive education on key concepts in self-management, judging severity of the exacerbation, identifying triggers, the basic pathology, peak flow monitoring, medications, deep breathing exercises, problem solving, and follow-up care.

Initially, all inpatient nursing staff were requested to implement the educational plan. Inservices were presented by the pediatric asthma case manager to the nursing staff on patient/family teaching form usage and how to teach the concepts. However, 30-, 90-, and 180-day chart audits indicated little usage of the form. Thereafter, the asthma case manager assumed the role of educating all patients to provide a more consistent and proficient education. The model has evolved to one expert who educates the majority of patients. Simultaneously, the physician and nursing staff are educated.

Although the case management program reduced LOS, the educational program was not achieving all of its intended outcomes. For example, it was expected that patients and their families would be adequately prepared and educated during hospitalization, as reflected in the outcome of fewer readmissions, but this was not being observed. A survey was performed by a pediatric resident physician on parental perceptions of asthma care at UTMB. Of the 29 parents who were asked if they felt they had received any education during their child's admission, 27 responded negatively.

A review of the 27 cases noted that they had all indeed received education during the admission. A possible explanation for this discrepancy was that education delivered in the acute setting may have been perceived as crisis intervention as opposed to crisis prevention.

The inpatient program was not abandoned but was revised to reflect these findings. The educational program was refocused to highlight the immediate posthospitalization period: medication and device usage, warning signs, and the importance of follow-up. This revision also had the unintended side effect of reducing the case manager workload and thus improved resource utilization. Also, an alternate location was used for teaching appropriate long-term self-management skills.

Focus on Outpatient/Home Education

Inpatient management involves management of an acute event, whereas outpatient management involves the day-to-day management of a chronic illness. One of the major management challenges is that asthma presents variably for many patients and is typically characterized by acute exacerbations on a background of either relatively mild disease (typical of infants with virus-associated asthma) or more severe chronic disease. The "triggers" or precipitating factors, if identified, lend themselves to behavioral control, unlike many illnesses in which the patient has little control over precipitating factors. Finally, emotional factors contribute to a significant amplification and/or precipitation of both chronic symptoms and acute exacerbations. Control of these emotional factors would have a significant impact on control of symptoms. To shift the majority of care and management to the home setting successfully, a carefully orchestrated education program was implemented.

The various topics of the educational program included triggers and environmental control, controlled breathing, and device usage. Although initially our educational program contained somewhat static or standard content, over time it was realized that for maximum efficacy, individualization and narrowing of the scope to only the most important facets of each child's disease were needed. Therefore, a standard program was developed with the philosophy that only those aspects of the program important to the care of each individual child would be emphasized. Overeducation was discouraged, and the educational program was altered spontaneously to accommodate the variable needs of these patients and their families.

Each individual participated in the development of his or her own educational program and was therefore given considerable freedom to take ownership in learning and altering health behaviors. Families were thus encouraged to experiment with their medications and behavioral techniques to prove for themselves the utility of these interventions. The ability to develop a management plan within the boundaries set by both patient/family and the health care team is paramount in developing an effective partnership. These partnerships evolve from a distinctly different style of medical management than traditional approaches.

Contrast of Leadership Styles

Traditionally, in outpatient clinics, the physician leads the clinic in directing patient care. The asthma management team differs. It shares the responsibility with the participants. This participative structure, when compared to the traditional autocratic management style, is more concerned with human relations, collaboration and teamwork, multidirectional communication, and concern with staff satisfaction and goal commitment.[3]

Respect between the disciplines fosters the dedication necessary to manage care across a continuum, from the hospital to the clinic and back out to the community. This care requires an abandonment of traditional work hours, for asthma is not a Monday through Friday, 9 AM to 5 PM disease. In fact, most exacerbations occur between the hours of midnight and 2 AM, weekends and holidays included. Thus, an on-call system had to be developed in which patients had maximum access to the same health care providers that most intimately understood that patient's self-management.

The asthma management team also differs from traditional medical management in that team members can perform many roles. For example, all team members perform spirometry, institute and evaluate the educational needs, complete vital signs, and do whatever it takes to ensure that patients receive expedient and quality care. The obvious exception is that the physician makes the diagnosis and determines medical therapy. Elemental to the treatment is the initiation of a written self-management medication plan. The "step-up, step-down plan" provides instruction on administering the maximum dose at the first sign of an exacerbation, then how and when to wean back. Families are encouraged to experiment with the minimum dose to determine the baseline. If symptoms return, the previous step is considered the new baseline.

Minimum treatment for some patients is no medications at all except during acute events or during their worst seasons. The written self-management plan also provides phone and pager numbers of physicians and the case managers to contact if patients do not feel they can manage the exacerbation alone. This 24-hour availability is often met with disbelief, and many test it by calling during the off hours. Families learn that the off-hour services are provided, and they are then guided through the process of managing the exacerbation at home.

Prior to the education, patients and families generally believed that asthma "just happened" and that they had little or no control over the progression of symptoms, much less management of the disease. Educational support returns an internal locus of control to the patient and family.

COMPREHENSIVE PROGRAM IMPLEMENTATION

The idea of a multidisciplinary asthma education program is not new. Several hospitals and HMOs have instituted similar programs to promote health and decrease resource utilization. Members of the original team were a physician pediatric allergy-immunology specialist, a case manager, and a pediatric pulmonary care specialist. Each discipline recruited more personnel until the resulting team consisted of two pediatric allergy-immunologists, a pediatric pulmonologist, two outpatient clinic nurses, a case manager, a respiratory therapist, and a nurse assistant.

The team developed on a three-module program with components from the original patient teaching form. Module 1 instructed families about medications and devices, how to judge severity of the exacerbation, decision making, and how to track symptons and events prior to the exacerbation. Module 2 covered medications to use for acute illness and medications to use for prevention. Peak flow training was also implemented to provide families an objective measure to judge severity. Trigger identification training included diary keeping. The third module consists of an evaluation of all previous education to assess if learning had occurred.

Families who complete module 3 graduate from the program when they can successfully implement the program. Positive reinforcement for each concept learned empowers families to control asthma instead of the reverse. Reinforcement of the program is instituted on a six-month to one-year schedule depending upon the level of competence of the family/patient and the presence or absence of close follow-up by a primary care physician.

PROGRAM EVALUATION

The program was implemented in April 1995. Approximately 171 patients were seen in the first year. Asthma severity demographics for year 1 revealed 52 mild, 74 moderate, and 40 severe cases, 4 cases with isolated exercise-induced asthma, and 1 case of a patient eliminated with a diagnosis other than asthma. All patients were staged on the basis of criteria from the National Asthma Education Program for disease severity[4] (Figure 10–3).

During the first year, a total of 13 patients dropped out of the program. Outcomes to determine effectiveness of the program measured frequency of emergency department usage and number of hospitalizations after entering the program. In the remaining 158 patients, a total of four emergency department visits occurred. Of these, one occurred after module 1, two occurred after module 2, and one occurred after module 3. Hospitalizations totaled three: one after module 1, none after module 2, and two after module 3.

Comparison figures were obtained for these same patients by parental history. These data revealed 550 emergency department visits and 71 hospitalizations in the year prior to entering the program, for an average of 3.6 visits or hospitalizations per patient. Comprehensive disease management did result in decreased consumption of health care resources and improved quality outcomes.

A case study illustrates this point (Exhibit 10–1). J.G. is an 11-year-old Hispanic male with moderate to severe asthma and allergic rhinitis. One year prior to

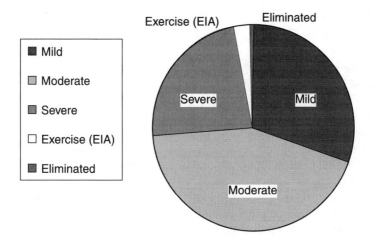

Figure 10–3 Asthma Severity Demographics, 1995–1996. Courtesy of University of Texas Medical Branch at Galveston, Galveston, Texas.

participation in the program, he had six acute care visits, six emergency department visits, and one hospitalization. Seven months after program participation, he had no pediatric walk-in clinic visits, emergency department visits, or hospitalizations. This patient and family had progressed from an illness-centered focus to a health focus. At this review, it would appear that the program has accomplished what it set out to do, but evaluation remains an ongoing process.

FUTURE DIRECTIONS

New members to the team, a psychologist and home health nursing, bring valued expertise in their individual fields to enrich the program offering. To meet the growing demand for this educational intervention, the team has begun seeking different methods to see patients more effectively. Proposed solutions have been a peer support group for teenagers. This is developmentally appropriate and could prove to be more effective in managing this age group.

Another group identified with higher recidivism is a small percentage of patients and families who have less than an eighth-grade reading level. Materials aimed for low literacy levels with an increased number of visual messages are being evaluated for effectiveness to be used with this subset of patients and families.

Continued measurement of outcomes is essential to understanding the impact of specific interventions on patient and family outcomes. The program content will continue to evolve and respond to empirical evidence of improved outcomes.

Exhibit 10–1 Case Study—J.G.

Triggers
  Weather changes
  Upper respiratory infections
  Exercise

Pattern
  Shortness of breath
  3–4 exacerbations per week
  Symptoms every morning

Management
  Nonsteroidal inhaled anti-inflammatory medication as preventative management
  Inhaled corticosteroids as both preventive and crisis management
  $_2$Agonists for crisis management
  Inhaled nasal steroids for allergic rhinitis
  24-hour availability of staff to coach family on appropriate management of acute
    exacerbations

Goal of Intervention
  To decrease emergency department visits and hospitalizations through home
    management

Environment
  City in close proximity to refineries
  Home 50+ years old
  Heated by natural gas with space heaters

Impact of Disease on Patient/Family
  Missed 28 days of school the prior year
  3 times per week of nocturnal awakenings
  Decreased activity related to exercise-induced asthma
  Increased parental anxiety

Outcomes
  No missed school days 7 months after enrollment in program
  Very infrequent nighttime problems
  Increased participation in sports without exercise-induced bronchospasm
  Decreased parental stress related to perception of better control of symptoms

Courtesy of University of Texas Medical Branch at Galveston, Galveston, Texas.

NOTES

1. S.K. Powell, "Utilization Management," in *Nursing Case Management: A Practical Guide to Success in Managed Care,* ed. S.K. Powell (Philadelphia: Lippincott-Raven, 1996), 77–141.

2. *St. Anthony's DRG Working Guidebook* (Alexandria: St. Anthony's Publishers, 1994).

3. R.L. Jenkins and R.L. Henderson, "Motivating the Staff: What Nurses Expect from Their Supervisors," *Nursing Management* 15, no. 2 (1984): 13.

4. National Asthma Education Program, *Executive Summary: Guidelines for the Diagnosis and Management of Asthma,* U.S. Department of Health and Human Services Pub. No. 94-3042 A (Washington, DC: 1994).

CHAPTER 11

The University of Connecticut Health System's Evolving Model of Clinical Resource Management

Gloria J. Opirhory and Anthony E. Voytovich

Chapter Objectives

1. To describe an evolving model of clinical resource management.
2. To describe the Univeristy of Connecticut Health System (UCHS) patient care delivery model.
3. To discuss the development and implementation of care paths at UCHS.

Founded in 1961, the Health Center is Connecticut's only publicly supported academic health center. It consists of three main units: the School of Medicine, the School of Dental Medicine, and the University of Connecticut Health System. The University of Connecticut Schools of Medicine and Dental Medicine educate the new generation of physicians, dentists, and other health care professionals and pass on the benefits of advanced research to patients.

The University of Connecticut Health System (UCHS) was created in 1994 to enhance the "environment of exemplary patient care" to fulfill the Health Center's mission and serve Connecticut's citizens. This system includes the 204-bed John Dempsey Hospital, which provides routine and specialized inpatient, outpatient, and emergency services; Internal Medicine Associates, the system's primary care practice, which focuses on prevention, wellness, and ongoing management of medical problems; and University Physicians and Dentists, the integrated multispecialty group practice of more than 200 physicians, dentists, and other health care professionals. UCHS has approximately 300,000 outpatient visits per year.

EVOLVING MODEL OF CLINICAL RESOURCE MANAGEMENT

Since November 1994, multiple approaches have been initiated within UCHS to reduce and contain costs. These include operational restructuring, work redesign, and care path development. These efforts are part of our aggressive management of clinical resources, which is essential in achieving significant cost reduction. Increased emphasis on decreasing length of stay (LOS), increasing efficiency in delivery of care, and reducing unnecessary use of services on the inpatient units will significantly improve the management of clinical resources. Unlike larger hospitals, our medical/surgical units provide a wide variety of patient populations. The size and nature of these units make it difficult to identify a definitive set of care paths. This presents some interesting challenges and opportunities.

Our unit team approach is unique and has been successful in its early stages. The newly created clinical governance committee of the School of Medicine faculty is a full partner in these endeavors.

Unit Teams

The medical department that generally manages the majority of patients on a given unit assists directly in the management of the clinical resources used by patients on that unit. The clinical chairs were asked to identify a lead physician on each unit. The lead physician for a unit works closely with the nursing manager and advanced-practice nurses (either nurse practitioners or clinical nurse specialists). Together, they constitute the unit-based triad (clinical resource management unit team) who are responsible for clinical resource management. Goals are to shorten the length of stay and decrease clinical resource consumption where appropriate. This is particularly important with those patients who are neither case managed nor on a care path.

Ongoing, prospective interactions with residents and support services can achieve significant results even before redesign and/or care paths are totally implemented. Units with high cost or high volume, diagnosis-related groups (DRGs) with side variations in resource consumption, and high length of stay or services critical to managed-care negotiations are the first to be reviewed. The financial focus of care paths, redesign, and the case management process is at the unit level. Opportunities to reduce costs and/or enhance patient care services are also available through the systematic review of physician practice patterns and the resources used to provide that care to various patient groups (DRGs).

Assumptions that underlie the review of physicians and use of resources are as follows:

- A major cost reduction strategy involves decreasing clinical resource utilization/consumption to complement the ongoing work redesign/cost reduction activities underway in all clinical departments throughout UCHS.
- The control and standardization of clinical resource utilization/consumption are generally desirable to enhance positive patient outcomes while reducing the cost of care; standardized practices must be evidence based.
- Analysis of physician practice patterns must involve the leadership of qualified, respected physician colleagues in a spirit of discovery and improvement.
- Most physicians (and other providers) are willing and able to modify their practice when provided with valid and reliable data suggesting better methods.
- UCHS possesses or has access to valid data illustrating variances in patient care services and resources consumed as compared to internal and/or external benchmarks.
- UCHS has the necessary staff expertise and related resources to analyze the data in a meaningful way.

After a patient group has been identified, the best available data are reviewed, analyzed, and summarized. The forms shown in Exhibits 11–1 and 11–2 are used to collect data, which are then summmarized and communicated to the appropriate persons, including physicians, care path teams, and care managment teams. The communications strategy includes one-on-one meetings with identified physicians to review the data, answer questions, and discuss practice changes deemed beneficial and feasible. The need for development of a care path is also considered during these discussions, although this may not always be an appropriate solution. The role of the physician colleague in ensuring the success of clinical resource management cannot be overemphasized. The UCHS medical director and the faculty clinical governance committee (CGC) also have responsibility for managing clinical resources. Specific strategies that have been employed by the unit teams to improve the management of clinical resources are as follows:

1. Select top DRGs or procedures based on volume, costs, LOS, and financial risk for institution.
2. Review and evaluate all current and planned care paths.
3. Coordinate selection with redesign activities.
4. Select physicians for each unit.
5. Obtain data/cost outcomes.
6. Adjust data for severity.
7. Develop resource consumption profile by department.
8. Graph data: LOS, severity, cost, mortality.
9. Summarize current practice patterns.
10. Review benchmark data.
11. Identify opportunities for improvement.

Exhibit 11–1 Clinical Resource Utilization Unit Team Plan

Unit: _____

I.   A.   What opportunities have you identified for clinical resource utilization?

     B.   What data (sources) did you rely on to research and identify these opportunities?
          (Use attached form for I.A. and I.B.)

II. Summarize the approach you expect to pursue to address these opportunities.

III. What are the major barriers to the proposed plan?

IV. Projected next steps:

V.   Comments/additional information:

Courtesy of University of Connecticut Health Center, Farmington, Connecticut.

12. Select improvements for action.
13. Implement actions.
14. Establish time for evaluation and follow-up.

UCHS Patient Care Delivery Model

Redesign is the UCHS's call to change. Like health care in general, we are confronted with belt-tightening economic conditions and are challenged to reduce our costs, improve efficiency, and enhance both the quality of patient care and customer satisfaction. Competition is fierce in the health care industry, and the nature of academic health centers does not always lend itself to cost-effective practices.

John Dempsey Hospital holds a unique position in the state of Connecticut. We are the state academic health center, with educational, research, and clinical imperatives. We are well established as a university hospital and state institution and are in the process of developing and expanding our health system. Consequently, there are both internal and external expectations that the UCHS serve as a leader in health care delivery, education, and research. To do so, we have created an en-

Exhibit 11–2 Clinical Resource Utilization Plan Opportunity Statement Form

We Have the Opportunity To:	By/Through	Data Source(s)

Date _____

Courtesy of University of Connecticut Health Center, Farmington, Connecticut.

tirely different way of delivering patient care. Processes are being streamlined and barriers broken. Patient care and customer service will be seamless and user friendly across the entire continuum of care. Traditional roles and functions are being revisited. We are asking if the right people are in the right place, doing the right thing, in the right way, for the right cost.

Our patient care delivery model not only reduces costs, increases efficiency, and enhances customer satisfaction, but it is professionally rewarding for staff and promotes the mission triad of education, research, and clinical excellence. Our model has been not imposed upon us but designed by us.

The delivery model is a reflection of the philosophy and values inherent in the UCHS culture. Our model focuses on wellness and the appropriate use of UCHS resources. Excellence in patient care includes continuous improvement that is systematic and cost-effective. We are creating meaningful, satisfying professional roles for all employees, as well as a system that is caring and compassionate and that satisfies the needs of patients, their families, and staff.

The patient care delivery model redesign team was called upon to create a vision for the UCHS care delivery model and to design a patient care delivery model that would enhance the quality of patient care throughout the UCHS while decreasing the overall cost of delivering patient care. An essential criterion was the applicability of the model to both inpatient and outpatient settings and flexibility within the model to meet the needs of various units, departments, and practices.

The UCHS ambulatory services are changing focus toward minimal inconvenience to patients and maximum efficiency in the use of resources. Key planning principles enhanced or built into the model include

- low number of patient stops, interactions
- care and support components available at single points of service wherever possible
- care sites organized within multidisciplinary clinical clusters
- high degree of resource sharing and flexibility for resource use
- elimination of non–value-adding steps and tasks
- accountability for outcomes assigned and authorized at the practice sites

Coordination of patient care, case management, and care paths are the tools used to ensure and control appropriate resource utilization. The patient care delivery model is shown in Figure 11–1.

At the center of the model is the patient/family. Immediately surrounding the patient/family is the care management team. This team is composed exclusively of professionals who plan, manage, and deliver patient care. They act as the patients' anchor to the UCHS. The team also functions as the point of contact for community physicians or affiliated systems who refer patients to the UCHS for episodic testing or consultation. Members of the team generally include physicians, advanced-practice registered nurses (APRNs) and staff RNs, other health professionals, and professional students. Case management responsibilities are assigned to the most appropriate team member. The core care teams and the referring community physicians/affiliated systems intersect with each other and the care management team and interact with the patient/family. The core care team is composed of professionals and assistive personnel who provide direct, hands-on patient care. The specific composition and staffing level of a team will depend on the patient population for which the team is providing care, as well as the patient acuity, volume, and throughput. While the RN often functions as the direct link, the team also includes physicians, other health professionals, care associates, and professional students. Supporting both the care teams and the patient are the clerical/administrative and environmental staff. The foundations of the model are case management, care paths, and clinical resource utilization.

CASE MANAGEMENT

Case management has been defined as a collaborative process that assesses, plans, implements, coordinates, monitors, and evaluates options and services to meet an individual's health needs through communications and available resources to promote quality, cost-effective outcomes.[1] The goals of the case management process are to improve outcomes and reduce costs. These goals are detailed in Exhibit 11–3.

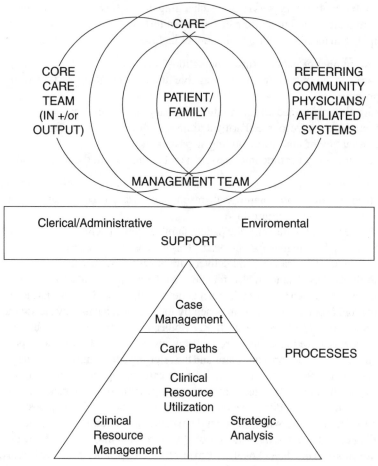

Figure 11–1 Patient Care Delivery Model. Courtesy of University of Connecticut Health Center, Farmington, Connecticut.

Exhibit 11–3 Goals of Case Management

- Improve
  1. Patient outcomes
  2. Quality
  3. Links with community resources
  4. Standard of care
  5. Coordination of services
  6. Organizational performance
  7. The use of data as a means to measure impact of case management
  8. The evaluation of the achievement of goals
  9. Monitor progress
- Decrease/Reduce
  1. LOS—appropriately
  2. Cost
- Increase
  1. Satisfaction
     a. patient
     b. family
     c. payer
     d. staff/physician
  2. Revenue—as appropriate
  3. Effective clinical resource management
     a. appropriate level of service
- Care will be:
  1. Standardized yet appropriate for each individual patient
  2. Seamless

Courtesy of University of Connecticut Health Center, Farmington, Connecticut.

The six major components found in the definition have been used to categorize the functions/activities. These functions/activities are described in Exhibit 11–4. All functions/activities become the responsibility of the care management team and are not solely the responsibility of the care managers. The one notable exception is the coordination of financial counseling, which may include the team social worker but the ultimate responsibility for which remains with the financial counselors.

Decisions about which patients are case managed are based on a number of screening criteria (Exhibit 11–5). All UCHS patients meeting any one of the criteria are screened by the care management team. The care management team decides when a patient must be case managed and assigns that responsibility to the most appropriate team member.

Exhibit 11–4 Care Management Team Activities/Functions

- Assesses
  1. Initial patient review before precertification
  2. Assess intensity, severity, diagnosis, and level of care and services
  3. Review case management risk criteria
- Plans
  1. Assigns patient to care path if appropriate
  2. Scheduling—tests, procedures, equipment needed for procedures or home
  3. Continuum of care
- Implements
  1. Case management process if appropriate
  2. Plan of care
  3. Notifies appropriate staff
  4. Arrange for appropriate level of care and services
- Coordinates
  1. Education
     a. prevention
     b. patient/family responsibilities in coordinating services
     c. preop teaching
     d. support to patient and family
  2. Financial counseling
  3. Changes in levels of care
     a. transfer
     b. discharge
     c. episodic care
     d. services no longer needed
- Monitors
  1. Compliance with plan of care
  2. Compliance with care paths
- Evaluates
  1. Present and future resource needs
  2. Aggregate data to improve
     a. care paths
     b. processes
     c. resource utilization
     d. organizational performance

Courtesy of University of Connecticut Health Center, Farmington, Connecticut.

CARE PATH UTILIZATION, DEVELOPMENT, AND IMPLEMENTATION

Among the many tools available to improve efficiency, clinical pathways or care paths are the most effective if employed appropriately. Contemporary management philosophy recognizes that variation (within a process or outcome) re-

Exhibit 11–5 Case Management Screening Criteria

- Clinical or Patient Risk Factors
  1. Age
     a. 65 or older, living alone or with an incapable caregiver
     b. Mentally retarded, regardless of age
     c. Pregnant minors
  2. Residence
     a. Transfers from other facilities, including nursing homes, group homes, and other hospitals
     b. Unclear, or no known place of residence
  3. Behavioral Factors
     a. History of noncompliance with health care plan
     b. Readmissions within 15, 30, or 60 days, except in cases of readmission per chemotherapy protocol
     c. Attempted suicide
     d. Possible/active substance abuse
  4. Social/Familial/Cultural
     a. No identification
     b. No next of kin and/or a guardianship need
     c. Cultural/language barriers
     d. Single parents (minors at home)
     e. Obstetrics—minor patient, adoption, infant loss
  5. Handicapped/Disabled
     a. Abuse, suspected abuse, failure to thrive, neglect, substance abuse, accidental drug ingestion
     b. All psychiatric patients
     c. History of multiple hospitalizations within a short period of time
     d. Joint replacement
     e. AIDS
     f. Bone marrow transplants
     g. Newly diagnosed insulin-dependent diabetes mellitus (IDDM)
     h. Orthopedic trauma
  6. Nursing Care/Social Work
     a. Patients with teaching needs
     b. Patients with inadequate financial resources
     c. Patients being currently served by other agencies
     d. Patients who may require special equipment in their homes; e.g., oxygen, ventilator, apnea monitors, parenteral or enteral feedings
     e. Patients with changes in body image (stomas, plastic repair, burn)
- Institutional Financial Risk Factors
  1. High volume
  2. High length of stay
  3. High cost

Courtesy of University of Connecticut Health Center, Farmington, Connecticut.

flects a system that is in less than optimal control. For example, a thermostat that allows room temperature to vary from 60 to 80 degrees achieves a mean of 70 but only transiently visits the optimum temperature. Similarly, in health care settings, variations in the care process and the lack of agreed-upon plans make it nearly impossible to optimize our approach. Oncologists have known this for years and have established protocols that enable us to know the often slim margins offered by the various chemotherapeutic regimens. Clinical pathways represent multidisciplinary plans that establish, on a day-to-day basis, what is expected by way of studies, interventions, and outcomes.

Our care path process began with the careful analysis of our high-cost, high-risk, and high-volume activities. This analysis was performed by senior clinical leaders and members of the UCHS administration. Given the investment in personnel in conducting a proper care path process, it makes little sense to devote energies to diagnoses that occur infrequently or are relatively straightforward. Initially, we chose eight DRGs encompassing such activities as total hip replacement, open heart surgery, acute myocardial infarction, extreme prematurity, and stroke. A team cochaired by a physician and a nurse established a multidisciplinary group who met and formulated a plan of management. The most difficult part of the care path process was to arrive at a consensus across the disciplines. Each member of the team carried the plan to his or her respective department for endorsement, which was a major challenge in some cases. Although it is possible to establish a care path process as a grassroots bottom-up enterprise, support from senior leadership is critical to maintain the momentum and to make available the required resources.

Care path development was monitored by an implementation team chaired by the chief of staff and the director of quality resource management (QRM), with representation from each team as well as each discipline. Progress in care path development was tracked carefully within the QRM committee, executive board meetings, and meetings held by administration. As the plans were developed, extensive education occurred in clinical department meetings as well as hospital department meetings to clarify goals and objectives.

We found it essential to establish an infrastructure to guarantee a consistent approach and to facilitate the ultimate flow of data on variance into our systems. We insisted upon a consistent format for team composition, documentation, and reporting. This was accomplished by creating a handbook with examples and clearly established rationales for each step of the process. We have purchased and begun to implement a software package that allows us to record and document each pathway; print the required forms and documents; and record, track, and analyze data that augment information on resource use, cost, and LOS from elsewhere within the system.

Some institutions claim to have large numbers of critical pathways in place. However, upon careful examination, one may discover preprinted care plans with

* Improve quality—through work redesign and process improvement activities to enhance patient care satisfaction outcomes.
* Manage change—create a proactive and positive approach to change to increase flexibility and ability to respond to market changes.
* Reduce costs—to maintain competitive status in the challenging health care marketplace and stay in business.
* "Do No Harm"—ensure that cost reductions do not come at the expense of patient care, and maintain our focus on the core missions.

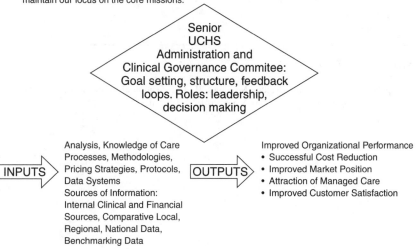

Figure 11–2 UCHS Performance Improvement. Courtesy of University of Connecticut Health Center, Farmington, Connecticut.

little evidence of local multidisciplinary buy-in or connection to the data systems, all so important to make full use of this tool. We elected to work initially with a limited number of teams, and to build carefully the infrastructure that would allow us to establish consistent practices, minimize variation, and gradually improve our processes and outcomes. The urgency of appropriately using, developing, implementing, and tracking compliance with care paths has increased as we have begun to implement all of the above changes. These activities are moving from an academic pace to a faster proactive pace.

CONCLUSION

UCHS is still an evolving system. Daily progress is made in bringing together what were once divergent enterprises into a singular health care system. The once separate and distinct department-based physician faculty practices are becoming one multispecialty ambulatory group practice. At the same time, the operations of all components are undergoing massive change and integration.

Progress is made slowly but surely as we move to integrate fully ambulatory and acute care services. The greatest resource is the talent of all the component players. The mission of education, research, and patient care in an exemplary model is always at the core of these changes.

The case studies that follow exemplify the collaborative efforts of the professionals who work together to ensure the success of the UCHS. The singular goal of performance improvement is the focal point that brings it all together, as depicted in Figure 11–2.

NOTE

1. *CCM Certification Guide* (Rolling Meadows, IL: Certification of Insurance Rehabilitation Specialists Commission/Certified Case Manager, 1993), flyleaf.

CHAPTER 12

Case Study in Total Hip Arthroplasty: A Patient-Centered Model of Care

Karen Livingston, Anne Horbatuck, and Courtland G. Lewis

Chapter Objectives

1. To delineate the evolution of one process improvement plan at the University of Connecticut Health System (UCHS).
2. To describe the implementation of a total hip arthroplasty patient-centered model of care.
3. To define the ongoing modification and refinement of the patient-centered quality improvement process.

Total hip arthroplasty has been embraced in many institutions across the United States as an early candidate for care path development. It is a frequently performed, relatively expensive, and elective procedure (performed primarily on the elderly population). In this context, it has been the focus of considerable attention by the Health Care Financing Administration (HFCA).[1] By its nature, there is a large associated procedure effect, and the impact upon quality of life and the overall cost-effectiveness of the procedure have been established.[2] Moreover, given the need for a patient who is both reasonably healthy and cognitively intact, there is arguably more homogeneity within the patient population for this procedure than for many others. For these reasons, total joint arthroplasty has been identified as an ideal focus for care path development.

In 1985, the senior author (CGL) became interested in examining the variance in satisfaction of patients undergoing total hip and total knee arthroplasty. A study of this patient cohort demonstrated that expectations and satisfaction could be related to the patient's psychological profile using the standardized Symptom Check

List-90 instrument.[3] To minimize the risk of complications, patients undergoing total joint arthroplasty require compliance with positioning, exercise, and deep-vein thrombosis prophylaxis regimens. In 1988, a grant funded through the Multipurpose Arthritis Center at the University of Connecticut (NIH Grant #AR 20621) was obtained to study various forms of pre- and perioperative patient education. This study, performed at the University of Connecticut Health System (UCHS) and Hartford Hospital, required consistent nursing and rehabilitation algorithms that served as a starting point for the development of a patient-centered model of care in total joint arthroplasty at UCHS.

Concurrent market analysis demonstrated that despite median length of stay below the mean average for our service area, patient charges were approximately 15 percent higher than average, although less than the HCFA reimbursement to our institution for diagnosis-related group (DRG) 209.

PATIENT PROCESS MODEL

Conceptually, the care model was envisioned from its inception as being an "episode of care" approach. Hence, once a patient had fulfilled subjective and objective criteria for hip arthroplasty, preoperative planning was implemented. This was carried directly into the hospitalization component and into long-term follow-up.

Schematically, the model is represented in Figure 12–1. The patient enters at a lower level of function and achieves a sustainable improvement in the long term followed out over a several-year course. The return loop, as diagrammed and discussed later, ensures that each patient's experience contributes to process improvement.

Preoperative Care Process

Since its inception, the total joint care path team has been driven by the acute care nurse practitioner/case manager (KL) and a single surgeon (CGL). Other interdisciplinary team members include the surgical/orthopaedic inpatient nursing manager (AH), the surgery scheduler in the medical practice office, a nurse from the same-day surgery unit, designated total joint arthroplasty physical therapists, the operating room total joint primary nurse, the clinical coordinator anesthesiologist, and the designated surgical social worker. This group meets three times a year to take an overall look at progress and areas for improvement.

At the time of surgery scheduling, as depicted in Figure 12–1, a series of necessary activities are triggered. These include notification of the admitting office, the operating room, rehabilitation services, the American Red Cross autologous donation unit, social services, the dedicated orthopaedic inpatient nursing unit, the

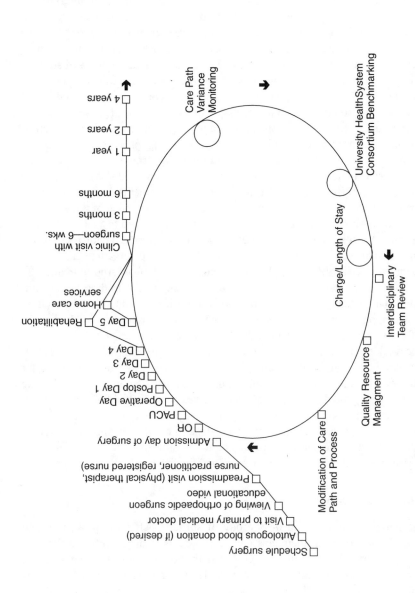

Figure 12–1 Total Joint Arthroplasty Patient-Centered Model of Care. Courtesy of University of Connecticut Health Center, Farmington, Connecticut.

nursing manager, and, most important, the acute care nurse practitioner/case manager. A list of upcoming patients is distributed monthly with the ability to broadcast by voice mail any changes if a patient postpones or reschedules. Approximately three weeks prior to surgery, the patients are seen by the operating surgeon in the outpatient office. At that time, they review an educational videotape of their surgeon outlining the course of treatment as well as risks and benefits of surgery. This approach was found in a previous study[4] to be as effective as or more effective than face-to-face patient education by a surgeon, commercially available videotapes, a home computer teaching program, or a computerized telephone education program in terms of patient knowledge retention around issues such as positioning and deep-vein thrombosis prophylaxis compliance.

Patients are given admission history and physical forms to be completed by their primary care physician preoperatively to ensure completeness of the medical database and identification of potential perioperative problems. Following discussion with the surgeon, an education booklet that duplicates much of the videotape information is supplied to the patient. The patient is instructed to keep the booklet in his or her possession during hospitalization, because discharge instructions are incorporated as well as the date of the six-week follow-up outpatient clinic visit.

During this visit, discharge-planning needs are identified. Approximately 20 percent of patients will require rehabilitation placement due to their home environment. The patient who requires rehabilitation is instructed to visit the facility, complete application packets, and ensure that there is a rehabilitation bed available for his or her projected date of discharge (postoperative day 4).

One week prior to surgery, patients are seen on an outpatient basis in the rehabilitation gym located on the dedicated orthopaedic unit. There they undergo fitting for assistive devices and preoperative explanation of the rehabilitation regimen. They are then seen in the same-day surgery unit by the acute care nurse practitioner/case manager to discuss intraoperative anesthesic options and postoperative pain management. A review of the patient's medical history is done to ensure that specific needs are addressed. At this time, questions pertaining to the procedure and hospital stay are discussed, and discharge plans are reviewed and finalized.

Inpatient Care Process

The patients are admitted on the day of surgery. After the procedure and postanesthesia care unit, their inpatient care process is documented in the care path (Appendix 12–A), which is supported by nursing protocols, educational flowsheets, standard postoperative orders, and rehabilitation protocols. Documentation by exception is performed by physicians, nurses, and rehabilitation therapists (sample in Appendix 12–B). Overall care path variance monitoring is performed by the acute care nurse practioner/case manager. The patient's progression on the care path is monitored daily. To maintain continuity, the acute care nurse practitioner follows the patient at the bedside and assists with identifying and incorporating specific needs in order to maintain the patient on the care path.

Patients remain on the care path until discharged either to a rehabilitation facility on postoperative day 4 or home on postoperative day 5; patients are routinely seen at six weeks, three months, six months, one year, two years, four years, and so on for follow-up.

Outcomes Measures

Four dimensions of outcomes are routinely captured on total joint patients at UCHS. As part of the hospital's postdischarge protocol, inpatient (and sampled outpatient) satisfaction questionnaires are submitted and reviewed on the basis of the Press-Ganey methodology. Routine clinical parameters (physical examination and X-ray) are obtained by the surgeon at follow-up. Functional outcomes measurements at this time include the SF-36 and Western Ontario and McMaster (WOMAC) Universities Osteoarthritis Index at six months and one year. Cumulative and comparative financial data using the Connecticut Hospital Association database (CHIME) and the University HealthSystem Consortium Information Management System (IMS) are reviewed by the care team.

CLOSING THE LOOP

Philosophically, it is our contention that while standardizing care helps to improve expectations by both patients and care providers, clinical care paths have limited impact as isolated tools. Once care paths are developed or, if necessary, reengineered, "closing the loop" is an essential feature. Said differently, the process of data-driven continuous quality improvement is essential to optimizing any patient-oriented care process. The charge to the interdisciplinary care path team, once the pathway is established, is not monitoring per se but rather identifying opportunities for process improvement. Potential data sources include ongoing analysis of care path variances, outcomes data as delineated above, and benchmarking comparisons. Such comparative data, derived from two rounds of clinical benchmarking as part of the University HealthSystem Consortium project on total hip arthroplasty, have been invaluable in both norming against the experience at other academic health centers and identifying areas for substantive improvement.

FUTURE DIRECTIONS

As noted in the introduction, total hip arthroplasty has several inherent advantages as a focus of patient-centered process improvement. One of these advantages, the predictable and dramatic procedure effect of the surgery itself, is a limitation in designing process improvement studies. Specifically, with a relatively small cohort of patients, we have been unable to identify significant impact on overall patient satisfaction, clinical results, or functional outcome as an end point to incremental process improvement. However, measurable improvement in various process parameters (Figure 12–2) has been realized. Maintaining quality while supplying lower cost care in a competitive marketplace does have the poten-

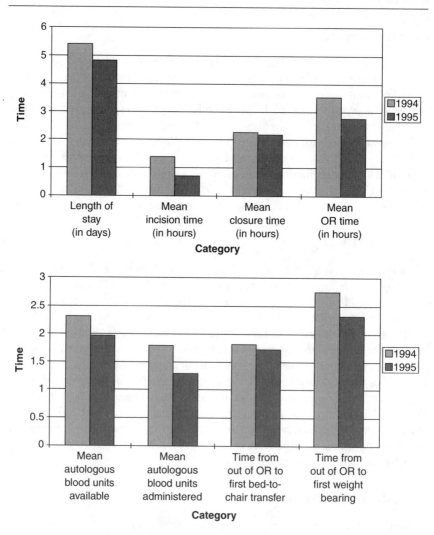

Figure 12–2 Patient-Centered Process Improvements in Total Hip Arthroplasty, 1994/1995. Courtesy of University of Connecticut Health Center, Farmington, Connecticut.

tial for increasing the value of care provided and hence offers a common, relatively expensive, and elective procedure as an ideal focus for further cost-effectiveness research.

At the University of Connecticut, current initiatives include identification of a minimal data set to track patient progress as well as efforts to validate current patient satisfaction techniques. A pilot project to severity index *within* CPT codes is underway, an issue of significant impact on tertiary care practices.

Formal inpatient cost accounting is currently in the early implementation stage at the University of Connecticut; once UCHS's ability to identify costs both early and late in the hospital course has matured, it should be possible to structure contracts with payers such that the impetus to transfer patients early to a rehabilitation setting will be neutralized. Through such efforts, less disruption of the patient's relationships with physician, nursing, and rehabilitation can be realized.

NOTES

1. Health Care Financing Administration, *Center of Excellence in Total Hip Arthroplasty* (request for proposal, Washington, DC: 1996).

2. R.W. Chang et al., "A Cost-Effectiveness Analysis of Total Hip Arthroplasty for Osteoarthritis of the Hip," *Journal of the American Medical Association* 275 (1996): 858–865.

3. L.F. Derogatus, "SCL-90-R," *Archives of Physical Medicine and Rehabilitation* 64 (1983): 359–363.

4. C.G. Lewis et al., "Patient Education in Total Joint Arthroplasty: Impact upon Compliance and Patient Satisfaction," unpublished manuscript, 1996.

Appendix 12–A
Total Hip Arthroplasty Care Path

	Prehospital	OR Day Inpatient Day 1	Postop Day 1 Day 2	Postop Day 2 Day 3
Outcomes	Patient/family verbalize understanding of plan of care Patient/family will identify posthospital destination Patient satisfied with process of preparation Abnormal labs are identified/addressed Patients who want short-term rehab have completed application Anesthesia plan in place Presurgical evaluation through patient survey: SF-36, WOMAC	Anesthesia plan consistent with preop plan Adequate pain control	Patient progressing per PT protocol Adequate pain relief Stable HCT	Patient progressing per PT protocol Adequate pain relief Stable HCT
Consults needed	Nurse practitioner Physical therapy Anesthesia as needed Blood bank	Anesthesia	PT OT Anesthesia (if regional)	PT OT
Diagnostic studies	Blood work Urinalysis EKG Chest X-ray Other studies as needed	X-ray in PACU Hgb in PACU	HCT in AM Other labs as needed	HCT in AM Other labs as needed

Courtesy of University of Connecticut Health Center, Farmington, Connecticut.

216

	Prehospital	OR Day Inpatient Day 1	Postop Day 1 Day 2	Postop Day 2 Day 3
Treatments (procedures)		Pain assessment per appropriate pain protocol VS & CSM checks q 4 hr Foley to closed drainage TEDS stockings/PAS Hemovac to suction IS q hour while awake Monitor primary dressing. Reinforce as needed	Pain assessment per appropriate pain protocol VS q 4 hr CSM checks q 8 hr Foley to closed drainage TEDS stockings/PAS Hemovac D/C IS q hour while awake Monitor primary dressing, reinforce as needed D/C regional catheter as appropriate	Pain assessment per appropriate pain protocol VS & CSM checks q 8 hr D/C foley at 8 AM per nursing protocol TEDS stockings/PAS IS q hour while awake Primary dressing changed by MD then dressing/incision care per MD order
Treatments (medications)		IV fluids Antibiotics Tx Stool softeners Pain medications Anticoagulation Tx Routine meds	D/C IV fluids when PO adequate Antibiotic therapy Stool softeners Pain medications Anticoagulation therapy Routine meds	Stool softeners Pain medications Anticoagulation therapy Routine meds
Diet		Clear liquids or diet as ordered	Regular, or special diet as needed	Regular, or special diet as needed
Activities allowed		Bed rest in abduction pillow	Dangle with PT BID, OOB as tolerated Abduction pillow while in bed	Progressive activity per PT protocol: OOB to chair, ambulate as tolerated Regular pillow between legs while in bed/chair
Patient education	Patient education video Patient education booklet	Nursing patient education protocol Patient education booklet	Nursing patient education protocol Patient education booklet	Nursing patient education protocol Patient education booklet
Discharge-planning efforts	Application for short-term rehabilitation completed as needed		Social work if referral to rehab	Social work if referral to rehab

	Postop Day 3 Day 4	Postop Day 4 Day 5	Postop Day 5 Day 6	Postdischarge
Outcomes	Patient progressing per PT protocol Adequate pain relief Stable HCT Patient/family/MD confirm discharge plan	Patient discharged to rehab as appropriate Patient discharged to home if appropriate with home care referral as needed Patient verbalizes understanding of home education program Adequate pain relief	Patient discharged to home with home care referral as needed Adequate pain relief	Outcome evaluation through patient survey: SF-36, WOMAC (6 months postop)
Consults needed	PT OT	PT	PT	Patient at home or rehab
Diagnostic studies	HCT in AM Other labs as needed	Other labs as needed	Other labs as needed	Lab work per MD order
Treatments (procedures)	Pain assessment per appropriate pain protocol VS & CSM checks q 8 hr TEDS stockings/PAS IS q hour while awake Dressing/incision care per MD order	Pain assessment per appropriate pain protocol VS & CSM checks q 8 hr TEDS stockings/PAS Dressing/incision care per MD order IS q hour while awake	Pain assessment per appropriate pain protocol VS & CSM checks q 8 hr TEDS stockings Dressing/incision care per MD order IS q hour while awake	Dressing/incision care per MD order
Treatments (medications)	Stool softeners Pain medications Anticoagulation therapy Routine meds	Stool softeners Pain medications Anticoagulation therapy Routine meds	Stool softeners Pain medications Anticoagulation therapy Routine meds	Pain medications Anticoagulation therapy
Diet	Regular, or special diet as needed	Regular, or special diet as needed	Regular, or special diet as needed	Regular, or special diet as needed
Activities allowed	Progressive activity per PT protocol: Ambulate as tolerated Regular pillow between legs while in bed/chair	Progressive activity per PT protocol: Stair climbing as appropriate Regular pillow between legs while in bed/chair	Progressive activity per PT protocol	Partial weight bearing × 6 weeks (cemented) Touch down weight bearing × 6 weeks (uncemented)

	Postop Day 3 Day 4	Postop Day 4 Day 5	Postop Day 5 Day 6	Postdischarge
Patient education	Nursing patient education protocol Patient education booklet	Nursing patient education protocol Patient education booklet	Nursing patient education protocol Patient education booklet	
Discharge-planning efforts	Social work if referral to rehab Home care referral is needed	Discharge summaries completed as needed Nurse PT OT MD Discharged to rehab as appropriate Discharged to home as appropriate	Discharged to home	

Appendix 12–B

Interdisciplinary Daily Progress Notes—Total Hip Arthroplasty—POD #1

✓ = Expected Response * = Variance ➔ = Unchanged from Previous Significant Entry		
DATE:		
PHYSICIAN:	YES	NO
Vital Signs WNL		
Lungs Clear		
Cardiac Status Stable		
Abdominal Exam Normal		
Neurovascular Status Stable		
CMS Intact		
Dressing Dry and Intact		
Pain Control Adequate		
PO Intake Adequate without N/V		
Urine Output >250 cc/8 hours		
HVAC Output Overnight: Removed ❑ Yes ❑ No HCT POD #1:		
Specific Plans/Actions:		
Clinical Course Thus Far: ❑ No variation, remains on care path		
❑ Variation has occurred, see progress note on back		
Patient remains on path ❑ Yes ❑ No		
Signature	MD/APRN	Time
I have: ❑ Seen the patient ❑ Examined the patient ❑ Agree with the above ❑ With the addendum as noted in progress notes on back.		
Signature	Attending MD	Date Time
NURSING	YES	NO
	AM PM	AM PM

Courtesy of University of Connecticut Health Center, Farmington, Connecticut.

Vital Signs within Prescribed Limits		
CMS WNL per Protocol		
PO Intake Adequate without N/V		
Urine Output WNL per Orders		
Pain Control Adequate		
Primary Dressing Dry and Intact		
Teaching Plan Maintained		
Clinical Course Thus Far: ❑ No reportable conditions, remains on care path		
❑ Reportable condition has occurred, see progress note on back		
Patient remains on path ❑ Yes ❑ No		
Signature	RN	Time
Signature	RN	Time

CHAPTER 13

Care Path Design in the Neonatal Intensive Care Unit: Case Study for the Extremely Low Birthweight Infant

Terese Lynch Donovan and Marilyn R. Sanders

Chapter Objectives

1. To outline the steps taken in the development of the Care Path for the Extremely Low Birthweight Infant.
2. To describe the utility of baseline and pilot data in the creation of the Care Path for the Extremely Low Birthweight Infant and in the identification of opportunities for improvement in care.

The Neonatal Intensive Care Unit (NICU) at John Dempsey Hospital, University of Connecticut Health Center, is the designated level 3 regional perinatal referral center for northern Connecticut. Approximately 400 infants are admitted annually to the 30-bed NICU. Infants who no longer require intensive care may be transferred to our special care and newborn nurseries or transported back to their referral hospitals. The special care nursery (SCN) contains 10 beds and treats predominantly infants who require supplemental oxygen and pharmacotherapy for bronchopulmonary dysplasia (BPD). The newborn nursery (NBN) contains eight monitored beds for growing preterm infants who are breathing room air and who are able to tolerate full-volume intermittent feedings.

John Dempsey Hospital is an academic medical center. Primary medical care in the NICU is provided by pediatric house officers and 13 advanced practitioners (neonatal nurse practitioners [NNPs] or physician assistants [PAs]). Neonatal fellows and seven attending neonatologists complete the neonatal medical team. Additional team members include the disciplines of nursing, dietary, social work, occupational therapy/physical therapy, pharmacy, and respiratory therapy. With the exception of a limited number of rotating house officers, medical care in the NICU is governed by a relatively small and consistent group of professionals.

Annually, between 50 and 60 infants are admitted to the NICU who are designated as "extremely low birthweight" (ELBW). These infants weigh less than 1,000 grams (2 pounds, 3 ounces) at birth and are usually born between 23 and 28 weeks' gestation. In an examination of populations of hospitalized infants who might benefit from a case management model of care delivery, this group of patients stands out because of the prolonged length of hospitalization and the high cost of care. While as a proportion of total patients, ELBW infants are relatively few, they use a disproportionately large amount of health care resources, including total hospital days, total ICU days, and percentage of total hospital charges. For example, our 1994 data show that while infants weighing less than 1,000 grams at birth represented 12.7 percent of NICU admissions, their total hospital days constituted 35 percent of total NICU patient days.

These tiny infants require the best that neonatal technology has to offer, including assisted ventilation, sophisticated monitoring devices, total parenteral nutrition, pharmacotherapy for respiratory distress syndrome, infection and hypotension, and equipment for thermal control. This care also necessitates frequent laboratory and radiological interventions because many complications of preterm delivery, such as hyperbilirubinemia, hypoglycemia, hyperglycemia, and periventricular/intraventricular hemorrhage, exhibit few overt clinical symptoms to assist with accurate and definitive diagnosis. Staffing levels for nursing personnel must be appropriately matched to the needs of these infants to optimize outcomes. In addition to frequent assessments and evaluation of the effects of the disease processes and treatments, meticulous attention to details regarding fluid balance, thermoregulation, skin care, and developmental support is required. Adequate time and attention must also be allotted to the provision of the intense emotional support required by families who experience the delivery of one or more infants who may be surviving at extremely low birthweights.

DEVELOPMENT OF THE EXTREMELY LOW BIRTHWEIGHT INFANT CARE PATH

When the John Dempsey Hospital care path implementation team recognized that opportunities for improved delivery of care and cost savings might exist with ELBW infants, our efforts at care path development began. Relating our population of ELBW infants to the case management model was a challenge because published literature provided little guidance to our efforts to create a clinical plan of care based on a predictable sequencing of events. Care paths reported in the adult literature often involved short-term hospitalizations related to surgical procedures. Our data for 1994 demonstrated that infants weighing less than 1,000 grams remained in the neonatal units for an average of 90 days. We initially questioned whether it was possible to create such a guideline for medical care given the uniqueness of this patient population. Ultimately, we recognized that while clearly outliers would exist who would "fall off" the path, there was a reasonably predictable sequence of events over the first two weeks of life from which we might structure a standardized approach to care for the "average" patient. Subsequent to this first two weeks, there is substantial heterogeneity in hospital course until the time closer to discharge. Thus, we have devised an additional care path to address the discharge needs of infants diagnosed with bronchopulmonary dysplasia. In the future, as our experience and sophistication increase, we hope to fill in this temporal gap with other care paths reflecting the needs of both long-term ventilated patients and healthier, growing preterm infants.

The steps followed in developing our care path for the ELBW infant are summarized in Exhibit 13–1. An initial limited retrospective chart review of ELBW infants was performed to identify current practice in the NICU. This chart review provided data that permitted the identification of time frames for and sequencing of predictable events in the early hospitalization of ELBW infants. It also allowed us to clarify and define our population further. We elected to exclude those infants born at less than 24 weeks' gestation and/or less than 500 grams because of their small numbers, very high mortality rate, and lack of predictability. Because the

---

Exhibit 13–1 Steps in Development of the Extremely Low Birthweight Infant Care Path

1. Review of existing literature
2. Retrospective chart review
3. Draft of care path to medical team for review
4. Care path revision
5. Revised draft to nursing team for review
6. Identification of "case managers"
7. Development of data collection tool
8. Initiation of prospective baseline data collection
9. Interim data review
10. Revised draft to multidisciplinary team for review
11. Care path revision
12. Summary of baseline data reported to multidisciplinary team
13. Final revisions of care path
14. Education of caregivers regarding care path use
15. Pilot implementation of care path
16. Ongoing support and education of caregivers
17. Care path evaluation

chart review brought us to the realization that it was unrealistic to create a care path mapping out predictable events during a three-month hospitalization, we elected to focus our attention on the first two weeks of NICU hospitalization, a time when interventions and changes in medical condition are frequent.

Physician Support for the Extremely Low Birthweight Infant Care Path

Using the template provided by the care path implementation team, an initial draft of the Extremely Low Birthweight Infant Care Path was developed and presented individually to each of the attending neonatologists and to the advanced practitioners for review. Although not conforming to the ideal and philosophy of care path development as a multidisciplinary effort, this approach was taken for a number of reasons. First, unlike many care path development models, our care path team chairperson was a neonatologist who felt that physician buy-in was critical to the success of this project. This care path was our physicians' first exposure to the concept of case management. This concept can be threatening because it represents change in general and also because it may be perceived as threatening the individual's practice philosophy. Physicians may feel as if *they* are being "managed" by the path. The neonatologists needed to be reassured that in the case management model the patient remains the central focus of care. Some individual personal preferences and biases toward care needed to be negotiated to ensure collaboration from all.

The time spent allowing discussion and input to creation of the path was required to ensure buy-in from the physicians as a prelude to successful implementation. The neonatologists were reassured that the path would not be implemented without the collection of prospective data to validate subsequently the path's outcomes. An additional concern for academic physicians relates to their teaching role. Academic physicians work diligently at teaching house officers to solve problems, given clinical, laboratory, and other data, in working out a plan of care. Concern has been expressed that care paths promote a "cookbook" approach to patient care and that with the steps outlined, caregivers no longer need truly to think about the patient. It was important to emphasize that patients' individual health care needs do take precedence over the care path. Education of the attendings also needed to occur regarding patient selection for the path and conditions that promote exclusion from the path.

Advanced Practitioner Support for the Extremely Low Birthweight Infant Care Path

Review and critique of the care path by the neonatal advanced practitioners was also a critical step in development of this care path. In our NICU, NNPs and PAs perform primary bedside medical care that is overseen by the neonatal attending physicians. Our NICU has a long history of using advanced-practice roles. Because of their experience and expertise, our advanced practitioners function very independently, with little supervision required. Therefore, feedback from those individuals working "in the trenches" was crucial to the development of a care path based on actual and projected real clinical practice.

Nursing Support for the Extremely Low Birthweight Infant Care Path

Once suggestions from the attending physicians and the advanced practitioners were incorporated into the care path, the care path was presented to the two neonatal clinical nurse specialists (CNSs) for review. Feedback was also solicited from several nursing staff members who had developed expertise and interest in caring for these tiny infants. As with the advanced practitioners, we deemed it necessary to obtain input from bedside caregivers early in the process of care path development. At the same time, the clinical nurse specialists, who had been designated as case managers, and the attending neonatologist who chaired our care path team began to develop our data collection tool for variance monitoring and to discuss the role of the case manager for the care path.

Data Collection Tool for the Extremely Low Birthweight Infant Care Path

As part of our quality management program for the nurseries, the data collection tool was designed to target areas of medical and nursing practice related to common clinical problems for this population of infants: for example, thermoregulation, fluid and electrolyte imbalance, acid-base imbalance, hyperbilirubinemia, and skin integrity and care. We attempted to focus on resource utilization by investigating the number of laboratory tests and diagnostic procedures performed and relating these tests to the infant's clinical condition. Because we saw this as a valuable opportunity to monitor and potentially to improve our practice, we also included a number of data collection items pertaining to family support. Once the care path is implemented, the case manager will communicate directly with the family about the adequacy of information and support provided. Items related to parental interaction with the infant were added to provide us with information on balancing the infant's developmental need for careful handling with the parents' desires and needs to interact with their infant. We also elected to include some nursing department "systems issues." These items had been previously identified in our quality assurance monitoring as potential areas for improvement in practice.

Identifying the Case Manager

Currently in our institution, there is no dedicated position entitled "case manager." It is anticipated that personnel at many levels will perform case management functions and that the case manager for each care path will be determined individually by the nature of the pathway and the team members involved. At the outset, the two neonatal CNSs were identified as appropriate case managers for the Extremely Low Birthweight Infant Care Path. This decision was based on the following:

1. Attributes of the CNS role are congruent with the case manager role.
2. CNSs' length of service at the John Dempsey Hospital NICU facilitates their effective communication with the neonatal attendings regarding their practice within the framework of the care path.
3. CNSs have the support of the unit's nursing manager and director for necessary redefinition of role performance.
4. CNSs' removal from direct caregiving means that they can be objective team members with no conflict of interest.
5. CNSs have an ongoing relationship with nursing staff in a supportive role to guide them through transition to the case management model.
6. CNSs' certification as NNPs means that they have an understanding of the medical decision making for this population of infants.
7. CNSs' established role of providing education and support to antepartum patients enables them to be viewed as part of family support network.

We also discussed the possibility of using the advanced practitioners or primary nurses as case managers for this care path. It may be advantageous to use direct bedside caregivers as case managers because of their intimate knowledge of the patient and family and their accountability for the plan of care. However, we felt that given the operation of our unit, this patient population, and the purpose of this care path, it was unfair to expect primary nurses to assume case management functions at this time. We are concerned about creating adversarial relationships (with nurses monitoring the frequency of diagnostic studies) when the care path is expected to promote collaboration and teamwork.

For the advanced practitioner, our primary concern was conflict of interest between the need to manage the patient clinically and the need to monitor the path. Our Extremely Low Birthweight Infant Care Path is time limited, representing a fraction of the total hospital stay of these infants. We were also very concerned about the family's need to adapt to seeing caregivers in multiple roles during a time of intense emotional upheaval.

Baseline Data Collection

Baseline data collection for the Extremely Low Birthweight Infant Care Path occurred for six months. This prospective data collection was important to us for a number of reasons. At the time that we initiated this project, benchmark data from other institutions were not available to us. Although retrospective data from chart review were helpful in drafting the care path, data from the medical record exist within a vacuum; they are removed from the patient. Prospective collection of data is also central to the concept of hypothesis generation and testing in scientific inquiry. We are committed to ongoing data generation and analysis as we further refine this care path and, most important, monitor the frequency of procedures as well as potential adverse outcomes. Collection of prospective data allowed us to appreciate the subtleties and nuances involved in the care of these patients. Connecting the data to existing patients enabled us to better identify opportunities for improvement in care and exclusions from the care path. Ongoing data collection also permitted us to demonstrate that we were serious about designing our path on the basis of substantive information rather than individual preference. Two tools were used for data collection: the care path data collection tool, which targeted variances from the care path, and a tally sheet for the collection of demographic data and frequency monitoring of laboratory and other diagnostic studies and tests as well as potential adverse outcomes. The data were collected by the two neonatal CNSs. Data collected were used to modify the path in order truly to define normative practice recommendations for this population in our unit.

MULTIDISCIPLINARY TEAM INPUT INTO THE EXTREMELY LOW BIRTHWEIGHT INFANT CARE PATH

As the baseline data collection progressed, the care path team expanded to include the nurse manager, a neonatal social worker, a neonatal dietitian, an occupational therapist, the discharge planner, and our data systems manager. A representative of the respiratory therapy department was not included because in our unit respiratory therapists have limited hands-on patient care responsibilities. We also added three nursing staff members (representing all shifts) who are core members of the care path team. We will continue to involve additional nursing staff with special expertise and/or interest in specific populations during future care path development. On the basis of the multidisciplinary team's input, the care path was revised to reflect practice.

We also decided to add two sections to the neonatal care paths that distinguish them from other care paths in our institution. A separate "Psychosocial" section was added because care for the family is such a crucial part of caring for hospitalized infants. Although some items in this section are specific interventions that are performed by the neonatal social worker, there is overlap among disciplines in the performance of other items.

The "Developmental" section was added because of our unit's commitment to individualized developmental care and support for preterm and sick infants. There may be overlap in completion of developmental responsibilities between the developmental specialists and the neonatal nursing staff.

While we included expected interventions of other team members, it was crucial to set realistic time frames because 24-hour coverage for routine psychosocial, dietary, or developmental specialist involvement is not currently available in our NICU. The final revision of the care path is exhibited in Appendix 13–A.

INCORPORATION OF BASELINE DATA

At present, we have complete baseline data for 25 ELBW infants, including data for three infants who would not have met initial criteria for the path by virtue of gestational age (<24 weeks) or weight (<500 grams). In terms of medical expectations, we made very few changes in the initial care path. We did, however, identify opportunities for improvement based on our baseline data. We were able to identify situations in which laboratory testing could be minimized—particularly in measuring electrolyte and bilirubin levels beyond the first few days of life. We found repetitive sampling with normal levels of electrolytes and very low bilirubin levels. We were somewhat surprised by the rarity of electrolyte imbalance and found no infant with hyperbilirubinemia approaching exchange transfusion level. Reducing the frequency of laboratory draws has other potential implications. These tiny infants usually require transfusions to replace iatrogenic blood loss. Consequently, fewer transfusion exposures is a very positive outcome that is not captured by the path. Frequency of therapeutic drug level monitoring for aminoglycosides and Theophylline was also identified as an opportunity for improvement.

Multidisciplinary team meetings called to discuss care path revisions often resulted in lively discussions as we related some of our "standard" recommended practices to actual practice. For example, our feeding protocol recommends labs to assess bone mineralization status at two weeks of life. According to our baseline data, these labs were not done for any infant. Clinician rationale for not performing these tests was the historical lack of yield for concrete identifiable problems at this time and the desire to limit blood draws. Our baseline data showed that nearly 50 percent of patients were receiving 50 percent or more of their fluids by the enteral route and that by two weeks of age they were progressing nicely toward full feedings. We hope to define better those situations in which the need for long-term total parenteral nutrition is projected and in which lab monitoring is warranted. In this way, we will recommend a more individualized approach to screening labs rather than adopting a standardized approach.

The baseline data also helped us to define conditions that would create exclusions from the path. These conditions are listed in Exhibit 13–2. All of these conditions may dramatically increase resource utilization and the potential for additional complications.

Exhibit 13–2 Exclusions to the Extremely Low Birthweight Infant Care Path

- Death prior to day 14
- Necrotizing enterocolitis requiring surgery
- Cardiovascular support required for more than 48 hours
- Patent ductus arteriosus requiring ligation prior to day 14
- Steroids for severe pulmonary insufficiency prior to day 7
- Gross pulmonary hemorrhage
- Air leak syndrome requiring two or more chest tubes
- High-frequency oscillatory ventilation plus pulmonary air leak

THE EXTREMELY LOW BIRTHWEIGHT INFANT CARE PATH: THE NEXT STEPS

Prior to implementation, staff education of all disciplines about the care path is required. Emphasis will be placed on the purposes of the care path, the role of the case manager, communication with families about the care path, how to use the path (including multidisciplinary documentation), and the opportunity for evaluation of the care path. Because this path represents a limited portion of the hospitalization of these infants, other aspects of documentation will not change at present. We will continue to use our current system for patient progress notes and our standard nursing care plan. About 75 percent of our patients currently receive their primary medical care from an advanced practitioner who generates a comprehensive daily note using a computer template. In the future, we hope to be able to link data collection and variance monitoring for these infants to our overall data system, thus decreasing workload for the case manager. Other modifications in documentation may be forthcoming as we have more experience with the path.

Development of the case manager's role is also crucial to the implementation of the path. For the neonatal CNSs, assuming the functions of the case manager represents a role change. Because of role redefinition, other traditional responsibilities and aspects of the CNS role will, of necessity, be revised or eliminated. The overall impact of this change on the unit warrants examination.

It is imperative to recognize staff responses to implementation of the path, because this represents change in practice at a time when additional changes related to patient care redesign are forthcoming. Supporting staff during the implementation of this practice change is essential to ensure successful implementation as well as opportunities for feedback and evaluation. A formal plan for evaluation and staff support is ideal.

Our next task will be to pilot this care path for 20 to 25 ELBW infants, a process that we expect will require approximately six months to complete. Included in our safety monitoring for this pilot will be data collection on common neonatal morbidities such as sepsis, necrotizing enterocolitis, patent ductus arteriosus, intraventricular hemorrhage, and retinopathy of prematurity. We will also gather data about days to regain birthweight, time to full feedings, and other monitors of clinical progress.

ADDITIONAL CONSIDERATIONS FOR THE NICU

Some specific issues related to care path development in the NICU deserve attention. Our Extremely Low Birthweight Infant Care Path was devised on the basis of weight criteria. Others may argue that using gestational age–specific criteria is more meaningful because infants who are small or large for gestational age will have different clinical problems than infants who are appropriately grown. It is important to look separately at the effects of birthweight and gestational age on outcomes, and both our baseline and pilot data collections will allow us to do so. The infants for whom we collected pilot data ranged in gestational age from 23 to 31 weeks with an average of 26.2 weeks and a median of 26 weeks. Some of the more mature infants exceeded the expectations of the path, while others did not. Our data collection will allow us to generate predictors of which infants may be expected to vary significantly from the care path.

Unlike adult patients, infants in the NICU do not have a single doctor. Due to service rotations, infants with prolonged hospitalizations may be managed by seven different attendings. With each service rotation, there is a transitional period in which the attending gets to know the patient and the family. While we currently have mechanisms in place to facilitate communication among the attendings about patients in the NICU, even minor alterations in a communicated plan of care can be disconcerting and frustrating to families who are attempting to cope with the impact of their infant's NICU hospitalization. Care paths may be very advantageous for this population as we attempt to improve the consistency and the continuity of care.

CONCLUSION

This case study represents an important "work in progress" in that a large NICU with no previous experience in design and implementation of a care path is striving to develop a more standardized yet flexible approach to care that will meet the needs of our critically ill patients, their families in crisis, and a diverse multidisciplinary health care team. Our experience to date has taught us that inclusion of representatives from all aspects of the health care team is vital to the success of a care path. We encourage other units embarking on this path to designate a broad multidisciplinary team under the combined leadership of medical and nursing personnel to ensure optimal health care team buy-in.

Be respectful of your own neonatal intensive care unit—while there may be a relatively predictable sequence of events in the lives of extremely premature infants, units have unique cultures and methods for approaching such infants. Look at the work of other units, but be realistic about what will work in your own unit given its history, personnel mix, and unit philosophy and values.

Allow time for data collection, reflection, and revision, because you may be surprised at how your actual practice varies from your "idealized" practice. Use existing data collection mechanisms where possible, and if you must design new data collection tools, do so with a mind toward progressing toward interfacing with your current (or "idealized") data collection systems.

Understand that your care path is a dynamic document. Because we all prioritize the best interests of our patients, health care workers will be understandably fearful and perhaps inflexible if you design a system that forces them to ignore patient data or signals. Stress to everyone involved that you will be constantly gathering data, evaluating it, and seeking feedback regarding the daily workings of the care path. Encourage the team to view the care path not as a rigid protocol that denies individualization to their patients but as a dynamic, flowing guideline that is flexible enough to accommodate patients of variable severity of illness but that has some generalized expectations regarding interventions and therapies.

Developing a care path for extreme prematurity is analogous to caring for such a tiny, critically ill infant. In the beginning, the uncertainty and the task ahead may appear almost overwhelming. Furthermore, there is no guarantee of a happy outcome at the end of a tremendous combined multidisciplinary effort. However, in the same way that we put our uncertainty and anxiety temporarily aside in caring for such infants, we must put it aside in the development of a care path and recognize that we will give the best combined effort of our team to design a workable, systematic approach to care for our most vulnerable patients.

Appendix 13–A

Extremely Low Birthweight Infant Care Path

Pathway outcome: Completed _____ Clinical Exclusion _____ Transferred to other pathway _____

D.O.B. _____ Day 1 ends 11:59 pm _____ Gestational age: _____ Birthweight _____

	Prehospital	Day 1	Date/Initial	Day 2	Date/Initial	Day 3	Date/Initial	Day 4	Date/Initial	Day 5	Date/Initial
S T U D Y	Maternal Serology HBsAg	Blood C+S, CBC, T&C, Ca+ lytes qd to tid ABG prn		Lytes qd to bid Bili prn ABG prn		Lytes qd, Bili prn ABG q 6°–8° as indicated per clinical condition. Antibiotic levels if continuing Rx		Lytes q day Bili prn ABG q 6°–8° as indicated per clinical condition. CF screen/1st PKU		Lytes qod Bili prn ABG q 6°–8° as indicated per clinical condition.	
P R O C E D U R E S		Initiate procedures as indicated: 1. Ventilation a. HFOV b. CMV c. CPAP d. Ambient O$_2$ 2. a. UAC b. UVC 3. Phototherapy 4. Echocardiogram 5. LP if meningitis suspected 6. a. CXR b. KUB Plot growth parameters		As indicated: 1. Ventilation a. HFOV b. CMV c. CPAP d. Ambient O$_2$ 2. a. UAC b. UVC 3. Phototherapy 4. Echocardiogram 5. LP if meningitis suspected 6. a. CXR b. KUB		As indicated: 1. Ventilation a. HFOV b. CMV c. CPAP d. Ambient O$_2$ 2. a. UAC b. UVC 3. Phototherapy 4. Echocardiogram 5. LP if meningitis suspected 6. a. CXR b. KUB		As indicated: 1. Ventilation a. HFOV b. CMV c. CPAP d. Ambient O$_2$ 2. a. UAC b. UVC 3. Phototherapy 4. Echocardiogram 5. LP if meningitis suspected 6. a. CXR b. KUB		As indicated: 1. Ventilation a. HFOV b. CMV c. CPAP d. Ambient O$_2$ 2. a. UAC b. UVC 3. Phototherapy 4. Echocardiogram 5. LP if meningitis suspected 6. a. CXR b. KUB 7. CUS #1	

Courtesy of University of Connecticut Health Center, Farmington, Connecticut.

	Prehospital	Day 1	Date/ Initial	Day 2	Date/ Initial	Day 3	Date/ Initial	Day 4	Date/ Initial	Day 5	Date/ Initial
MEDICINE		Surfactant Vitamin K IM Erythromycin OU Antibiotics as indicated Pressors as indicated		Surfactant Antibiotics as indicated Pressors as indicated		D/C antibiotics if C + S neg, mother not pretreated/no clinical suspicion of infection Indomethacin as indicated		Antibiotics only if previous criteria not met Indomethacin as indicated		Antibiotics only if previous criteria not met Indomethacin as indicated	
DIET		NPO/IV fluids		NPO/IV fluids		Start TPN if fluid status stable		TPN Evaluate tolerance of nutrition support		FPP started TPN	
ACTIVITY	Tour NICU	RD SCP		RD SCP Infant positioned appropriately with special equipment		RD SCP		RD SCP		RD SCP	
DEVEL										Infant identified/ history reviewed Primary DT/S identified Initial observations & consult	
EDUCATION	Neonatal consult if possible	GA appropriate Support/equipment Unit orientation teaching plan initiated BF teaching plan initiated		Update status by 1° caretakers Breast pumping initiated Unit orientation teaching plan BF teaching plan		Update status by 1° caretakers Unit orientation teaching plan BF teaching plan		Update status by 1° caretakers Unit orientation teaching plan BF teaching plan		Intro to infant development Unit orientation teaching plan BF teaching plan MD/AP met with family to discuss initial CUS	

	Prehospital	Date/Initial	Day 1	Date/Initial	Day 2	Date/Initial	Day 3	Date/Initial	Day 4	Date/Initial	Day 5	Date/Initial
P S Y C H O S O C			Neonatologist met with family after delivery								Psychosocial assessment completed, and parents have met all 1° caretakers	
D / C			Start database Anticipated LOS		Complete database							

	Day 6	Date/Initial	Day 7	Date/Initial	Day 8	Date/Initial	Day 9	Date/Initial	Day 10–14	Date/Initial	Day 14–21	Date/Initial
STUDY	Lytes qod Bili prn ABG q 6"–8" as indicated per clinical condition		ABG qod Lytes qod		ABG prn Lytes qod		ABG prn Lytes qod		Lytes twice/wk 2nd PKU day 14 HCT			
PROCEDURE	As indicated: 1. Ventilation a. HFOV b. CMV c. CPAP d. Ambient O_2 2. a. UAC b. UVC		As indicated: 1. Ventilation a. HFOV b. CMV c. CPAP d. Ambient O_2 2. a. UAC b. UVC		As indicated: 1. Ventilation a. HFOV b. CMV c. CPAP d. Ambient O_2 2. a. UAC b. UVC		As indicated: 1. Ventilation a. HFOV b. CMV c. CPAP d. Ambient O_2 2. a. UAC b. UVC		As indicated: 1. Ventilation a. HFOV b. CMV c. CPAP d. Ambient O_2 2. a. UAC b. UVC Assess IV access when removing UAC/UVC CXR if indicated CUS #2			
MEDS	Antibiotics only if previous criteria not met		D/C antibiotics unless meningitis or blood cx +						D/C antibiotics unless meningitis Assess need for diuretics/nebs/steroids		Antibiotics only if previous criteria not met	
DIET	TPN FPP		TPN FPP		TPN FPP		TPN FPP		TPN FPP		TPN FPP Nutrition and growth assessment Evaluation of feeding adequacy	
ACT	RD SCP		RD SCP		RD SCP		RD SCP		RD SCP		RD SCP	

	Day 6	Date/Initial	Day 7	Date/Initial	Day 8	Date/Initial	Day 9	Date/Initial	Day 10–14	Date/Initial	Day 14–21	Date/Initial
DEVELOPMENTAL					Infant observed during care and additional needs identified; Family meets DT/S; Recommendations discussed with family and staff; Individualized developmental plan completed							
EDUCATION	Unit orientation teaching plan; BF teaching plan		Introduce parent to parent; Introduce parent meetings; Complete unit orientation teaching plan		BF teaching plan		BF teaching plan		If BF, milk supply/pumping regimen established. Introduce kangaroo care and offer when appropriate; Parents' goals for involvement in infant's care clarified		Contact with family to discuss progress; Initiate discharge teaching plan	
PSYCHOSOC			SSI and insurance initiated; Plan for regular parent communication established						Weekly psychosocial contact			
D/C											Multidisciplinary team meeting to discuss care	

Signature	Initials	Signature	Initials	Signature	Initials

Exclusions to path:
1. Surgical NEC; 2. HFOV for air leak; 3. Steroids ≤ day 7; 4. Gross pulmonary hemorrhage; 5. Cardiovascular support >48°; 6. Death ≤ day 14; 7. PDA requiring ligation ≤ day 14; 8. ≥ 2 chest tubes

Key to abbreviations:
1°, primary; ABG, arterial blood gas; AP, advanced practitioner; BF, breast-feeding; bid, two times a day; Bili, bilirubin; Blood C+S, blood culture and sensitivity; Ca+, calcium; CBC, complete blood count; CF, cystic fibrosis; CMV, conventional mechanical ventilation; CPAP, continuous positive airway pressure; CUS, cranial ultrasound; cx +, culture positive; CXR, chest X-ray; D/C, discontinue/discharge; DOB, date of birth; DT/S, developmental therapist/specialist; FPP, feedings per protocol; GA, gestational age; HBsAg, hepatitis B surface antigen; HCT, hematocrit; HFOV, high-frequency oscillatory ventilation; IM, intramuscular; IV, intravenous; KUB, kidneys, ureter, bladder; LOS, length of stay; LP, lumbar puncture; Lytes, electrolytes; nebs, nebulizers; NEC, necrotizing enterocolitic; neg, negative; NICU, neonatal intensive care unit; NPO, nothing by mouth; O₂, oxygen; ou, both eyes; PDA, patent ductus arteriosus; PKU, phenylketonuria (newborn metabolic screen); prn, as needed; qd, daily; qod, every other day; RD SCP, respiratory distress standard care plan; Rx, treatment; SSI, Social Security income; T&C, type and crossmatch; tid, three times a day; TPN, total parenteral nutrition; UAC, umbilical artery catheter; UVC, umbilical venous catheter.

CHAPTER 14

The Center of Coordinated Care: The St. Luke's Episcopal Hospital Model for Clinical Quality and Resource Management

Rosemary Luquire, Susan Houston, and Karlene Kerfoot

Chapter Objectives

1. To define outcomes management and research.
2. To discuss resources necessary for implementing an outcomes management program.
3. To describe the steps and associated activities in the outcomes management process.

Health care is now the second-largest industry in the United States and accounts for 14 percent of the gross national product. In comparison to other countries, the United States spends more on health care than Canada, Germany, Japan, and the United Kingdom combined. Additionally, health care in the United States costs more than what is being spent on public education and defense of our country.[1] Despite this, outcomes of our health care, such as life expectancy and infant mortality, have not improved in comparison to other industrialized nations. To help address some of these important issues, today's providers are challenged to begin the process of health care redesign and develop a system that values consumer-driven services.

The rapidly evolving mandate for fiscally responsible health care with substantiated quality results has led to new models for delivery and measurement of health care services. One such model is the Center of Coordinated Care at St. Luke's Episcopal Hospital, whereby case management and outcomes management models complement and support each other to achieve significant improvements in quality of care and cost-effectiveness.

CASE MANAGEMENT VERSUS OUTCOMES MANAGEMENT: REAL DIFFERENCES OR SEMANTICS?

An important distinction should be made between outcomes management (OM) and case management. The nursing case management (NCM) movement that arose in the 1980s pioneered a restructuring of *nursing* care delivery to include an emphasis on cost efficiency and utilization management. In fact, in an early publication, Zander referred to NCM as "second-generation primary nursing."[2] Nursing case management in the acute care hospital arose purely as a nursing strategy to facilitate care coordination.

Case managers have been used extensively by third-party payers to handle catastrophic or high-cost cases as part of the payer's utilization management strategy. Insurance case managers work with patients, providers, and insurers to coordinate health services and resources so that the patient receives appropriate medically necessary health care. These case managers may negotiate discounted fees for ancillary services such as medical equipment, hospice care, and pharmaceutical products.[3]

Case management models have historically focused on the management of individual patients using tools such as critical pathways that are consensus based or guidelines for length of stay. Outcome measures studied by early nursing case managers were rudimentary and limited to descriptive statistics reflecting length of stay, cost of care, and patient satisfaction (Exhibit 14–1).

In 1988, OM was theorized by Paul Ellwood as a mechanism to redesign and continually enhance interdisciplinary health care processes through the use of outcomes measurement. Ellwood defined OM as a "technology of patient experience designed to help patients, payers and providers make rational medical care-related choices based on better insight into the effect of these choices on the patient's life."[4(p.1549)] Four key principles were cited by Ellwood for inclusion in an OM program:

1. an emphasis on standards that physicians can use to select appropriate interventions
2. the measurement of patient functioning and well-being along with disease-specific clinical outcomes
3. a pooling of clinical and outcome data on a massive scale
4. the analysis and dissemination of a database to appropriate decision makers[5]

OM provides a mechanism to foster development of patient-driven services through revision of practice based on the measurement of health outcomes. It allows providers to begin redesigning health care delivery to meet the needs of patients.

At St. Luke's Episcopal Hospital, OM is defined as the enhancement of physiologic and psychosocial patient outcomes through development and implementation of exemplary health practices and services, as driven by outcomes assessment.[6] OM uses a quality and research perspective to improve patient outcomes,

Exhibit 14–1 Comparison of Case Management and Outcomes Management

Case Management	Outcomes Management
Process	*Process*
Reviews individual patient's progress	Questions care practices related to a defined patient population (e.g., asthma, congestive heart failure)
Facilitates/expedites progression of care based on a defined plan of care	
Reviews appropriateness of care and determines appropriate level of care (acute, skilled, custodial, hospice, rehabilitation)	Measures clinical and financial results of practice (links processes to outcomes while recognizing effect of comorbidities)
Actively negotiates reimbursement with payer based on level of care. Negotiates payment for discharge needs (home care)	Redesigns care on the basis of research literature, professional society recommendations (e.g., American College of Cardiology), benchmark data, and descriptive and predictive models that measure outcomes on own population
	Develops and implements tools for guiding care on the basis of the above review (pathways, algorithms, order sets, guidelines)
	Measures effect of changed process on outcomes
	Redesigns tools as needed and as new information becomes available
Results	*Results*
Reduced length of stay and costs	Reduced length of stay and costs
Decreased number of retrospective reviews requested by payers	Decreased complications
Reduction in insurance denials	Increased satisfaction
	Enhanced expertise of staff via knowledge and use of research-driven protocols
Focus	*Focus*
Business	Clinical
Utilization management	Quality enhancement

Courtesy of St. Luke's Episcopal Hospital, Houston, Texas.

thus balancing the cost/quality ratio. This model recognizes the relationship between interdisciplinary practices, patient conditions, and the production of health outcomes; it provides a mechanism to test interventions toward achievement of *best* interdisciplinary health practices.[7]

The sophisticated level of outcomes measurement and standardization of interdisciplinary practice advocated by Ellwood were not a part of the nursing case management movement.[8] Many institutions have developed case management models with unsatisfactory results. The St. Luke's model of coordinated care recognizes the value of both case management and OM in improving care and lowering costs. In fact, we believe that OM provides a foundation for case management. OM identifies specific areas that need improvement and develops tools to guide and measure practice. Case management provides a mechanism for the use of site-specific standardized tools on an individual patient basis and promotes coordination of that patient's care.

PRINCIPLES RELATED TO OUTCOMES MANAGEMENT

Several principles must be embraced for an institution to recognize and engage in an OM effort. The first principle is that the culture of the institution must support and embrace risk taking to bring about significant changes in clinical practice. Changes in practice come only from creating a safe environment where everyday clinical practice can be questioned. All health care practitioners in the institution must be willing to ask, "Why do we do things the way we do?" or, of greater importance, "Is there a better way?" A good example is related to the old adage "Once a Caesarean section, always a Caesarean section." Research is substantiating that this is not necessarily best practice.[9] Obviously, for practitioners to question practice, a safe environment that encourages risk taking and creativity is necessary. Administration is foremost in creating this open milieu in which it is safe to question.

The second principle thus recognizes the importance of administrative and physician involvement. Administrative support is necessary for enacting change required to alter and improve standards of care while decreasing costs. Authority and responsibility must be provided to those who engage in the development of structured care methodologies (SCMs) such as pathways, standing orders, algorithms, and guidelines. Other examples of administrative support include engaging in product evaluation, providing monies for literature review and research, and ensuring the time necessary to engage in quality activities. Medical staff support is also a necessity. Physicians must be an instrumental part of the creation of SCMs, as well as serving as champions in enlisting fellow physicians' adherence to the SCMs and practice improvement activities. Without physician involvement, OM becomes an impossible task.

The third principle recognizes that change is a continuous process within an OM effort. Resultant changes may be slow and often time consuming. The key to successful change is dependent on health care teams' recognizing that practice improvement based on accurate data can result in increased efficiency and cost savings. This increased efficiency and quality of care enhances the institution's ability to compete in a managed-care market. The belief that there is always room for improvement must be the foundation of this program. Overall, OM can benefit individual practitioners and the institution at large because of this continual search for ways to improve.

The fourth principle related to OM is the recognition that while the processes driving outcomes can be managed, total control of all factors affecting outcomes may be initially and continually difficult. The medical outcomes model provides an excellent example of the many variables that may affect one particular outcome.[10] This model highlights structural and care process components that can account for variations in outcomes. The key to influencing outcomes is the recognition of those variables that lend themselves to manipulation and control. For example, existing comorbid conditions often interfere with achieving optimal outcomes. However, many practitioners are working to reduce the impact of these conditions on the patient's health status. In ischemic stroke patients, dysphagia contributes to an untoward outcome of aspiration pneumonia. Early identification and adherence to a dysphagia protocol may reduce the incidence of pulmonary complications, thus reducing cost while improving the quality of care provided.

The fifth and last principle recognizes that OM is a continuously evolving process that adapts SCMs frequently according to the demands of new technology and research. This necessitates frequent appraisal and feedback of process/practice changes and resulting clinical and fiscal outcomes. Frequent sharing of information and accomplishments fosters widespread acceptance and testing of OM activities in diverse patient populations. Additionally, this sharing creates competition among health care providers to pursue marketable quality in a cost-effective manner.

Additionally, many institutions engaging in an OM effort are using advanced-practice personnel to spearhead the work necessary for affecting outcomes.[11] These personnel, often called *outcomes managers,* are generally held accountable for the development, implementation, and evaluation of OM programs for a defined patient population. Both clinical nurse specialists and advanced nurse practitioners may occupy this position. Most outcomes managers are required to function in five roles: clinical practice, consultation, administration, research, and education.[12] The competencies of an outcomes manager include analytical skills, clinical expertise, problem-solving and risk-taking abilities, collaborative skills, fiscal finesse, leadership skills, group facilitation, research, and the ability to operate from a holistic perspective. This holistic approach encompasses not only the patient and family or the continuum of care but also the mechanics of today's health care industry. Outcomes managers must be knowledge specialists who are able to grasp the vision needed to affect patient outcomes and engage in the work necessary to improve them. Because OM has an interdisciplinary focus, other types of health care providers, such as physicians or social workers, may function as outcomes managers.

NECESSARY RESOURCES FOR MANAGING OUTCOMES

Several resources are necessary for engaging in a successful OM effort. These include the use of collaborative practice teams (CPTs); outcomes assessment expertise; information systems (ISs), including data analysis; SCMs; research and quality programs; and educational systems.

Interdisciplinary CPTs are assembled to help manage and improve outcomes. Their goal is to develop and ensure the quality, cost-effective, and research-based clinical care that is necessary to provide patient care throughout the continuum. These CPTs may include medical staff, nursing staff, diabetes specialists, physical therapists, dietitians, respiratory therapists, social workers, financial administrators, case managers, and pharmacists. Team composition differs according to the needs of the patient population. CPTs help determine and develop the processes and practice patterns that contribute to population-specific outcomes. Collaborative work is then necessary to implement measures that will continually enhance the quality of care provided by the institution. To be successful, CPTs supporting an OM effort are required to engage in research utilization, analyze current care practices, conduct pilot studies to identify best practice, and measure the impact of changes made in both the care practices and system processes.[13] Concurrently, successful CPTs market their accomplishments by extensive communication and educational programs in vehicles such as service meetings, thereby enticing a broader range of participation from their peers. Collaborative practice teams within an OM effort model the Joint Commission on Accreditation of Healthcare Organizations (Joint Commission) standards. These standards now address the need for performance improvement activities to be carried out collaboratively throughout the organization and across multiple structural and staffing components as appropriate.[14]

A second necessary resource for engaging in OM is the expertise and infrastructure to assess outcomes. *Outcomes assessment* is defined as the measurement, monitoring, and analysis of an outcome associated with specific care processes.[15] Ultimately, outcomes assessment assists in identifying the processes that drive a particular outcome. The overall goal of an outcomes assessment process includes the ability to describe the impact of routinely delivered care on patients' lives. The outcomes assessment process has been well described in a recent publication by the Joint Commission.[16] Exhibit 14–2 identifies the 12 steps related to this process.

Initially, outcomes of interest are selected and defined by CPTs. Outcomes of interest may include quality outcomes (such as infection, readmissions, Caesarean section rates, vaginal birth after Caesarean, and mortality), satisfaction outcomes

Exhibit 14–2 Outcomes Assessment Process

1. Select a condition or procedure.
2. Assemble a collaborative practice team.
3. Define the purpose.
4. Narrow the scope.
5. Explain the logistics of collecting data.
6. Identify instruments.
7. Ensure quality control of data.
8. Collect data.
9. Enter the data into the computer.
10. Analyze the data.
11. Provide feedback and interpretation.
12. Connect the outcome to the process.

Source: Data from *A Guide to Establishing Programs for Assessing Outcomes in Clinical Settings,* © 1994, Joint Commission on Accreditation of Healthcare Organizations.

(patient, payer, and provider), and financial outcomes (cost, length of stay, and resource utilization).[17] Health care providers should ask, "What outcomes are currently measured and available to us?" This process helps prevent redundancy in data collection, because some outcomes data have been collected for years. The assessment of outcomes is best done from an interdisciplinary perspective to ensure the expertise necessary for analyzing processes that drive the outcome.

An outcomes assessment effort yields quantitative outcome measures as well as variance data related to specific outcomes. The data collection effort produces large databases specific to patient populations (Exhibit 14–3). One data set contains data on patients' demographic characteristics, history of previous illnesses, and existing comorbid conditions. Another data set includes variances associated with outcomes. These variances may include patient problems, system problems, or practice problems. A last data set offers valuable outcome measures such as quality of life, readmission, and mortality. These data can be used to establish a baseline, identify problems, monitor impact of changing practice patterns, and trend long-term outcomes. The data also serve as a foundation for marketing best practices in the community.

The third resource necessary for engaging in an OM effort is informatics, inclusive of statistical software. Informatics supports health care professionals in their outcomes assessment and management efforts.[18] Traditionally, ISs have been

Exhibit 14–3 Data Sets for Outcomes Assessment in Coronary Artery Bypass Graft Patients

Patient Information
Emergent versus nonemergent
Age
Gender
Prior heart surgery
Diabetes
Smoking history
Chronic obstructive pulmonary
  disease (%)

Variances
Pump time (mean minutes)
Reexplore for bleeding
Intraop IABP insertion
Intubation time
Delay in discharge
Pulmonary complications
Arrhythmias

Outcomes
Functional (Preop, 1, 3, and 6 months)
    Physical function
    Mental function
    Role—physical
    Role—mental
    Bodily pain
    Vitality
    General health
    Social function
Clinical
    Mortality
    Readmissions
    Sternal infection or dehiscence (%)
    Leg infection (%)
    Cerebrovascular accident (%)
Patient Satisfaction
    Satisfaction with services
Cost and Utilization
    Total charges
    LOS
    Postop LOS
    Postop ICU
    Preop LOS
    Cath same admit
    Cath to coronary artery bypass graft

Courtesy of St. Luke's Episcopal Hospital, Houston, Texas.

viewed as hospital-based systems for automation of care processes such as order entry, results reporting, and admission/discharge/transfer. This view provides a limited dimension of what ISs truly are and will need to be in the future.

Ledly and Lusted characterized an IS as having three essential parts: a system for organizing or recording the data, a process for locating the data, and a process for storing the data.[19] Lindberg described a medical IS as a set of orderly arrangements by which facts about health and health care of individual patients are stored and processed by computers.[20] This description leads one to the realization that a medical IS is a complex structure encompassing data from multiple sources. This structure will be further complicated in a disease management program in which additional data elements will be captured. Today, IS experts are charged with developing a single, integrated patient record from birth to death. This is in contrast to the current fragmented record, which focuses on specific care episodes. Information technology provides the framework for developing comprehensive databases required for OM[21] and is essential to the measurement and management of outcomes due to its ability to assist in collection, storage, aggregation, and segmentation of data.

Information technology is also key to statistical analysis of data necessary for large patient populations. Both descriptive and inferential statistics must be used to answer questions and make inferences regarding a particular patient population. When OM programs do not include statistical analysis of data, it is impossible to determine the effect of any programmatic changes. Using the correct statistics to answer questions regarding the outcomes of a specific patient population is absolutely essential. A statistician certainly facilitates the analysis and interpretation of data but is not necessarily required. Today, abundant software packages make the use of statistics easier. Additionally, graphical software allows for the presentation of process and outcomes data to health care professionals in an understandable and meaningful way. Graphic presentations facilitate health care professionals' interpretation and use of data and bring great value to presentations.

The fourth resource necessary for engaging in an OM effort is the use of SCMs. SCMs allow for the standardization of care processes, thus contributing to the management of outcomes. These SCMs include pathways, algorithms, guidelines, protocols, and standing orders.[22] All of these SCMs contribute to identifying and stabilizing care practices and system processes that are designed to improve outcomes. SCMs, to have an observable impact, should be executable, specific, designed for homogenous patient populations, amenable to constant scrutiny, and updated on the basis of new research findings.

The fifth resource necessary is quality and research programs that allow for the development of programs and projects affecting outcomes. Quality processes such as COMIT[23] (Exhibit 14–4) or SERIAL V[24] provide a systematic method of selecting a particular outcome or variance, engaging in the work necessary to affect that

Exhibit 14–4 Continuous Outcomes Measurement and Improvement Technique

1. Measure outcome or variance.
2. Select team members.
3. Determine associated care processes.
4. Determine causative factors.
5. Select high-impact causative factors.
6. Determine performance measures.
7. Implement plan for change.
8. Remeasure the outcome or variance.

Courtesy of St. Luke's Episcopal Hospital, Houston, Texas.

outcome or variance, and ultimately improving an outcome or eliminating or reducing a variance. These processes allow for a thorough assessment as well as identification of factors that contribute to a specific outcome or variance and also promote the development of action plans and remeasurement of the outcome or variance.

Outcomes research (OR), another vehicle for affecting outcomes, can help identify best practices for specific patient populations. OR can be defined as any research that attempts to link the structure and/or the process of providing care to outcomes at the community, institutional, or patient level. Much debate exists regarding what OR is specifically; however, many researchers agree that certain hallmarks of OR exist. OR is interdisciplinary, capturing the health care contributions of many disciplines. Often it uses large existing databases to identify best practices at the institutional or community level. Outcomes research tends to be macro-level research, in which the continuum of care accessed and utilized by the patient is examined. Last, OR attempts to focus on identifying best practices in hopes that the results will contribute information needed by patients, payers, and consumers in making rational health care decisions. Numerous research designs facilitate conducting OR. Hard research, such as experimental research, and much softer research, such as evaluative or descriptive research, both make a contribution to identifying best-practice approaches used by health care providers. There are advantages and disadvantages to OR. Advantages include the opportunity to improve patient outcomes, develop an understanding of the work necessary to redesign systems that ultimately affect outcome, and formulate new standards to increase the value of health care provided. Disadvantages include the fact that research, generally, is long term and requires patience and fortitude. The required changes in practice often make OR difficult due to the necessity of continually changing supporting system processes. Outcomes research can also be labor intensive, often requiring the support of research assistants, statisticians, and researchers.

The last resource required for managing outcomes is a supporting educational structure. Health care professionals within an institution managing outcomes will require education regarding the goals, need, work, potential benefits, and job responsibilities of the various disciplines. Roberta Abruzzese's evaluation model[25] allows for simple to complex evaluation of the impact of educational programs designed to educate professionals about OM. This process involves five types of evaluation: *process,* which examines the general happiness with the learning experience; *content,* which examines change in knowledge and behavior; *outcome,* which examines a change in practice that results as a product of education; *impact,* which examines institutional results such as the impact on patient outcomes; and *total program,* which examines the consistency of the education program with the goals and objectives of the institution. Education within an OM program is not a single event. Education of all health care professionals regarding the work of OM and its impact on outcomes needs to be continuous to enhance constantly the OM effort. Continuous education (such as describing outcomes relevant to a specific patient population), profiling health care workers, and benchmarking the institution at the local or national level all help to educate health care professionals continuously regarding their contributions to specific patient outcomes.

MANAGING OUTCOMES

OM is actualized through a process model. The model first highlights the need for explicit values related to supporting quality and research activities, overall impact on cost, and the work effort that must be conducted to affect outcomes (see Exhibit 15–1 for St. Luke's Episcopal Hospital outcomes management model). Use of educational resources to inform all health care practitioners about OM tenets, resources, process, and impact on both outcomes and work ethic is a necessity. The next step in the model is the collection and assessment of population-specific short- and long-term outcomes, variances, and process data. Selection of the identified patient population is usually based on revenue loss or high volume. Not all patient populations require management, due to existing positive outcomes. Collection and assessment of related outcomes data are necessary for determining results of care practices and system processes. A multidisciplinary CPT is charged with analysis and evaluation of the data and determining which care processes drive particular outcomes. The third step of the OM model identifies the CPT work in determining relationships between process and outcome. The use of quality and management tools promotes dissection and identification of the positive and negative care practices and processes. On the basis of reliable outcomes assessment and process analysis, the CPT targets areas of practice change and related outcomes data for measurement. Through quality, research, or change projects, methods for improving care practices are implemented, the fourth step in the OM model. Often, structured care methodologies such as guidelines, pathways, algorithms, standing orders, and/or standards of care representing best practice provide direction to practitioners and assist in stabilizing change. After implementation of process and practice changes, outcomes-related data are once again analyzed and evaluated for impact. IS support can facilitate analysis and understanding of results. Statistical and quality software facilitates data manipulation for the CPT and promotes interpretation of findings. Additionally, meaningful presentation of findings is required for reevaluation and education of practitioners regarding the effect of the OM effort. Finally, further education on OM activities and effects on outcomes promotes the continued valuing of an OM effort.

CASE STUDIES

The percutaneous coronary angioplasty (PTCA) patient population was selected for OM due to high volume and opportunities for cost reduction. Outcomes assessed included coronary artery reocclusion, functional status, cost, and other complications such as hematomas. In examining the outcome of cost, process analysis revealed that costs in this patient population are primarily driven by cath lab resources and immediate care post intervention. Additional process analysis revealed inappropriate utilization of critical care for stable PTCA patients. Placing stable PTCA patients in appropriate levels of care such as telemetry reduced costs by approximately $1,700 per patient and facilitated appropriate usage of ICU beds for the critically ill. Reevaluation of outcomes showed no difference in quality measures such as hematomas, recatheterizations, and postprocedural myocardial infarction rates for patients recovered on the telemetry unit. Additionally, patient and physician satisfaction improved. This comprehensive approach ensured a balance between cost and quality measures.

Another case study explains how a program was developed for elective bowel surgery patients in conjunction with a multispecialty physician group, as well as the outcomes obtained. In 1994, discussions were initiated between St. Luke's Episcopal Hospital and a multispecialty physician health maintenance organization to identify opportunities for both parties to reduce cost of care and improve patient outcomes. A CPT consisting of physicians, administrators from both facilities, an operating room manager, a clinic case manager, and an outcomes manager was developed. The purposes of the program were to improve patient flow through the hospital system, reduce hospital cost and hospital days, and provide consistent patient education.

A process analysis was done to determine current practice patterns and to identify opportunities for change. After a detailed analysis of the current processes, several recommendations were made to the CPT. These recommendations included initiation of a same-day admission for elective bowel surgery cases and standardization of preoperative bowel preparation.

The program was developed over a five-month period. During this time, delineation of responsibilities of the physician, office staff, clinic case manager, outcomes manager, and home health agency was completed. In addition, a critical pathway for this physician group was developed along with a patient plan of care. By developing a patient plan of care, consistency in patient information was obtained. This also provided the patient and family with an outline of the hospital experience and expectations for patient involvement with care.

Since initiation of the program in August 1994, 92 patients have been managed through this process. This has resulted in a cost savings of 60 percent and a reduction in length of stay of 46 percent. No increase in infection, readmissions, or mortality has occurred. Also, informal patient interviews have demonstrated high patient satisfaction with the program.

In addition, communication channels between the outpatient setting and the inpatient setting have increased. The clinic case manager and the outcomes manager identify high-risk patients and implement a plan of care that can be initiated in the clinic and carried over into the hospital setting. At discharge, the outcomes manager provides the clinic case manager with a status update in addition to the discharge plan. The patient is then followed by the clinic case manager.

Using an interdisciplinary approach to manage elective bowel surgery patients, the multispecialty clinic was able to reduce hospital days without reducing quality of care. The hospital was able to reduce cost through cooperative efforts in operating room standardization. The patient benefited through improved prehospital education and evaluation by both the clinic and hospital staff. Through efforts such as this, all parties involved were able to accomplish their established goals. Cooperative initiatives are essential in today's health care, especially within nonintegrated delivery systems.

BENEFITS OF OUTCOMES MANAGEMENT

The benefits of OM are numerous and are not limited to the improvement of patient outcomes. Institutions observe an improvement in system processes, such as the flow of patients through the institution, thus increasing their efficiency. Payers, such as health maintenance organizations (HMOs), benefit from OM through the resulting cost reductions. Additionally, the focus on improved continuity of care provides adequate health care resource utilization by consumers.

Overall benefits recognized by an organization or health care system include improved patient outcomes, increased scientific-based practice, improved collegiality and collaboration, increased expertise of health care providers, improved quality enhancement programs, and improved continuity of care.

CONCLUSION

OM will succeed if the commitment can be made to build the program with collegial synergistic collaborative practice teams that are focused on improving quality, building an evidence-based practice environment focused on "best practices" that continually keeps a "patients first" philosophy. The St. Luke's model has evolved a collaborative practice environment that reaches beyond the boundary of OM. The ideal of collegial/collaborative practice can be realized in programs similar to the St. Luke's model.

NOTES

1. Congressional Budget Office, *Trends in Health Spending: An Update* (Washington, DC: 1993).
2. K. Zander, "Second Generation Primary Nursing," *Journal of Nursing Administration* 15, no. 3 (1985): 18–24.
3. M. Fazen, *Managed Care Desk Reference* (Dallas, TX: HCS Publications, 1994).
4. P. Ellwood, "Outcomes Management: A Technology of Patient Experience," *New England Journal of Medicine* 318 (1988): 1549–1556.
5. Ibid.
6. L.S. Houston et al., *Outcomes Management: A User's Guide* (Houston, TX: St. Luke's Episcopal Hospital, 1992).
7. A.W. Wojner, "Outcomes Management: An Interdisciplinary Search for Best Practice," *AACN Clinical Issues* 7, no. 1 (1996): 133–145.
8. Ellwood, "Outcomes Management"; Wojner, "Outcomes Management."
9. D.A. Miller and F.G. Diaz, "Vaginal Birth after Cesarean: A 10-year Experience," *Obstetrics and Gynecology* 84 (1994): 255–258.
10. A.R. Tarlov et al., "The Medical Outcomes Study," *Journal of the American Medical Association* 262 (1989): 925–939.
11. M. Terhaar and S. O'Keefe, "A New Advanced Practice Role Focused on Outcomes Management in Women's and Children's Health," *Journal of Perinatal and Neonatal Nursing* 9, no. 3 (1995): 10–21.
12. G.F. Grady and A. Wojner, "Collaborative Practice Teams: The Infrastructure of Outcomes Management," *AACN Clinical Issues* 7, no. 1 (1996): 153–158.
13. Ibid.
14. A.B. Hamric and J.A. Spross, eds., *The Clinical Nurse Specialist in Theory and Practice* (Philadelphia: W.B. Saunders, 1989), 243.

15. Joint Commission on Accreditaiton of Healthcare Organizations, *1996 Comprehensive Accreditation Manual for Hospitals* (Oakbrook Terrace, IL: 1995).

16. Joint Commission on Accreditation of Healthcare Organizations, *A Guide to Establishing Programs for Assessing Outcomes in Clinical Settings* (Oakbrook Terrace, IL: 1994).

17. Ibid.

18. N.M. Lang and K.D. Marek, "The Classification of Patient Outcomes," *Journal of Professional Nursing* 6, no. 3 (1990): 158–163; J.G. Osbolt and J.R. Graves, "Clinical Nursing Informatics: Developing Tools for Knowledge Workers," *Nursing Clinics of North America* 28 (1993): 407–425; T. Singarella, "Health Informatics and Biocommunications," *Journal of Biomedical Computing* 18, no. 1 (1991): 12–13.

19. Cited in M. Collen, "A Brief History Overview of Hospital Information System (HIS) Evolution in the United States," *International Journal of Biomedical Computing* 29 (1991): 169–189.

20. Ibid.

21. P.B. Batalden et al., "Linking Outcomes Measurement to Continual Improvement: The Serial "V" Way of Thinking about Improving Clinical Care," *Journal of Quality Improvement* 20 (1994): 167–180.

22. E. Green and J.M. Katz, "Practice Guidelines: A Standard Whose Time Has Come," *Journal Nursing Care Quality* 8, no. 1 (1993): 23–30; P.A. Hofman, "Critical Path Method: An Important Tool for Coordinating Clinical Care," *Journal on Quality Improvement* 19 (1993): 235–246; C. Mosher et al., "Upgrading Practice with Critical Pathways," *American Journal of Nursing* (January 1992): 41–44.

23. P.E. Windle and S. Houston, "COMIT: Improving Patient Outcomes," *Nursing Management* 26, no. 9 (1995): 64AA–64II.

24. Batalden et al., "Linking Outcomes Measurement."

25. R.S. Abruzzese, *Nursing Staff Development* (St. Louis, MO: C.V. Mosby, 1992).

CHAPTER 15

Reducing an Institutional Caesarean Section Rate

Robin G. Fleschler and Kenneth J. Moise, Jr.

Chapter Objectives

1. To describe the need for reducing a Caesarean section rate.
2. To describe the process for evaluating and changing the Caesarean section rate within an outcomes management (OM) framework.
   a. To describe the process for enlisting physician support for the Caesarean reduction initiative.
   b. To describe the strategies implemented for reducing the Caesarean section rate.
   c. To describe ongoing approaches for reevaluating the Caesarean section rate.
3. To describe development of an antepartum risk scoring tool to predict risk for Caesarean section.

Hospitals have been under tremendous pressure in recent years to evaluate the appropriateness and subsequently to reduce their rate of Caesarean delivery. Caesarean section is the most frequently performed major surgery in the United States.[1] The Caesarean section rate has risen from around 5 percent in the early 1970s to around 25 percent in the mid-1990s.[2] Since 1990, our hospital has striven to meet quality and financial goals within an outcomes management (OM) framework. OM is the enhancement of physiologic and psychosocial patient outcomes through development and implementation of exemplary health practices and services.[3] Challenging the Caesarean section rate of our hospital was addressed through this OM model.

REDUCING THE CAESAREAN SECTION RATE: THE ISSUE

Our institution began evaluating the number and appropriateness of our Caesarean section rate in 1994. For a few years prior to this time, the administrators and chief executive officer (CEO) received letters from third-party payers pointing out that the Caesarean section rate at our hospital exceeded the national average. Competition for obstetrical patients has been a reality in recent years. The rise of for-profit health care systems and the increase in patients choosing less expensive managed-care health plans has created an incentive for hospitals to develop less costly services while still maintaining quality of care. The reduction of postpartum lengths of stay in some health care systems has resulted in federal mandating of 48-hour postpartal stays for patients with a vaginal delivery and a 96-hour postoperative stay for patients who undergo a Caesarean section.[4]

Caesarean section rates were always an important part of the hospital's medical quality process and were reported in comparison with similar hospitals in the Maryland Hospital Indicator Project. Caesarean sections are reviewed monthly by peer physicians as part of the quality assurance process. When questioned about the higher-than-average Caesarean section rate at our institution, the obstetricians and perinatologists felt that this could be explained by the disproportionate presence of high-risk patients.

Our hospital is a 946-bed tertiary care institution in the Texas Medical Center. The annual number of deliveries has ranged from 2,500 to 4,000 yearly for the past five years. Twenty-five percent of the obstetricians who practice at our institution are maternal-fetal medicine specialists. Our location is immediately adjacent to level 2 and level 3 neonatal nurseries at a pediatric hospital, Texas Children's Hospital. The maternal-fetal medicine specialists comprise both full-time and clinical academic faculty of a local medical school. Monthly deliveries of these specialists vary from 25 percent to 35 percent of the total volume. The institution serves as a referral center for patients with obstetrical complications and provides nursing services in specialized antepartum, intermediate care, and labor and delivery areas to care for these women. In the past year, the obstetrical population has become more skewed to complicated perinatal patients. They are transferred to the care at our hospital even from neighboring institutions who advertise tertiary care services.

As the reimbursement for health-related services declines, quality is becoming more of a factor in differentiating care between institutions. OM has become one vehicle for change in the institution. Research-based changes in practice have resulted in both enhancement of quality and reduction in costs in many patient populations.[5] This strategy has enabled the hospital to remain competitive in an aggressive managed-care environment. The outcomes of the perinatal population have been excellent. Complicated perinatal patients have such diagnoses as preterm labor, idiopathic thrombocytopenia purpura, incompetent cervix, multiple gestation, and Phesus isoimmunization. Quality is difficult to identify and measure, as evidenced by a recent series supporting this contention in the *New England Journal of Medicine*.[6] The Caesarean section rate represents an easy but nonrepresentative method for assessing the quality of care for an obstetrical population. This parameter is commonly used by by payers to assess quality. Because the institution places great value on the outcomes of these high-risk mothers and their infants, an effort began to evaluate the rate of Caesarean delivery.

EVALUATION AND CHANGE WITHIN OUTCOMES MANAGEMENT

The success of various programs in the institution in identifying, implementing, and evaluating changes driven by patient outcome was possible through the OM framework. This framework was applied to decrease the number of patients who required a Caesarean section.[7]

The Outcomes Management Model

OM is illustrated by the model shown in Figure 15–1. This model identifies the need to express the institutional values related to quality and cost that affect patient

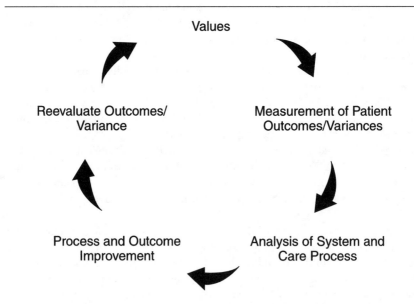

Figure 15–1 St. Luke's Episcopal Hospital Outcomes Management Model. Courtesy of St. Luke's Episcopal Hospital, Houston, Texas.

outcomes. The next step in the model emphasizes the collection and assessment of population-specific outcomes data. Examination of system and care processes that drive the outcome must then be performed. Using sound outcomes assessment and process analysis, quality improvement then provides the method for alteration of a specific outcome. After quality or research strategies have been implemented, outcomes are reevaluated to identify the impact of the changes in patient care processes.

USING THE OM FRAMEWORK TO MEASURE AND CHANGE THE CAESAREAN SECTION RATE

Step 1: Values

The first phase of the OM process is the identification of institutional values. The goal of high quality at the lowest cost includes two values previously addressed. Quality for an obstetrical population is the first absolute value. This means that there is *zero* tolerance for poor maternal and neonatal outcomes. Not only is this an institutional value, but the legal climate for caring for obstetrical patients makes this an essential aspect of any program.

The second value relates to cost. As previously mentioned, cost is driving health care choices. Being adversely selected as a high-risk center for complicated patients makes cost a problematic issue. Reimbursement systems are not always designed to pay for the complex care needed by these patients. Especially challenging is the prolonged hospitalization for such patients with an incompetent cervix and hourglassing membranes or preterm premature rupture of the membranes at 22 weeks in a multiple gestation. Private and governmental third-party payers do not always reimburse for these prolonged stays, even though suboptimal care might result in neonatal candidates for the level 3 nursery. Infants in neonatal intensive care units face the initial challenge of survival and then continue their challenges with long-term developmental and disability issues. Although quality is the primary factor driving the care, the institution cannot remain solvent if that care is not reimbursed. If ongoing assessment of the fetus portends compromise, then delivery is affected. Imminent delivery often necessitates a Caesarean section.

A third value supported by the institution is that of collaborative decision making. This value is one of the tenets of a system that supports an OM philosophy. All members of the health care team contribute to the optimal outcomes of the patients. Physicians, nurses, pharmacists, anesthesiologists, administrators, and pathology personnel all have a role in these optimal outcomes.

Step 2: Measurement of Patient Outcomes

Caesarean section and vaginal birth after Caesarean (VBAC) rates are the quality outcomes being measured. National rates for Caesarean sections are approximately 22 to 24 percent.[8] Primary and repeat Caesarean section rates are also reviewed and reported historically in an institution. Primary Caesarean sections are those performed on women who have never previously delivered by Caesarean section. A repeat Caesarean section is performed on a woman who has undergone a Caesarean section to deliver a child.

Caesarean section rates at our institution prior to 1994 exceeded the national average. VBAC rates were lower than desired.

Step 3: Analysis of System and Care Process

Caesarean section is undertaken in accordance with the judgment of the attending physician. He or she makes this decision on the basis of his or her expertise and previous experience. To reduce the Caesarean section rate, physician buy-in was necessary. Discussions were held between physician leaders of the service and hospital administrators. Physician leaders were aware that third-party payers were seeking Caesarean section rates as evidence of quality in awarding competitive managed-care contracts to our hospital.

Two presentations were made at the monthly OB-Gyn service meetings to illustrate and explain the importance of the Caesarean section rate to the hospital in terms of quality and benchmarking. Information about the rising rates, regional variations, and indications for the high Caesarean section rates was given. One presentation was given to the obstetrical collaborative practice group by the outcomes manager and the quality utilization nurse. A second presentation was given by the chief of maternal/fetal medicine at the monthly OB-Gyn physician service meeting.

The physician leaders then formed a Caesarean section task force to make recommendations for changing practice. The Caesarean section task force was comprised of a physician leader, several perinatologists, the clinical nurse specialist/outcomes manager, and the hospital administrator responsible for women's services. The group met several times. After reviewing current research, a plan of action was developed, consisting of (1) a VBAC information form required before all elective repeat Caesarean sections, as presented in Exhibit 15–1; (2) an active management of labor policy and protocol; (3) VBAC classes (offered at no cost to the participants); and (4) biannual peer review of individual Caesarean section rates published by name for the physicians with more than three deliveries per month. These rates were distributed at the OB-Gyn service meeting and then retrieved as confidential information.[9]

Step 4: Process and Outcome Improvement

During the several months required for program development, the Caesarean section rate decreased, probably as a result of awareness of the program. This is

Exhibit 15–1 VBAC Information Form

Information Form for Women with a History of Previous Caesarean Section

I, _____, have been counseled by _____
　　　　(Patient Name)　　　　　　　　　　　　　　　　　　(Doctor, Midwife, Nurse)

concerning a vaginal delivery after a previous Caesarean (surgical) delivery. I had a Caesarean section for the birth of my last child and understand that, based on studies by the National Institute of Child Health and Human Development and the American College of Obstetrics and Gynecology, my health care provider advises that vaginal delivery after Caesarean birth is a reasonable option for my next pregnancy.

I understand that during a Caesarean section an incision is made on my womb. This incision may be classical (high on my womb), vertical (low on my womb), or low transverse (horizontal). If my incision was the transverse (horizontal) type, it may be possible for me to deliver vaginally at the conclusion of my current pregnancy. Overall, there are usually fewer complications after a successful vaginal delivery compared with those experienced from a repeat Caesarean section. I understand that for women like myself who attempt a vaginal birth with a previous low transverse uterine incision, a 60 to 80 percent success rate in delivering vaginally may be expected.

The benefits of a successful vaginal delivery usually include the elimination of the need for an operation, postoperative complications, and a reduction in the length of time for recuperation in the hospital. The average hospitalization after a vaginal delivery is one day, compared with the average length of hospitalization after a Caesarean section, which is two or more days.

I understand the main risk of attempting a vaginal birth after a previous Caesarean section is that the scar on the uterus may separate during labor. The separation of the scar may be small and insignificant and occurs in only 2 percent of patients who have attempted a vaginal delivery after a Caesarean section. The risk for uterine scar separation that requires an urgent repeat Caesarean section is less than 1 percent. I understand that in the majority of cases where an urgent repeat Caesarean section is needed there will still be no ill effects to myself or my infant but occasionally urgent surgery may result in increased blood loss that requires administration of a blood transfusion. In rare cases the removal of my womb may be necessary.

I understand that because of the risks mentioned above, my labor will be observed in the hospital and special monitoring may be used during this labor to help the doctor evaluate my uterine contractions and my baby's well-being. I understand that if the incision on my uterus was a classical (vertical) type, it is not advisable for me to attempt a vaginal delivery, and I will need to have a repeat Caesarean section for the delivery of my current baby. The rate of uterine scar separation in a woman with a classical incision who attempts a vaginal birth in the next pregnancy may be as high as 8 percent.

continues

Exhibit 15–1 continued

I certify that this form has been fully explained to me, that I have read it or have had it read to me. I understand the contents of the form include the risks and benefits for a vaginal birth after a Caesarean section and that all my questions have been adequately answered by the staff.

I, _____DO desire to attempt a vaginal birth after a previous
    (Patient's signature)   Caesarean section.

I, _____DO NOT desire to attempt a vaginal birth after a
    (Patient's signature)   previous Caesarean section.

Date _____ Time _____

_____
(Witness' signature)

Source: Adapted with permission from M. Gabay and S.M. Wolfe, *Unnecessary Cesarean Sections: Curing a National Epidemic,* © 1994, Public Citizen's Health Research Group.

commonly known as the Hawthorne effect. In the following six months, the Caesarean section rate remained near the national average. Approximately a year after the initiation of the program, a shift in the population occurred. A large number of patients cared for by a health maintenance organization moved to a different institution, and a group of six private obstetricians moved their practice to our hospital. Subsequent to this change, the Caesarean section rate began to fluctuate again. It became evident that the tertiary care center was being adversely selected by physicians for the care of the high-risk obstetrical patients. Approximately 60 to 75 percent of the patients were noted to be at risk.

The process improvements were implemented during the following year. Caesarean section and VBAC rates continued to be reported at the monthly physician service meeting. VBAC rates were also reported in accordance with the recommendations of a recent committee opinion for the American College of Obstetrics and Gynecology.[10] During this time, the physicians asked for calculation of a rate more reflective of the patients who could safely choose a trial of labor—the *attempted trial of labor rate*—and a *VBAC success rate* indicating the rate of vaginal delivery in those patients who were considered good candidates. Examples of conditions that precluded a trial of labor included a history of two Caesarean sections, breech presentations, and placenta previa. The committee recommended that the *VBAC rate* be defined as the number of VBACs divided by the total number of women with prior Caesarean deliveries and that the *VBAC success rate* be defined as the number of VBACs divided by the total number of women who had a trial of labor after Caesarean delivery.

Step 5: Reevaluation of Outcomes

The Caesarean section rate decreased below the national rate in the first six months of the program development. It returned to the level that was noted prior to our interventions after the large managed-care group left our instituion and the smaller private obstetrical group shifted most of their clients to the institution. The Caesarean section rate remained at this level for several months, then began decreasing slowly. Attempted trial of labor rates quickly increased to levels exceeding the national norms. VBAC success rates also are excellent when compared to national norms of 60 to 80 percent.[11] Patients with a history of previous Caesarean section are now routinely educated by their physicians regarding their options for delivery and the active management of labor protocol. Peer review of rates at the physician service meeting is conducted every six months, and all patients undergoing a Caesarean surgery are reviewed by the continuing quality improvement committee.

Education was an integral part of the process and continues to play an important role. Physicians continue to question the rates and review their practice. Nursing is aware of the quality initiative as well and reports the rates as a nursing quality measure. Current literature is reviewed on an ongoing basis to identify measures to continue lowering the rate while maintaining good maternal and neonatal quality outcomes.

ANTEPARTUM SCORING SYSTEM TO PREDICT RISK FOR CAESAREAN SECTION

During the development of the program to lower the Caesarean section rate, a risk assessment tool for predicting the Caesarean section rate was formulated from a population of 9,300 deliveries at an associated inner-city teaching hospital. The scoring system was developed in response to our desire to associate a Caesarean section rate higher than national average with an obstetric population that was perceived as being more at risk than the average population. Patients with risk factors that precluded vaginal delivery were excluded. These patients included those with a history of prior classical Caesarean section, placenta previa, and abnormal fetal presentation. This same scoring system was then prospectively applied in a blinded fashion to 2,691 births at our tertiary care medical center hospital. Chi-square analysis was performed. Exhibit 15–2 indicates the risk factors and their respective scores.

The Caesarean section rate for patients with no known risk factors exceeded the parameter noted for risk-free patients identified at the inner-city teaching hospital. However, the Caesarean section rate increased for patients with an increasing risk score. The antepartum Caesarean section risk score continues to be calculated to assess risk relative to Caesarean section rate. Table 15–1 identifies risk scores and

Exhibit 15–2 Antenatal Caesarean Section Risk Factors Used in Patient Cumulative Risk Scores

	Score		Score
Age >35 or <15 years	2	Nulliparous	2
Ethnicity = non-Caucasian	1	Prior Caesarean section	4
No prenatal care	2	>1 preterm delivery	3
Fetal weight <1000 g or >4,500 g	6	Gestational age >42 weeks	4
Fetal weight 1,000–1,800 g or 4,000–4,500 g	3	Abruptio placentae	4
		Illicit drug use	2
Third-trimester bleeding	3	Preterm premature rupture of membranes	3
Diabetes (any class)	3		
Preterm labor	3	Intrauterine growth retardation	2

Courtesy of St. Luke's Episcopal Hospital, Houston, Texas.

corresponding Caesarean section rates. This antepartum Caesarean section risk system continues to be evaluated at the current time.

CONCLUSION

Analysis and evaluation of the patient population are ongoing. Caesarean section rates, VBAC rates, attempted trial of labor rates, and VBAC success rates continue to be monitored and reported. Consequences of trials of labor and Caesarean sections are monitored for quality of care. However, optimal maternal and newborn outcomes remain the final deciding factors in the method of delivery.

Table 15–1 Antepartum Risk Scores and Corresponding Caesarean Section Rates Based on 9,300 Deliveries at an Inner-City Teaching Hospital

Risk Score	C-Sec. No. (Rate)	Total Deliveries
0	2 (2.5%)	79
1–4	574 (8.4%)	6,856
5–9	337 (15.6%)	2,158
≥10	47 (21.6%)	218

Courtesy of St. Luke's Episcopal Hospital, Houston, Texas.

NOTES

1. U.S. Department of Health and Human Services, *Health United States* (Washington, DC: 1993).
2. *Morbidity and Mortality Weekly Report* 42 (1991): 86–89.
3. S. Houston et al., "Outcomes Management: A User's Guide" (unpublished document, St. Luke's Episcopal Hospital, 1996).
4. R. A. Rosenblatt, "Congress Expands Requirements for Health Insurance: New Moms Get 48 Hour Hospital Stays; Coverage for Mental Illness Increased," *Houston Chronicle,* 25 September 1996: 10A.
5. Houston et al., "Outcomes Management."
6. D. Blumenthal, "Quality of Care—What Is It? (Part I)," *New England Journal of Medicine* 335 (1996): 891–894; R.H. Brook et al., "Measuring Quality of Care (Part II)," *New England Journal of Medicine* 335 (1996): 966–970; M.R. Chassin, "Improving the Quality of Care (Part III)," *New England Journal of Medicine* 335 (1996): 1060–1063; D. Blumenthal, "Origins of the Quality-of-Care Debate (Part IV)," *New England Journal of Medicine* 335 (1996): 1146–1149.
7. Houston et al., "Outcomes Management."
8. Medical Leadership Council, *Coming to Term: Innovations in Safely Reducing Cesarean Rates* (Washington, DC: Advisory Board Co., 1996).
9. P. Boylan et al., "Effect of Active Management of Labor on the Incidence of Cesarean Section for Dystocia in Nulliparas," *American Journal of Perinatology* 8, no. 6 (1991): 373–379; G.R. Cohen et al., "A Prospective Randomized Study of the Aggressive Management of Early Labor," *American Journal of Obstetrics and Gynecology* 160 (1987): 1174–1177; B.L. Flamm et al., "Vaginal Birth after Cesarean Section: Results of a Multicenter Study," *American Journal of Obstetrics and Gynecology* 76 (1988): 750–754; S.A. Myers and N. Gleicher, "A Successful Program To Lower Cesarean-Section Rates," *New England Journal of Medicine* 319 (1988): 1511–1516; J.A. Lopez-Zeno et al., "A Controlled Trial of a Program for the Active Management of Labor," *New England Journal of Medicine* 326 (1992): 450–454; R.P. Porreco, "High Cesarean Section Rate: A New Perspective," *Obstetrics and Gynecology* 65 (1985): 307–311; E.J. Quilligan, "Making Inroads against the C-Section Rate," *Contemporary OB/GYN* (1983): 221–225; A.J. Satin et al., "High-Versus Low-Dose Oxytocin for Labor Stimulation," *Obstetrics and Gynecology* 80 (1992): 111–116; M.L. Socol et al., "Reducing Cesarean Births at a Primarily Private University Hospital," *American Journal of Obstetrics and Gynecology* 168 (1993): 1748–1758; R.S. Stafford, "Alternative Strategies for Controlling Rising Cesarean Section Rates," *Journal of the American Medical Association* 263 (1990): 683–687.
10. American College of Obstetricians and Gynecologists, *Committee Opinion: Rate of Vaginal Births after Cesarean Delivery,* no. 179 (Washington, DC: 1996).
11. Ibid.

CHAPTER 16

Case Study in Stroke Outcomes Management

Anne W. Wojner and Michael E. Newmark

Chapter Objectives

1. To identify the significance of descriptive research in measuring clinical opportunities for practice improvement within a population of patients.
2. To discuss multidisciplinary interventions that may improve stroke patient outcomes.

Stroke is the third leading cause of death in the United States and the leading cause of disability among adults. Although the term *cerebral vascular accident* (CVA) evolved in the 1900s, the original term *stroke* has since replaced CVA due to the nonaccidental nature of the disease process.[1] Stroke costs U.S. citizens approximately $30 billion annually. An estimated $17 billion is attributed to direct care costs, and the indirect costs of stroke have been estimated at $13 billion annually, related to lost societal productivity by the stroke victim and often family caregivers.[2] Data from the National Stroke Association (NSA) have revealed that the public is unaware of the warning signs for stroke, confusing these important clinical findings with well-publicized cardiac symptoms such as chest pain and shortness of breath. Additionally, the NSA found that only two of five study participants indicated that they viewed stroke as an emergency.[3]

Approximately 25 to 50 percent of stroke survivors experience partial or total functional dependence in their ability to perform activities of daily living.[4] Currently, there is limited acute care therapy available to combat stroke. The introduction of rtPA as an acute intervention aimed at halting ischemic stroke shows promise but carries a narrow therapeutic window of only three hours from onset of symptoms for treatment initiation.[5] Without aggressive public education, the use of rtPA for the treatment of ischemic stroke will remain limited. Finally, Medicare reimbursement for the diagnosis-related group (DRG) covering stroke, DRG 14, is limited nationally to an average of $3,300 per case for acute care hospitalization. This limited reimbursement, coupled with expensive rtPA therapy at close to $2,200 per dose, will continue to challenge acute care providers to develop new and innovative care delivery systems that enhance patient outcomes, improve provider practice, and reduce financial risk.

THE ST. LUKE'S EXPERIENCE: A STROKE COLLABORATIVE PRACTICE TEAM

In 1990, DRG 14, "Specific Cerebrovascular Disorders, Except Transient Ischemic Attack," was targeted for outcomes management by St. Luke's Episcopal Hospital (SLEH) administrators. Management of DRG 14 is complex due to the inclusion of both hemorrhagic and ischemic stroke in this diagnostic group. In 1990, average length of stay (LOS) for DRG 14 was 21 days at SLEH, with a Medicare reimbursement of $4,500 per case (Figure 16–1).

In 1991, a collaborative practice team (CPT) was formed consisting of members from each discipline involved with stroke care; the purpose of the CPT was to "reinvent" stroke care at SLEH. A descriptive study of the SLEH stroke population was undertaken for the first year of the program, providing a profile of the hospital's typical stroke case. Findings revealed a patient population that was predominately female, with the majority of stroke lesions occurring in the right cerebral hemisphere. A statistically significant difference in LOS by location of infarct

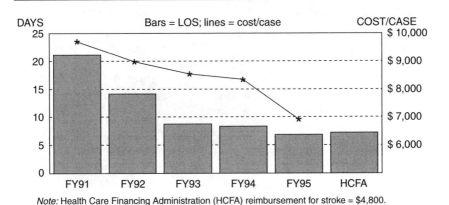

Note: Health Care Financing Administration (HCFA) reimbursement for stroke = $4,800.

Figure 16–1 Length of Stay and Cost per Case in the SLEH Stroke Population. Courtesy of St. Luke's Episcopal Hospital, Houston, Texas.

was measured by Student's *t*-test (Figure 16–2). These initial data promoted development of a high-risk profile for stroke patients: (1) multiple brain infarcts, average LOS of 21 days, $p = .0009$; and (2) brainstem infarcts, average LOS of 34 days, $p = .0001$.[6]

Using these descriptive data, the stroke CPT members came together to identify patient outcomes as quality targets to frame an outcomes management stroke initiative. Figure 16–3 illustrates the continuous quality improvement (CQI) process used by stroke CPT members. Intermediate and long-term outcomes were targeted in phase 1. During phase 2, members worked toward development of structured care methodologies (SCMs; pathways, protocols, order sets) that would be used to standardize practice across multiple disciplines caring for stroke patients. In phase 3, new practice standards were introduced, and in phase 4, outcomes were measured. In keeping with the CQI concept, when outcomes measurement fell short of achieving a targeted outcome, the stroke CPT members returned to phase 2 to revise and create additional SCMs aimed at population outcomes attainment.[7]

The first outcomes worksheet and critical pathway for stroke emerged in 1992 with a targeted LOS of eight days (Exhibit 16–1). A research question generated by a staff nurse from the neuroscience intensive care unit led CPT members to incorporate

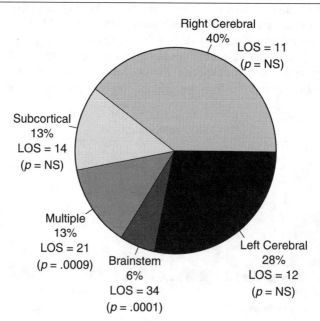

Figure 16–2 Length of Stay by Location of Stroke. Courtesy of St. Luke's Episcopal Hospital, Houston, Texas.

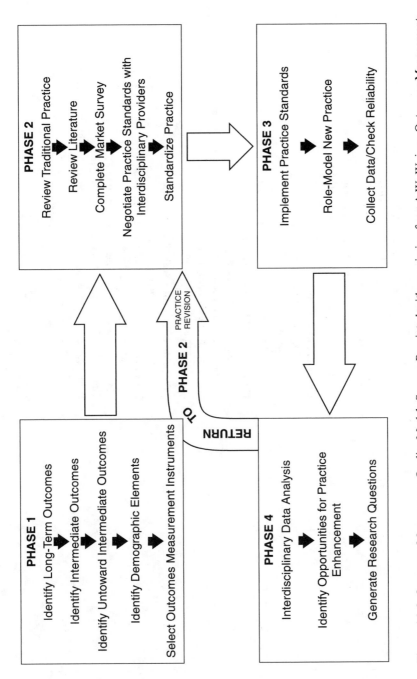

Figure 16–3 Outcomes Management Quality Model. *Source:* Reprinted with permission from A.W. Wojner, Outcomes Management: The Search for Best Practice, *AACN Clinical Issues*, Vol. 7, No. 1, p. 142, © Lippincott-Raven.

Exhibit 16–1 Outcomes Worksheet and Critical Pathway for Stroke

ADDRESSOGRAPH AND TRIAGE
TIME STAMP

ST. LUKE'S EPISCOPAL HOSPITAL
DRG 014: STROKE

Check one of the following:

___ Hemorrhagic (without craniotomy or coil embolization)
___ Ischemic   ___ Embolic   ___ Thrombotic

Check one of the following:

___ Not entered in drug study
___ rtPA Study
___ Lubeluzole Study

Check the INITIAL anticoagulation order below:

___ No anticoagulation therapy
___ Heparin bolus/heparin infusion/warfarin started following day
___ Heparin bolus/heparin infusion
___ Heparin infusion (no bolus)

Admission NIH Stroke Scale Score:

Emergency Department Use Only:

Time to hospital from onset of stroke symptoms _____
     Arrival: EMS_____   Private_____
Time from Neurologist notification to arrival in ED _____
Time from CT order to start of CT _____
If applicable: Total time from onset of symptoms to initiation of rtPA
     infusion _____

LOS: ____

                                        Total

continues

Exhibit 16–1 continued

PLACE A CHECK MARK IN THE BLANKS BELOW FOR ALL FINDINGS THAT APPLY TO THE PATIENT. USE "NA" IF UNABLE TO TEST.

Dysphagia Assessment Profile:

PO Diet: Dysphagia _____

  Other _____

  Pocketing food _____

Tube Feedings _____

Water Swallow Test:

  Coughs on H_2O _____

  More than 1 swallow to empty mouth _____

  Wet voice after swallow _____

  Drooling _____

Cranial Nerve VII (Facial):

  Weakness _____

  Incomplete oral closure _____

Cranial Nerve XII (Hypoglossal):

  Unable to protrude tongue _____

  Unable to move tongue side to side _____

  Unable to move tongue upward (Abnormal or absent "L" sound) _____

Cranial Nerve IX & X (Glossopharyngeal & Vagus):

  Absent gag reflex _____

  Absent or abnormal "K" sound _____

Communication:

  Expressive Aphasia _____

  Receptive Aphasia _____

  Global Aphasia _____

  Dysarthria _____

PMH:

  Previous stroke _____

  Atrial fibrillation _____

Location of Stroke(s):

  L cerebral _____

  R cerebral _____

  L cerebellar _____

  R cerebellar _____

  Subcortical _____

  Brainstem _____

Discharge Information:

  Home _____

  Rehab Center _____

  Subacute Care _____

  SNF _____

  Death _____

continues

Exhibit 16–1 continued

DATE	DAY 1: _____	DAY 2: _____	DAY 3: _____	DAY 4: _____	DISCHARGE TARGET DAY 5: _____
CONSULTS	Neurology; CNS Social Service; Dietitian	Physical & Occupational Therapy	PM&R Consider Speech Pathologist		Consider Gastroenterologist (PEG)
DIAGNOSTICS	CXR; CT Scan; ECG Chem 7 & 12; CBC; PT/PTT Consider prealbumin	Carotid Doppler PT/PTT (if on anticoagulation)	PT/PTT (if on anticoagulation) Consider Modified Barium Swallow	PT/PTT (if on anticoagulation)	PT/PTT (if on anticoagulation)
TREATMENTS	Neuro VS q 2–4 hours I&O; IV therapy	Neuro VS q 2–4 hours Continency program	Neuro VS q 2–4 hours Continency program prn	Neuro VS q 2–4 hours Continency program prn	Neuro VS q 2–4 hours Continency program prn
ACTIVITY	Bed rest	Up in chair 2–4 times/day Begin self-grooming/feeding	Up in chair 2–4 times/day Increase self-care	Increase OOB activity Identify max self-care potential	Increase OOB activity Self-care discharge plan
NUTRITION	RN completes Dysphagia Assessment Profile Consider Dysphagia Protocol	Soft diet Dysphagia diet Tube feeding	Soft diet Dysphagia diet Tube feeding	Soft diet Dysphagia diet Tube feeding	Soft diet Dysphagia diet Tube feeding (consider PEG)
PT/FAMILY EDUCATION	Stroke booklet & video	Nutrition/diet/dysphagia	Incontinence	Self-care needs/ADLs	Self-care discharge plan
DISCHARGE PLANNING	RN gives NIH score to LMSW	LMSW completes assessment	Disposition planned	Support as needed	Discharge

continues

Exhibit 16–1 continued

UNTOWARD INTERMEDIATE OUTCOMES WORKSHEET

Privileged and confidential medical peer review communication generated pursuant to ad hoc review under V.A.T.S. 4495b, dec. 5.06; T.R.C.P. 166b(3)(d).

RECORD BY NUMBER BELOW THE APPLICABLE INTERMEDIATE OUTCOMES:

Physiologic Outcomes

1. Activity Intolerance: Unable to tolerate more than 2 hours of physical activity.
2. Decreased LOC: Lethargy or lower LOC that persists despite attempts to arouse for participation in ADLs.
3. FUO: Fever of unknown origin *not* present at time of admission.
4. UTI: Urinary tract infection *not* present at time of admission.
5. Pneumonia: Diagnosis of pneumonia made by X-ray, *not* present at time of admission.
6. Atelectasis: Diagnosis of atelectasis made by X-ray, *not* present at time of admission.
7. Skin breakdown, pressure related: The occurrence of new skin breakdown, *not* present at time of admission.
8. Ventilator dependency: Inability to wean from mechanical ventilation within 24 hours of initial wean attempt.
9. MBS aspiration: Aspiration witnessed on modified barium swallow.

10. Cerebral edema: Evidence of cerebral edema on CT scan.
11. Transformation: Evidence of ischemic stroke transformation to a hemorrhagic lesion as demonstrated by CT scan. (Initial CT scan must have reflected either ischemic stroke findings or have been negative.)
12. Disoriented to time.
13. Disoriented to time and place.
14. Disoriented to time, place, and person.
15. Seizures: New onset of seizures occurring following admission for stroke.
16. Urinary incontinence.
17. Bowel incontinence.

Psychosocial Outcomes

18. Code status: Family considering change in code status, but remain undecided for greater than 24 hours.
19. D/C indecisiveness: Patient and/or family undecided about discharge disposition for greater than 24 hours.

20. Patient D/C refusal: Patient refuses discharge plan but is incapable of independent living.

Provider Outcomes

21. Delayed nutrition intervention: Nutrition withheld for the first 72 hours following admission.
22. Inadequate nutrition intervention: Failure to administer sufficient calories and/or protein to meet patient's needs (can only be recorded by the nutrition support dietitian).

System Outcomes

23. No bed on 17 Tower.
24. No bed on 22 IMC.
25. No bed on 22 Tower.
26. No insurance coverage for rehabilitation.
27. Delay in insurance verification greater than 24 hours (include name of insurance carrier).
28. No Medicaid SNF bed available.

continues

Exhibit 16–1 continued

Date	Unit	Variance	Recorder	Date	Unit	Variance	Recorder	Date	Unit	Variance	Recorder

Courtesy of St. Luke's Episcopal Hospital, Houston, Texas.

variables for analysis of the impact of delayed nutrition intervention (withholding nutrition for greater than 72 hours) on intermediate-level stroke outcomes. Findings from this study included a statistically significant difference in LOS measured by Student's *t*-test for stroke patients with delayed nutrition intervention (LOS = 24 days, p = .0001). Further analysis revealed statistically significant relationships on chi square between delayed nutrition intervention and the following variables: inability to wean from mechanical ventilation (p = .001), fever of unknown origin requiring a septic workup (p = .001), incompetent swallow necessitating tube feeding (p = .001), and ICU management (p = .003). Analysis also revealed that stroke patients with an incompetent swallow requiring tube feeding had an average LOS of 24 days (p = .0001), those with fever of unknown origin averaged a 25-day LOS (p = .0001), and those with an inability to wean from mechanical ventilation within 5 days of intubation experienced a 31-day LOS (p = .0001). Additional relationships measured on chi square included incompetent swallow requiring tube feeding and development of pulmonary complications (p = .01), female patients and the occurrence of familial indecisiveness regarding discharge plan (p = .05), and cumulative stroke and the development of pulmonary complications such as aspiration pneumonia (p = .017).[8]

While not statistically significant (p = .06), a relationship between delayed nutrition intervention and inability to tolerate two or more hours of continuous rehabilitation therapy was also measured by chi square. Medicare inpatient rehabilitation criteria requires tolerance of three or more hours of continuous therapy; this finding alerted CPT members to the need to enhance nutritional management to optimize patient eligibility for poststroke rehabilitation.[9] This research supported further development of the high-risk stroke profile to include female patients and patients with dysphagia requiring tube feeding, patients requiring mechanical ventilation, and patients with cumulative brain infarction or delayed nutrition intervention.

The first protocol that emerged from the CPT was on standardized nutritional management for stroke patients (Appendix 16–A). The protocol included an automatic nutrition consult by a registered dietitian (RD) for all stroke patients admitted to the hospital, with provision of the RD's enteral nutrition recommendations within 24 hours of patient admission. Additionally, the stroke CPT's RD began following patients as they moved along the acute care continuum, departing from her previously geographically bound position. This provided consistent evaluation of the effectiveness of nutritional interventions in the population.[10]

Management of dysphagia was targeted next for protocol development (Appendix 16–B). The team's clinical nurse specialist (CNS) and speech and language pathologist (SLP) identified the need for a standardized approach to assessment of swallowing competency. A first draft of the CPT's Dysphagia Assessment Profile was developed in 1993 to assist interdisciplinary providers with early identification of "red flags" that may signal swallow incompetency. The Dysphagia Assessment Profile is now in its third revision, and preliminary findings using logistic regression indicate that it may be useful to predict the need for long-term tube feeding in stroke patients.[11]

The relationship between dysphagia patients requiring tube feedings and the development of pulmonary complications drove development of an interdisciplinary Dysphagia Protocol. The protocol emerged in 1993 as an intervention aimed at streamlining the approach to care provided by several disciplines working with dysphagia patients. The protocol automates a consult to the SLP for a bedside swallow assessment and a modified barium swallow study if indicated. Early tube feeding, as directed by the RD's and SLP's assessment findings, is also automated, with authority extended to the RD to determine appropriate formula and rate of delivery. Specific nursing care delivery techniques and occupational therapy standards are also driven by the protocol.[12]

Implementation and ongoing enhancement of the Dysphagia Assessment Profile and Dysphagia Protocol have produced dramatic results. Today, the incidence of delayed nutrition intervention, pneumonia, and atelectasis is rare among stroke patients managed by protocol at SLEH.

In 1993, use of the National Institutes of Health Stroke Scale (NIHSS) was added to the stroke program to provide a method for severity adjustment of stroke data. A relationship between the admission NIHSS score and acute care discharge site became apparent to providers within one year of implementation; analysis confirmed the existence of a statistically significant relationship between these two variables (Table 16–1).[13]

The admission NIHSS score is now routinely used to identify discharge-planning needs for stroke patients upon admission. The score is calculated by the neuroscience CNS, credentialed staff physicians, or nurses using a structured assessment panel to standardize the scoring procedure and reduce variability. Reliability assessment is conducted monthly. Tallied NIHSS admission scores are provided to the CPT's social worker, who then leads the family in the discharge-planning process.[14]

Table 16–1 The Relationship Between National Institutes of Health Stroke Scale (NIHSS) and Acute Care Discharge Site

NIHSS Score	Discharge Site	p Value
0–8	Home with outpatient rehabilitation therapy	.001
9–17	Inpatient rehabilitation candidate	.004
18+	Skilled nursing facility	
	Subacute facility	.001
	Home custodial care	

Note: N = 481 stroke patients.
Courtesy of St. Luke's Episcopal Hospital, Houston, Texas.

Additional NIHSS score analysis has identified statistically significant differences between NIHSS scores by gender: female stroke patients average scores of 13, while male stroke patients average scores of 10 ($p = .04$). A number of factors may be related to this finding, including the higher number of female stroke patients in the sample ($p = $ NS), the higher average age of women in the sample ($p = $ NS), or a potential reduction in lumen size of intracranial vessels among women, producing more proximal ischemic lesions with increased stroke severity.

In response to recent research findings indicating potential benefit derived from the early use of thrombolytic agents in ischemic stroke, the CPT implemented a rtPA stroke protocol in January 1996. Patients receiving thrombolytic therapy for the treatment of acute stroke are now followed longitudinally and compared with controls for several outcome indicators of interest (see rtPA Stroke Protocol, Appendix 16–C).[15]

Last, the SLEH stroke unit was developed to provide admission-to-discharge acute care for ischemic and hemorrhagic stroke patients. The unit is unique in that it can flexibly staff "up" to meet the needs of more critical stroke patients and flex "down" as patient acuity changes, allowing the patient and family to receive care throughout their hospitalization on one unit, by specialized, interdisciplinary stroke team members. The care provided on the unit is driven strictly by protocol, reducing practice variability among providers and facilitating outcomes measurement. Costly intensive care unit charges are prevented, reducing the overall cost of the stroke care provided.

Results of the neurology CPT's stroke outcomes management program have been dramatic. LOS for DRG 14 at SLEH has dropped significantly since the start of the program. There have been no readmissions secondary to complications post discharge, and there is an overall reduction in untoward intermediate outcomes, increased consultation between disciplines, increased interest in clinical research among grassroots providers, and increased provider and patient/familial satisfaction. Collaborative and collegial interdisciplinary practice is obvious in provider interactions, fostering an esprit de corps and trust among team members.

CONCLUSION

Stroke care will remain a challenging clinical practice area for health care providers. Traditional definitions for stroke care no longer serve the needs of patients, providers, and payers. Through a process of systematic clinical inquiry, interdisciplinary providers must measure the results of their interactions and continuously reinvent care delivery systems using outcomes data as their guide. Use of an outcomes management continuous quality improvement model provides powerful direction, and the assurance to interdisciplinary providers, patients, and payers that the pursuit of best practice is driven solely by patient outcomes.

NOTES

1. A.W. Wojner, "Optimizing Ischemic Stroke Outcomes: An Interdisciplinary Approach to Post-Stroke Rehabilitation in Acute Care," *Critical Care Nursing Quarterly* 19, no. 2 (1996): 47–61.

2. National Stroke Association, *NSA Newsletter* 11, nos. 3–4 (1994): 5.

3. National Stroke Association, "Cost of Stroke," *Stroke Clinical Updates* 5, no. 3 (1994): 11.

4. Agency for Health Care Policy and Research, *Post-Stroke Rehabilitation,* Clinical Practice Guideline, no. 16, pub no. 95-0662 (Rockville, MD: U.S. Department of Health and Human Services, Public Health Service, 1995).

5. Wojner, "Optimizing"; National Institute of Neurological Disorders and Stroke rt-PA Study Group, "Tissue Plasminogen Activator for Acute Ischemic Stroke," *New England Journal of Medicine* 353 (1995): 1581–1587.

6. A. Hedberg and A.W. Wojner, *Integrating Nutrition into Critical Pathways for Improved Outcomes* (Columbus, OH: Ross Products Division Abbott Laboratories, 1994); A.W. Wojner, "Outcomes Management: The Search for Best Practice," *AACN Clinical Issues* 7, no. 1 (1996): 133–145.

7. Wojner, "Outcomes Management: The Search"; A.W. Wojner, "Outcomes Management: From Theory to Practice," *Critical Care Nursing Quarterly* 19, no. 4 (1997): 1–15.

8. Hedberg and Wojner, *Integrating Nutrition*; Wojner, "Outcomes Management: The Search."

9. Hedberg and Wojner, *Integrating Nutrition.*

10. Ibid.; Wojner, "Outcomes Management: The Search."

11. Wojner, "Outcomes Management: The Search."

12. Ibid.

13. Wojner, "Optimizing"; Wojner, "Outcomes Management: The Search."

14. Wojner, "Outcomes Management: The Search."

15. Wojner, "Outcomes Management: From Theory."

Appendix 16–A

Interdisciplinary Stroke Care Program

SOCIAL SERVICES STROKE PROTOCOL

- All stroke patients will have a social service referral for patient/family assessment and discharge planning initiated on admission to the hospital.
- The order will be entered into the computer as follows:

Social Service Consult—Stroke Protocol

- The neuroscience social worker is responsible for initiating the assessment process within 24 hours of the consult date.
- The neuroscience social worker will use the National Institutes of Health Stroke Scale (NIHSS) score provided by the neuroscience CNS or credentialed RN staff to project discharge-planning needs for the stroke patient. The relationship between NIHSS scores and discharge disposition is as follows:

NIHSS Score	*Discharge Disposition*
0–8	Home with outpatient therapy
9–17	Inpatient rehabilitation program
18+	Subacute care, skilled nursing facility, or home with custodial care

- The neuroscience social worker will inform the neurology collaborative practice team (CPT) of his or her assessments, plans, and interventions through both direct communication and documentation in the chart progress notes.

NUTRITION SERVICES STROKE PROTOCOL

- All stroke patients will be automatically referred to the neuroscience nutrition support dietitian (NSD) for nutritional consult/risk screening on admission to the hospital.
- A nutrition risk screening will be conducted within 24 hours of admission.
- Results of the nutrition risk screening will be forwarded to the NSD. Findings from the screening process will be used by the NSD to determine the need for a nutrition consult and development of an individualized nutrition plan. If

Courtesy of St. Luke's Episcopal Hospital, Houston, Texas.

risk-screening findings indicate that a nutrition consult is not deemed necessary, the patient will not be charged for a consult.

- The NSD will use findings from the Dysphagia Assessment Profile provided by the neuroscience CNS or credentialed RN staff to determine the potential need for dysphagia-related nutritional interventions. Using the patient's medical history and current assessment, the NSD will identify interventions that meet 100% of the patient's nutrition and hydration needs.
- The NSD will inform the neurology collaborative practice team (CPT) of his or her assessments, plans, and interventions through both direct communication and documentation in the chart progress notes.
- In patients receiving tube feedings, the NSD will use the ongoing assessment of team members to project long-term tube feeding needs and the patient's ability to progress toward oral intake. The NSD's plan will include modification of enteral tube feeding rates in proportion to actual oral intake as the patient progresses.
- The NSD will include the patient and family/significant other in the development of a nutrition plan and provide ongoing education regarding all findings and interventions.

Appendix 16–B

Dysphagia Protocol

EXPECTED OUTCOMES

- Patient receives recommended referrals, therapies, medications, monitoring, and evaluations within 24 hours of protocol initiation.
- Neurology collaborative practice team (CPT) members, patients, and family are continuously updated on interdisciplinary assessment findings, recommendations, and interventions designed to optimize swallowing function and nutritional status.
- Patient does not aspirate food and/or beverage substances.

UNIT SECRETARY'S FUNCTIONS

1. Attach Dysphagia Protocol Nursing Order form to Kardex.
2. Enter orders for the following into the computer and record on Kardex:
   a. Nutrition assessment by registered dietitian (Dysphagia Protocol)
   b. Speech Language Therapy consult (Dysphagia Protocol)
   c. Suction apparatus to bedside; suction prn
3. Notify _____ of patient and Dysphagia Protocol order.

NURSING ORDERS

1. Assess swallowing using Dysphagia Assessment Profile; record findings on flowsheet.
2. Assess potential need for NPO status based on assessment findings and/or speech language pathologist's recommendations; notify physician/obtain order.
3. Monitor delivery of all oral substances, noting ability to successfully (without cough) swallow varying consistencies of food substances/liquids; assess for possible aspiration.
4. Maintain head of bed elevated to 30 degrees for a minimum of 30 minutes following delivery of oral intake or continually for patients receiving continuous tube feedings.

Courtesy of St. Luke's Episcopal Hospital, Houston, Texas.

5. Monitor intake and output every shift; complete calorie counts.
6. Monitor and record patient's weight twice weekly.
7. Assess/document breath sounds every shift and after oral intake; advise MD of findings and potential need for
   a. Portable chest X-ray
   b. CBC with differential
   c. Percussion and postural drainage tid; hold postural drainage with documented or suspected increased intracranial pressure
   d. Ultrasonic nebulization with sterile water
8. Suction apparatus at bedside; suction prn.
9. Provide patient and family education regarding dysphagia; record on patient education sheet.
10. Assess need for pharmacist to review medication regimen, considering the potential need for tube feedings.

SPEECH LANGUAGE PATHOLOGY ORDERS

1. The speech language pathologist (SLP) will determine a suitable route for delivery of enteral nutrition through use of a bedside clinical assessment, review of the Dysphagia Assessment Profile findings, and, when indicated, modified barium swallow.
2. Patients assessed for dysphagia may fall into one of three groups based on the SLP's bedside clinical assessment:

Category I: Candidates for Trial Oral Feeding

Descriptor: The patient lacks objective evidence of swallow dysfunction. There is no cough present on intake of water. The patient is alert and able to follow one-step commands. Silent aspiration cannot be ruled out.

- The SLP in collaboration with the RN will conduct a trial oral feeding using aspiration precautions. The patient's ability to competently swallow various consistencies of food will be assessed. Findings will be communicated by the SLP both directly and in the patient record on the progress note and will include recommendations for modified oral feedings, tube feedings, or modified barium swallow.

Category II: Candidates for Modified Barium Swallow (MBS)

Descriptor: The patient tests positive on bedside swallow evaluation for potential swallow dysfunction. This may include coughing on intake of water coupled with "successful" (no coughing) intake of thicker substances. The patient is alert and able to follow a one-step command.

- The SLP will assess the need for MBS and determine if the patient is an appropriate study candidate. A verbal order for the MBS will be obtained from the attending physician by the SLP. All MBS studies will be conducted and interpreted collaboratively by the SLP and radiologist. Findings will be communicated by the SLP both directly and in the patient record on the progress note and will include recommendations for modified oral feedings or tube feedings.

Category III: Noncandidates for Trial Oral Feeding or Modified Barium Swallow

Descriptor: The patient is unable to fully participate in clinical bedside assessment due to alterations in consciousness, cognitive status, gross motor dysfunction, or oral apraxia.

- The SLP in collaboration with the RN and MD will monitor the patient's progress toward potential candidacy for either trial oral feedings or MBS. The patient will receive tube feedings until oral feedings may be safely resumed.

OCCUPATIONAL THERAPY ORDERS

1. Assess trunk, neck, and head positioning to produce an effective swallow; if appropriate, provide adjunctive equipment to ensure proper or modified positioning. Communicate optimal positioning strategies to patient, family, and neurology collaborative practice team members directly and via patient record in progress notes.
2. Trial modified bolus placement techniques for patients cleared for oral intake. Determine effective strategies for feeding and communicate with patient, family, and neurology collaborative practice team members directly and via patient record in progress notes.
3. Assess perceptual and cognitive deficits that interfere with feeding; develop plan for environmental modification to enhance ability to work toward varying levels of independence with oral feeding, and communicate interventions with patient, family, and neurology collaborative practice team both directly and in patient record on progress note.

NUTRITION SUPPORT DIETITIAN (NSD) ORDERS

1. Review initial lab data, including electrolytes, prealbumin, and CBC with differential. Identify additional lab data necessary for assessment of nutritional status and communicate with physician/obtain verbal orders.

2. Complete nutritional assessment (see Nutrition Services Stroke Protocol) and communicate findings in patient record.

3. The NSD will utilize findings from the Dysphagia Assessment Profile provided by the neuroscience CNS or credentialed RN staff to determine the potential need for tube feedings. Using the patient's medical history and current assessment, the NSD will select a suitable enteral formula and calculate goal tube-feeding rate to meet 100% of the patient's protein and caloric needs.

4. The NSD will inform the neurology collaborative practice team (CPT) of his or her assessments, plans, and interventions through both direct communication and documentation in the chart progress notes.

5. The NSD will use the ongoing assessment of the speech language pathologist to project long-term tube-feeding needs and the patient's ability to progress toward oral intake. The NSD's plan will include modification of enteral tube feeding rates in proportion to actual oral intake as the patient progresses.

6. The NSD will include the patient and family/significant other in the development of a nutrition plan and provide ongoing education regarding all findings and interventions.

Appendix 16–C

rtPA Stroke Protocol

ELIGIBILITY ASSESSMENT INSTRUMENT

Inclusion Criteria:

_____ Age ≥18 and functionally independent prior to this acute stroke presentation

_____ Clinical diagnosis of ischemic stroke causing a measurable neurologic deficit presumed to be due to cerebral ischemia after CT excludes hemorrhage

_____ Ability to initiate thrombolytic therapy within 180 minutes from onset of stroke symptoms

Exclusion Criteria:

_____ Major symptoms that are rapidly improving by the time of treatment

_____ Evidence of intracranial hemorrhage on CT scan

_____ Acute hypodensity or mass effect suggestive of evolving infarction on CT scan

_____ Clinical presentation that suggests SAH, even if the initial CT scan is normal

_____ Seizure at onset of stroke

_____ Comatose at time of protocol initiation

_____ On repeated measurement, SBP greater than 185 or DBP greater than 110 at the time treatment is to begin

_____ Requires aggressive treatment (nipride) to reduce blood pressure to within acceptable parameters

_____ Blood glucose of less than 50 mg/dl or above 400 mg/dl (may be assessed by chemstrip)

_____ Platelet count less than 100,000

_____ Protime greater than 15 (If patient has *not* been on coumadin, may start thrombolytic before result returned)

_____ Patient received heparin within 48 hours and has an elevated partial thromboplastin time (greater than upper control limits of normal for laboratory)

Courtesy of St. Luke's Episcopal Hospital, Houston, Texas.

_____ Major surgery or serious trauma in the previous 14 days
_____ Serious head trauma in the previous 3 months
_____ History of GI or GU hemorrhage in previous 21 days
_____ Recent arterial puncture at a noncompressible site
_____ Lumbar puncture in the previous 7 days
_____ History of stroke in the previous 3 months
_____ History of an intracranial hemorrhage considered to put the individual at an increased risk for recurrent intracranial hemorrhage
_____ Clinical presentation suggesting postmyocardial infarction pericarditis
_____ Patient is a lactating female or known or suspected to be pregnant
_____ History suggestive of significant hepatic disease
_____ History suggestive of end-stage renal disease

TREATMENT ORDERS

1. Complete inclusion/exclusion criteria checklist.
2. Stat neurology consult.
3. Calculate NIHSS score.
4. Start 3 IV lines as follows:
   a. Dedicated rtPA infusion line
   b. Saline lock for blood draws
   c. KVO line for other fluid and medication administration
5. If unable to void, insert foley catheter prior to initiation of rtPA.
6. Administer intravenous rtPA 0.9 mg/kg as follows:
   a. Patient weight _____ kg × 0.9 mg = _____ **mg total rtPA dose.**
      (Total rtPA dose not to exceed 90 mg.)
   b. Administer 10% of total rtPA dose as an initial bolus:
      _____ mg total rtPA dose × .10 = _____ **mg bolus dose.**
   c. Administer the balance of the rtPA total dose over the next 60 minutes:
      _____ mg total rtPA – _____ mg bolus dose = _____ **mg infusion dose.**
7. Transfer to 22 Tower Stroke Unit.
8. Neuro vital signs q 15 minutes × 1 hour, then q 1 hour × 5 hours, then q 2 hours × 18 hours.
9. Cardiac monitoring via telemetry.
10. *Following rtPA infusion,* no nasoenteric/nasogastric tube insertions, foley catheter insertions, or invasive lines/procedures × 24 hours unless clinically indicated.
11. Repeat brain CT if patient shows signs of clinical deterioration.
12. Withhold anticoagulant or antiplatelet medications for a full 24 hours following rtPA administration.

MANAGEMENT OF INTRACRANIAL HEMORRHAGE (ICH) DURING OR POST RTPA INFUSION

1. If clinical suspicion of ICH, discontinue rtPA infusion if applicable.
2. STAT CT scan for any neurological deterioration.
3. Consider STAT lab studies: PT, PTT, platelet count, fibrinogen, and type/cross.
4. Consider administration of 6–8 units cryoprecipitated fibrinogen containing factor VIII.
5. Consider administration of 6–8 units of platelets.

OUTCOME MEASURES

Outcome measures will be assessed on admission, discharge from hospital, at 3 months post hospital discharge, and 6 months post hospital discharge.

1. Mortality
2. Morbidity (National Institutes of Health Stroke Scale scores)
3. Functional Status (Functional Independent Measures, Barthal Index)
4. Discharge Disposition
5. Quality of Life (Perceived Quality of Life Scale, Caregiving Burden Scale scores)
6. Hospital Cost/LOS

PROCESS MEASURES

Process measures will be assessed during the acute care phase of patient management.

1. Time from symptom onset to ED
2. Time from neurologist notification to arrival in ED
3. Time from CT order to start of CT scan
4. Total time from symptom onset to start of rtPA infusion

PART III

Information Systems and Redesign

Part Editors

Pamela Garrison, Debbie Olson, and Vivian West

CHAPTER 17

Information Systems for Operational and Clinical Process Reengineering

Dona E. Stablein and William L. Sheats

Chapter Objectives

1. To describe the relationship between process reengineering and information systems and technology.
2. To discuss the key enabling information systems and technologies that support two critical health care provider processes—care management and care delivery.
3. To identify and discuss the critical success factors related to integrating information systems and technologies with process reengineering.

Market conditions over the past five years have increased the pressure on hospitals and other types of care providers to reduce costs and increase customer—specifically, patient and physician—satisfaction. Various approaches, including continuous quality improvement/total quality management (CQI/TQM), value analyses, and operational benchmarking, have been employed as mechanisms for addressing these performance objectives. All of these approaches have produced results for organizations; however, not one of them has produced the dramatic improvement in performance that many executives believed was required for their organization to be successful.

In recent years, guided by the work of Michael Hammer and James Champy,[1] business process reengineering (BPR) leaders have developed an additional approach to address the cost and service quality balance. A common element among BPR, CQI/TQM, and value analysis approaches is the concept of a *process* as the basic building block for organizations. A process is defined by Hammer and Champy as "a collection of activities that takes one or more kinds of input and creates an output that is of value to the customer."[2(p.35)] By definition, processes represent a horizontal means of producing value and cross multiple functional areas. The focus is to eliminate the arbitrary division of work activities within a process that is created by an organizational structure based upon departments and divisions.

Applying a process perspective to an organization focuses us on what is required to produce value to the customer. A process perspective ignores the traditional organizational structure characteristics of operational departments/cost centers, functional divisions/silos, vertical management hierarchies, and job specialization. These characteristics are important only to the extent that they inhibit the ability to provide customer value. In this context, value represents the customer's perceived balance of cost and quality.

BPR has focused management's attention on how traditional ways of providing patient care and delivering services are affected by a process perspective. Process focus provides management the opportunity to eliminate hand-offs between individuals, departments, and divisions by defining new job classifications that result in responsibility for a larger part of the process's activities. The result is a reduced cycle time, fewer individuals involved in the process, increased accountability for value results, and reduced costs.

There are numerous operational process models to describe the hospital, integrated delivery system, or other care provider. No single one is the ideal or particular standard for all organizations. Organizations should identify their core business and the appropriate core processes that support their business (Exhibit 17–1). As long as they embrace the processes concept from the customer's perspective, it is difficult to define core processes inappropriately. Initial process identification should focus on approximately 6 to 10 organizationwide, broad processes. Once this is done, each process should be defined by its key subprocesses.

Acute care providers have applied the process concept to clinical activities in a number of ways. For example, clinical pathways represent a process definition of producing a value result to patients. By comprehensively identifying all of the assessment and care interventions required to achieve specific outcomes, the clinical pathway defines the process of what care should be provided in what sequence.

Exhibit 17–1 Sample Core Processes of a Health Care Provider Organization

• Lead Enterprise	• Manage Care
• Manage Administrative Infrastructure	• Deliver Care
• Manage Physical Infrastructure	

In conjunction with changing market and health care payment strategies, clinical reengineering has expanded the care process to well beyond the acute care setting. Concepts such as disease management and cross-continuum care management recognize the important role that self-care, home health care, and ambulatory care play in helping the patient achieve an optimal level of activity.

ROLE OF INFORMATION SYSTEMS IN REENGINEERING

With both operational and clinical process reengineering, the ability of information systems to enable the redesigned processes is critical for the organization to achieve a high level of performance improvement. Information systems enable process reengineering by increasing the effectiveness of information management along the process axis. Traditionally, information systems have been used to enhance staff and facility productivity with a departmental or functional focus. Using information systems to enable departmental needs will provide value to the extent that the department contributes to meeting overall customer needs.

The timing of when to apply information systems to operations to enhance productivity and effectiveness must be carefully considered to ensure that the full benefit of the information systems can be achieved. Experience has demonstrated that identifying and implementing operational changes, whether the changes are functional or process oriented, is required prior to using enabling information systems to ensure successful integration of both operational and system changes.

A number of organizations have reversed the order of implementing operational and information systems changes under the belief that information systems will drive the organization to initiate the required operational changes. Our experience has shown that operational changes initiated after the systems implementation rarely fully leverage the capability of the operational or technology improvement. Three reasons have been identified for the inability of systems to drive operational change.

First, allowing the operational process, procedural, or practice change to be implemented prior to the enabling technology forces the organization to ensure all aspects are meeting efficiency and effectiveness performance criteria. In essence, you have the opposite of "automating bad processes": that is, you ensure that the process being enabled by technology is operationally "good."

For example, a recent process reengineering client was preparing to implement the organization's redesigned materials management model to support the inpatient care division. Critical to the materials management model was the early identification of supplies and materials required to care for the inpatient. To meet the supply and materials need identification, the model required nurses to complete a 10-page needs document as a part of the initial clinical assessment of the patient. Their belief was that while it would be a struggle in the short term—that is, until the needs identification tool could be automated—the benefits of using the tool would prevail. As the tool was implemented, the nursing staff were quick to highlight that the size and complexity of the tool were not acceptable. And in actuality, even if the tool were automated, the workload associated with completing the tool would prevent it from ever becoming an effective, integral part of the processes of clinical assessment or supply and materials needs identification. The operational reality of applying the tool resulted in a significantly reduced size of tool and one that consisted of portions that were invisibly linked to already existing clinical assessment activities. This illustrates the value of having operational changes precede the implementation of enabling technology.

A second reason is that the considerable change resulting from an information systems implementation creates a subconscious expectation in users that the worst is behind them and that the solution will make their work lives easier and more productive. Therefore, attempting to revisit the operational process or procedure with the objective of initiating operational improvements once the problem has been "solved" with information systems is typically met with resistance. Information systems was the answer, so why are we continuing to make changes once the technology has been implemented?

The final reason is the prudence of allowing an information system or technology solution to define the operational and organizational requirements of a process, procedure, or function. By allowing system and technology solutions to precede operational changes, one is assuming that the manner in which the solution functions should drive the form of operations.

The importance of effectively integrating operations and information systems is illustrated by the story of an academic medical center that had installed one of the most highly functional surgical patient–scheduling information systems available on the market. As a part of our assignment to assess the causes for delays encountered by surgical patients on the day of surgery, we observed the surgical scheduling function.

Within 20 minutes of observation, the following process was documented for the booking of surgical suites and schedule times. The surgeon's office contacted the schedulers, who recorded the pertinent physician, patient, and procedure information on a 3 × 5–inch index card and booked the day, time, and room in the large 11 × 17–inch scheduling binders. When the number of scheduling calls lessened, the schedulers entered the same information into the automated surgical scheduling system.

The schedulers indicated that the automated surgical scheduling system was too slow to accommodate the limited time frames that the surgeons' office staff had on the telephone. They stated that the system was slow because there were long delays in the transition from one scheduling screen to the next and because the order in which the scheduling screens prompted the scheduler for data was inconsistent with the manner in which the scheduling telephone conversation proceeded.

Research into the concerns raised by the schedulers identified the following reason for the perceived slow responsiveness of the system and the duplicative scheduling process: delays in implementing the automated scheduling system significantly reduced the amount of time made available to integrate the technology with the operations and make any required changes. Likewise, the planned amount of user training was sacrificed in the name of expediency and to save implementation costs.

Our experience shows the importance of effectively integrating operations and information systems. Neither one by itself will provide the organization the full benefit opportunity. Conventional process reengineering principles and approaches reflect an integrated operations and technology methodology.

REDESIGN PRINCIPLES WITH A SYSTEMS FOCUS

Process reengineering practice and research over the past five years have produced a set of redesign principles that illustrate the significance of information systems within reengineering. These redesign principles represent a standard to which all process reengineering initiatives are compared to ensure that the new model embodies radical change.

Briefly, these redesign principles can be summarized as:

1. *Be flexible in anticipation of future needs.* This challenges the model design to provide the capability to predict the requirements of the process to achieve the expected outcomes or customer expectations. The accuracy of predictive tools is heavily dependent upon timely access to critical data that can be analyzed and provided for making decisions. Health care providers have developed a number of tools to facilitate the use of this redesign principle. For example, clinical protocols, clinical pathways, and demand management represent predetermined identification of the care needs of specific types of patients. Likewise, historical utilization of supplies is consulted to establish stock par levels, a variation of predicting future needs.

2. *Treat geographically dispersed resources as if they were local.* To define dispersed resources as a single one, the redesigned model will provide the capability to link all resources. Clearly, this link is represented by the ability to transfer data and information among all of the dispersed resources. An example of applying this principle is the design and implementation of a single process that allows patients to access care to an integrated delivery system from multiple locations. This process leverages information technology and systems infrastructure by providing staff in geographically dispersed locations access to the same patient or health plan member demographic, financial, and/or clinical data for purposes of facilitating access to

care. Without significant technology, the registrar would be limited to those data that had been previously collected at the particular site or the patient/ member would have to go to a central location to access care.

3. *Capture information once and at the source.* The inability of many health care providers to do this is a manifestation of traditional departmentally and functionally based organization structures. Data are collected to meet the identified needs of the specific department or function rather than the horizontal process that is addressing customer needs. This redesign principle has the most significance for reducing duplicative work efforts, enhancing data quality, and improving customer satisfaction.

4. *Put the decision point where the work is performed.* Meeting customer needs requires the ability to be responsive and act at the point of service delivery. With this challenge comes the requirement for the service provider to be an informed decision maker. Process reengineering models redefine the organizational parameters governing the ways in which services and care are provided. For example, the elimination of traditional departments or functions and the creation of multiskilled job positions enable customer needs to be met in a more responsive manner. To support the organizational infrastructure and permit service/care providers to make decisions, access to data will require information systems.

Applying these redesign principles to a process reengineering initiative will dictate a number of technology and systems infrastructure requirements. Specific requirements for two critical business processes will be discussed fully later in this chapter. At this point, the types of infrastructure that will be required are clear:

1. Connectivity within the delivery system as well as between the delivery system and key external providers and customers (e.g., major employers, insurers, and vendors)
2. Data repositories or warehouses that allow a common location for the storage, analysis, and retrieval of data
3. A standard user interface that allows multiple users with a wide range of computer skills to access and manipulate easily data from the information system

INFORMATION SYSTEMS AS ENABLERS OF REENGINEERING

Upon review of the redesign principles, it becomes readily apparent that a critical success factor of any reengineering initiative is the ability to provide information that will assist the end user in business and clinical decision making. While the specific tools and applications vary depending upon the process that is being reengineered, common building blocks can be found in any reengineering initiative. These include

- an *infrastructure* that allows information to flow across the system
- *applications* that capture data and subsequently feed them into data repositories or warehouses
- *integration tools* that combine various sources of data and transform data into information that is used to support decision making

As is the case with actual building blocks, all of the pieces play an important role in defining the architecture of the structure. If you attempt to build a structure without one of the foundation pieces, the building will collapse, and the same phenomenon can be evidenced in information systems. The identification and evaluation of the existing infrastructure, applications, and integration tools is a crucial component of any reengineering assessment. The result of the information systems assessment, in conjunction with the potential benefits identification, allows an organization to make an informed decision as to whether the benefits that can be achieved through reengineering will outweigh the information system investment that is often required.

Infrastructure

The infrastructure comprises those technologies that allow information to flow within an entity, from one entity to another, or to external entities outside of the delivery system. Essential elements of an infrastructure include the wide area network (WAN), local area networks (LAN), interface engines, and data security standards. As you will recall, one of the reengineering principles is to *treat geographically dispersed resources as if they were local.* A technology infrastructure that has been solidly designed and implemented enables the realization of this principle.

Applications

Applications, commonly known as software, capture data as steps in a process are being performed. The more sophisticated applications do it in a manner that is transparent to the user and require minimal intervention on the user's part. Through successful implementation of the applications and well-designed deployment of hardware devices, an organization can realize the redesign principle of *capture information once and at the source.*

Historically, providers have focused on the capture of billing and financial data; therefore, it is not uncommon to find these applications fully implemented. The area that has received less emphasis, until recently, is the capture of clinical information. Clinical information systems include order entry, registration, results reporting, clinical documentation, and charting modules and provide the foundation required to collect clinical data. In addition to the clinical information system, ancillary systems such as laboratory, radiology, pharmacy, and materials management provide important sources of "feeder system" data.

Information Integration

Provider organizations are beginning to differentiate themselves and gain competitive advantage based upon their ability to integrate information and make informed decisions. As a portfolio of applications is implemented, it becomes apparent that the departmental and divisional boundaries will inhibit the ability to integrate the data being captured. The existence of data by itself provides little value to the end user. Experience suggests that it is the ability to store data from the various feeder systems, extract those data from data repositories, and transform data into decision-supporting information that provides the value. Integration tools such as the enterprise master patient index, interface engines, data modeling, data repositories, and the permanent patient record have become essential elements as organizations seek to improve decision making through the use of clinical and financial information.

Once the foundation for information integration is in place, specific tools that support decision making can be evaluated. The redesign principle of *put the decision point where the work is performed* implies that the following questions must first be addressed:

- What decisions need to be made?
- What information is required to make that decision?
- Does that information exist?
- Where can that information be obtained?

Based upon the outcome of this exercise, information integration tools such as clinical decision support, ad hoc reporting, provider profiling, and cost accounting can be designed internally or purchased from an appropriate vendor.

Reengineering is one of the options available to health care organizations as they seek to improve dramatically the way work is performed As we have demonstrated, the ability to realize the reengineering principles is heavily dependent upon enabling information systems. To achieve the maximum benefit that can be attained through reengineering, large investments in new systems and upgrades to existing systems may be required. It is in the best interest of any organization to perform a solid assessment of the existing information infrastructure, applications, and information integration tools prior to initiating reengineering (Figure 17–1).

PROCESSES AS A CORE COMPETENCY

In the future, health care providers will be required to meet the clinical and financial outcomes that have been determined by the marketplace and regulatory

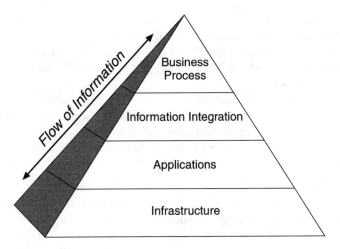

Figure 17-1 Flow of Information Throughout a Delivery System

agencies. The ability of the health care system to provide care within the confines of these outcomes will determine the viability of individual providers. In addition, those who wish to compete in the future health care market will be judged on the basis of their ability to produce information that demonstrates that capability.

Historically, we have delivered care and then focused on measuring and subsequently managing the outcomes of that care. Departments such as quality assurance and utilization management were designed to at best concurrently and in most cases retrospectively measure the outcomes of the care delivery process. The experience of other industries and current market forces suggest that this is no longer good enough. Imagine a car manufacturer attempting to sell a new model of automobile without knowing how much it costs to manufacture that automobile or how the quality of its design ranks compared to existing models. While that image may cause one to smile, the correlation between that image and the existing state of health care delivery is readily apparent.

We suggest that successful health care organizations will need to focus prospectively on two core competencies: the abilities to manage and deliver care. Emerging models of health care delivery suggest that to deliver care efficiently and effectively, one must actively manage the care delivery process.

CARE MANAGEMENT

The process of managing care is not to be confused with managed care and comprises the following subprocesses:

- enrollment into a health plan
- assessment of individual member health status
- segmenting the enrolled population on the basis of clinical and financial risk
- development of care management programs that meet the care requirements of each population segment
- access to the care delivery process
- measurement of how care management programs are performing in relationship to identified clinical and financial outcomes
- revision of care management programs on the basis of clinical and financial outcomes

While pieces of the care management process are currently in place, it is the rare health care provider who has developed the comprehensive care management process outlined above. The industry terms that describe these subprocesses include *case management, disease management, outcomes management,* and *demand management.* The underlying theme of these subprocesses is population-based care that seeks to match the degree of clinical resource utilization with the level of clinical and financial risk. A prerequisite to the development of a comprehensive care management process is the collection and effective use of member population-based information.

INFORMATION REQUIREMENTS OF THE CARE MANAGEMENT PROCESS

At the time of enrollment into a health care plan, information regarding demographics (e.g., age, sex, marital status), health history, and family risk factors has traditionally been collected. With the current focus on maintaining the health status of members, a baseline health status assessment that includes functional status information and members' perception of their health status is essential.

On the basis of the information collected during enrollment, the level of clinical and subsequent financial risk of the enrolled population can be identified. The methods for segmenting the enrolled population into clinical risk categories are numerous and include disease groups, demographics, comorbidities, and historical utilization data. The level of financial risk is determined by historical cost data and by payer and capitation rates.

As the enrolled population is segmented into risk categories, programs to control and reduce that risk are developed. The challenge of care management programs is to optimize the health status of the enrolled population while remaining within financial constraints.

For the high-risk members of the population, programs such as disease management are appropriate. Disease management has traditionally focused on those members who have a chronic disease and historically utilize a high level of health care resources. The disease groupings that have received the initial attention include diabetes, congestive heart failure, heart disease, AIDS, and asthma. From a resource utilization perspective, disease management programs require a high level of intervention and therefore are generally reserved for the high-risk segments of the population. Access to comparative databases, expert opinion, and providers that have implemented disease management programs provides guidance during development.

For the moderate levels of risk, programs such as continuum-based case management and tools such as clinical pathways and protocols have proven to be successful. Access to patient histories, active problem lists, utilization records, plans of care, medication profiles, and available community services support case management. Numerous professional organizations have developed clinical pathways and protocols. Experience suggests that for these tools to be implemented successfully, they must be modified to fit the organizational culture and delivery system capability.

The low-risk population, which includes the well population, has often been underserved. To reduce the level of high-cost interventions that are required, it would make sense to keep the member population healthy. Health status maintenance programs such as disease-specific risk factor identification, education, preventative screening, and immunization are essential to maintaining a healthy member population. Development of individualized education programs and preventative screening schedules with automatic reminders support a wellness focused program.

Throughout a lifetime, individuals can move from one level of risk to another. An example would be someone who has an episodic illness that requires a hospitalization. During that time in the hospital, he or she may fall into the moderate-risk category. As that illness is resolved, he or she would return to the low-risk category. Integration between care management programs is essential to ensuring continuity of care as members move throughout the delivery system and change levels of clinical risk.

To deliver efficient and effective care throughout a delivery system, members must be directed toward the appropriate level of care based upon current clinical need. In most organizations, members can access a health care system at multiple entry points. Once they physically arrive, we have a tendency to treat, regardless of whether it is the appropriate level of care. There should be one process and one central point of access to a health care delivery system. On the basis of a series of questions or clinical algorithms, the current clinical need and appropriate setting for intervention can be determined. The term used to describe these services is *demand management.*

Following the determination of need and associated interventions, services can be scheduled and the health care delivery team can be notified of the member's impending arrival. Access to the schedules of diagnostic testing areas, ambulatory services, physician's offices, and acute care services is required to support centralized scheduling services.

A comprehensive care management process eliminates duplication within the delivery system, establishes a clinical framework for achieving outcomes, and improves flow of both information and members through the system. In addition, care management provides the foundation for the care delivery process through the development of disease management programs, clinical pathways, and protocols.

When care management programs are implemented, a consistent process of care that reduces care variances based upon physician preference can be established. To determine if the care management programs are both effective and efficient, one must measure the clinical and financial outcomes. The mechanism to establish financial outcomes is quite simple: in a capitated environment, you will only receive a fixed amount, regardless of the services you provide. These capitated dollars become the target toward which you must lower the cost of care. Clinical outcomes are not quite as clear, and it is difficult to identify those that will eventually be chosen to evaluate a health care provider. Organizations to watch include the National Committee for Quality Assurance (NCQA), the Foundation for Accountability, and state and regional coalitions.

Despite the lack of a consistent set of outcomes to evaluate the care management and delivery processes, two themes are emerging:

1. There has been a clear shift in the focus of health care delivery from episodic interventions to continuum based services.
2. Clinical outcomes are becoming disease specific rather than using general measures such as mortality, which is reported in the aggregate.

As a result, the outcomes that will be important in the future are those that measure the ability to provide high-quality services across the continuum of care and are tailored to specific disease processes. Examples of continuum-based outcomes would include return to work, health status maintenance, and quality of life. The Foundation for Accountability, along with research-based organizations, is in the process of developing disease-specific clinical outcomes.

The capability to both measure and report clinical outcomes is dependent upon the ability to capture clinical and financial information across the continuum of care. While having the tools and technologies in place is essential, experience suggests that this is not enough. To improve clinical and financial outcomes, the information must be provided to those who have the greatest impact on these outcomes—the care delivery team.

CARE DELIVERY

If one were to sum up the capability of the future care delivery process, it could be stated as follows: *the care delivery team would be accountable for achieving the clinical and financial outcomes of the care delivery process.* At first glance, this makes perfect sense; however, the level of change that must occur within a health care delivery system is profound.

In the current task-oriented and departmentally focused delivery system, as one department completes its portion of a service, it hands the member off to the next department. As the member moves from one department to another, so does the accountability for that member. With the transition to continuum-based services, employees within a health care delivery system must shift their focus from maintaining separate departments, revenue centers, and entities to maintaining the viability of the delivery system as a whole. This translates into the need for service lines that incorporate the continuum of care, care teams that provide a majority of the services that are required, and the elimination of duplication that exists within current delivery system capability.

The care delivery process comprises the following subprocesses:

• create and maintain a member record
• test, evaluate, and diagnose
• provide treatment
• plan care

INFORMATION NEEDS OF THE CARE DELIVERY PROCESS

To support the delivery of care across the continuum, one must be able to identify patients and access their clinical record regardless of where they present within the delivery system. This common patient identifier, along with information that resides in a permanent record, ensures that a member of the care delivery team can access and view a consistent set of information on an as-needed basis. When care is delivered, it is documented in a standardized format designed to eliminate the duplication of information provided by clinical specialties, ancillary services, and members of the care delivery team.

With the implementation of care management programs, the need for testing can be predicted and service capability ensured. Once the testing is performed, results are delivered to the physician regardless of his or her location through remote physician access. Providing physicians with the ability to access the clinical record, specialty consults that have been obtained, and test results on demand enables physicians to evaluate a member's current status and identify the need for further services, regardless of physical location.

In addition to predicting the need for testing, care management programs allow the care delivery team to anticipate the need for personnel, clinical supplies, clinical consults, and therapeutics. This ensures that the care delivery team has at its disposal all of the resources required to provide treatment in an efficient manner. It also serves as a trigger to notify ancillary departments when and where their services will be required. Through the establishment of consistent processes for providing treatment, clinical outcomes measurement becomes meaningful and lends itself to subsequent evaluation and improvement.

Plans of care can include clinical pathways, protocols, disease management programs, and preventative screening schedules. Each member must have a plan of care that is appropriate for his or her level of clinical need. To support these plans of care, clinical information that is captured at the point of care must become dynamic. When variances from the plan of care occur, they must be identified and the care delivery team notified. This will allow the team to reevaluate and modify the plan if appropriate or to develop a new plan based upon individual need.

INFORMATION SYSTEM REQUIREMENTS FOR CARE MANAGEMENT AND CARE DELIVERY

To meet their clinical and financial outcomes, the processes of care management and delivery must act in concert with one another. To achieve this level of integration and coordination, a core set of clinical information must flow freely between the two processes. On the basis of our experiences in reengineering, we have identified the technologies and applications in Table 17–1 as the essential foundation that must be in place.

Once the foundation technologies and applications are in place, specific applications that support the care management or care delivery process can be evaluated and selected (Tables 17–2 and 17–3). When reviewing the various vendors that have developed these applications, it is critical to maintain the ability to integrate data from the proposed application with existing data sources.

CRITICAL SUCCESS FACTORS

The potential benefits associated with the successful integration of information systems and technology with process reengineering outweigh the challenges encountered to achieve the integration. As we have demonstrated, successful integration requires the appropriate sequencing of both operational and systems changes. The potential benefits include

- The ability to automate a high-performing operation. Allowing operational, process, and organizational changes to precede the implementation of enabling technology moves the organization up the performance improvement curve at a phenomenal pace
- Increased likelihood of the organization's maximizing the full capabilities, features, and functions of the acquired information systems and technologies. Operational, process, and organizational changes will reflect and support the capabilities of the technology

Table 17–1 Information System Requirements for Care Management and Delivery

Technologies and Applications	Capability
Networks	Provide the connectivity required to send information within an entity and between entities that compose the delivery system
Interface engines	Format and convert data between disparate systems and enable integration of information across applications
Data repositories	Provide a single central database or an integrated set of distributed databases that stores data from separate applications or feeder systems
Enterprise master patient index	Provides a common patient identification number throughout the delivery system
	Enables patient records and encounters to be linked and establishes the foundation for enterprise registration
Clinical information system	Supports the entry, retrieval, update, and analysis of patient care information
	Establishes standards for collection of clinical information and serves as the foundation for the permanent patient record
Permanent patient record	Allows a care provider to view a core set of patient information that generally includes demographics, payer, medical history, problem list, test results, medication profile, interventions, and plan of care
Remote physician access	Provides physicians with the ability to access pertinent clinical information regarding their patients from remote locations (e.g., home)
Common user access	Creates a common user interface that provides a consistent look and feel to initial system access
Data security standards	Define controls for access to information by type of user, affiliation status, function, and data type
	Establish and enforce consequences of security violations

- Significantly increased receptivity and use of both the operational and technological changes by truly increased efficiency and effectiveness of one's work and results

Experience has identified numerous critical success factors related to an integration initiative. Many of these factors are not unique to an operations and system integration initiative. The following four have been demonstrated to be key:

Table 17–2 Technologies and Applications for Care Management

Technologies and Applications	Capability	Role in Reengineering
Contract management	Identifies benefits and noncovered services, required authorizations, and referrals based upon payer and contract terms	Supports the decentralization of registration and ensures consistency in obtaining authorizations and referrals
Cost accounting	Provides the ability to identify, trend, and report costs associated with the delivery of care	Allows for the trending and reporting of performance in relationship to established financial outcomes Provides the care delivery team with information that allows for modification and improvement of the care delivery process
Clinical outcomes	Establishes the data sources, data modeling strategy, benchmarking strategy, and reporting requirements for clinical outcomes	Provides the delivery system with the ability to demonstrate performance in relationship to required clinical outcomes Provides the care delivery team with the information required to improve clinical practice
Demand management	Provides services such as "Ask a nurse" lines, clinical algorithms that determine the appropriate level of intervention, physician referral, and education tools regarding access to the system	Establishes controls for how members access the system and directs members to the appropriate level of care Provides guidance to members on how to get through the system Alerts providers of a member's need for service

continues

Table 17–2 continued

Technologies and Applications	*Capability*	*Role in Reengineering*
Enterprise scheduling	Provides an organizationwide scheduling capability that automates and manages patient/resource scheduling	In conjunction with demand management and contract management, allows personnel to determine the services that will be required and make arrangements for those services from one central location Provides the ability to identify scheduling or test sequencing conflicts in advance Allows the care delivery personnel to determine what volume and type of services will be required in advance
Electronic data interchange (EDI)	Allows for the transfer of information to vendors, suppliers, and payers in electronic format	Allows the system to obtain authorizations and referrals electronically
Ad hoc reporting	Allows the end user to establish standards for systemwide reports; these standards include timing, report content, and report format	Enables the system to produce reports that support the efforts of the care delivery team and demonstrate the system's ability to meet clinical and financial outcomes

Table 17–3 Applications for Care Delivery

Applications	Capability	Role in Reengineering
Clinical documentation/ clinical pathways	Define the timing and sequencing of care and services Provide decision points of care Identify expected outcomes and specify actions when diversions from the pathway are detected	Standardize the care delivery process, allowing the care delivery team to anticipate services and ensure that required resources are in place; when variances from the clinical pathway are identified, the care delivery team is notified, allowing for more rapid modification in the existing plan of care
Ambulatory patient record	Establishes functional requirements and data contents that support the delivery of care from multiple locations external to the hospital	When integrated with the clinical information system, provides standards for clinical documentation and supports enterprisewide development of the permanent patient record
Clinical decision support	Generates reminders and alerts based on organization-specific rules and patient-specific data in the repository	Provides reference information to the care delivery team regarding appropriate clinical management and the expected outcomes of clinical interventions
Ancillary department applications	Capture department-specific information based upon the application; applications such as laboratory, radiology, and pharmacy provide a source for critical clinical information to the data repository	Provide critical clinical information to the care delivery team such as laboratory results, X-ray, and interventional radiology results and medication profiles

1. *Senior leadership commitment.* If the organization's leaders are not the biggest champions of an integration initiative, failure is certain. A successful integration will require the dedication of significant resources and perseverance as both operational and technological changes are being made. Continual reinforcement of leadership's commitment to the initiative will establish the tone for the organization to achieve the benefits.

2. *Adequate internal resources.* An operational and technological integration requires significant staff and the right staff—that is, the organization's staff. While the number of staff will clearly determine the amount of time required to complete the integration initiative, the appropriate staff will determine the long-term success of the integration and the achieving of benefits. Heavy reliance on external resources can suggest that the initiative is someone else's, not the organization's. Ensuring that a proper balance of internal and external resources is used will help meet both short- and long-term needs.

3. *Discipline to benefits.* As difficulties and barriers arise with an integration initiative, it is easy to lose focus on the long-term requirement for benefits and focus on "getting the systems in." The organization's culture must reflect that benefits are *required* from such an initiative; they are not optional. With a strong discipline toward achieving benefits, the long-term focus can be maintained.

4. *Management of change.* Recognizing the human response to change is critical. Understanding and developing appropriate tactics to change and how people cope with change provides the organization with a competency that will never go unused. The management of change allows the organization to identify the resistance that is normal with this dramatic type of change and to deal with it on a real-time basis.

CONCLUSION

This chapter discusses the importance of integrating process reengineering and information systems and technology to achieve the maximum benefits from these initiatives. The specific information systems and technology requirements of two processes that are critical to a health care provider—care management and care delivery—are described. The chapter closes with a discussion of the requirements for a successful integration of process reengineering and information systems and technology.

NOTES

1. M. Hammer and J. Champy, *Reengineering the Corporation: A Manifesto for Business Revolution* (New York: Harper Collins, 1993).

2. Ibid.

CHAPTER 18

The Clinical Path Project at Northwestern Memorial Hospital

Anne M. Bolger, Marcia A. Colone, and Jean G. Crane

Chapter Objectives

1. To describe the development of clinical paths at Northwestern Memorial Hospital (NMH).
2. To discuss the process and communication strategies essential for full ownership by physicians and members of the clinical path teams.
3. To outline the next steps necessary for information systems integration.

Northwestern Memorial Hospital (NMH) is a nonprofit, 750-bed academic medical center located in Chicago that serves a densely populated urban area. Because of its urban location and reputation in the community as a health care leader, it serves a diverse patient population in a rapidly growing managed-care market.

It is the primary teaching hospital for the Northwestern University Medical School, with training programs in most specialties. The medical staff is composed of members of the Northwestern Medical Faculty Foundation, a multispecialty physician organization, and physicians who are in private practice. All physicians have academic appointments through the Northwestern University Medical School.

This chapter describes the development of clinical paths at NMH, including the process and communication strategies used to ensure full participation by physicians, nurses, and members of the health care team. Implementation of clinical paths is continually evolving at NMH, and future steps toward information system integration will be discussed.

RATIONALE

NMH has maintained a long-term vision of health care excellence for the populations served. In trying to link resources, quality of care, and cost to best serve patient care needs, hospital leaders recognized case management and clinical paths as important strategies for the future. Hospital administration clearly understood that health care organizations that demonstrated controls on resource utilization and length of stay would have an edge in negotiating managed-care contracts. In an era of managed care, an organization's financial viability hinges on its ability to change clinical practice in ways that improve patient care and reduce the costs of care.

The concept of case management was widely published and discussed in health care organizations in the late 1980s. NMH identified the need to develop structures to support the case management strategy. The goal of integrating professional disciplines in ways that would realign the focus on the care of the patient throughout the continuum and determine facts relative to cost and quality led to the organization of a formal case management department in 1992. A director of case management was hired to lead the effort of developing and initiating clinical paths and to integrate the disciplines of social work, nursing, and pastoral care.

In an effort to integrate the disciplines in the department of case management while still retaining professional identity with distinct functions, the director made the decision to develop a new role, the continuity-of-care nurse coordinator (CCNC). The outcome and expectations of this new role included cross-training the two nursing groups, which were made up of nurse discharge planners and utilization management nurses. The goal was to integrate these critical functions, thereby increasing the number of nurses able to conduct utilization management reviews and coordinate home care services. Social workers continued in their role of coordinating transfers to facilities and intervening in complex and conflictual patient and family situations. Pastoral care's focus was retained to provide spiritual counseling to patients, families, and staff.

The impetus for developing clinical paths as a case management tool at NMH arose from a desire to improve quality care, reduce costs, promote continuity of care, and change clinical practice patterns.

INITIAL EFFORT AT CLINICAL PATH DEVELOPMENT

One of the first efforts toward clinical path development was in 1992 by the joint reconstructive and implant service (JRIS) team to address the issues of length of stay and improve efficiencies in the delivery of patient care. This population represented an ideal scenario given the dedicated interdisciplinary team made up of physicians, nurses, physical therapists, and other ancillary staff. The JRIS team had nearly 10 years of experience in improving care to patients needing joint procedures. The decision to develop a clinical path was predicated on the fact that the length of stay for joint procedure patients was too long (9.5 days) as determined by data from regions of the country with high managed-care concentrations. In addition, the flow of activities for joint patients was not coordinated efficiently and effectively. The decision was made easier because these patients were cared for on one unit with a dedicated, experienced interdisciplinary team and because the treatment course was highly predictable.

The JRIS team targeted several areas of opportunities for improvement, including physical therapy methods, ambulation guidelines, and pain management. Over the next several months, two total joint replacement clinical paths (i.e., total hip replacement and total knee replacement) were developed by the orthopaedic clinical nurse specialist with input from the orthopaedic surgeons and all members of the JRIS team. As a result of the review of available data gleaned from chart analysis, review of the literature, and quality outcomes, an eight-day path was implemented in July 1992.

To date, application of these clinical paths has made significant improvements in patient care (cost and quality outcomes). The targeted length of stay has been reduced from 9.5 days to 4.3 days. The experience gained with this process validated to all clinicians that clinical paths do improve both quality and cost outcomes and also address patient satisfaction.

INTERDISCIPLINARY APPROACH

This organization's experience identified several critical success factors to the development of clinical paths: interdisciplinary approach, early and sustained physician participation, and accurate data to highlight current quality versus desired treatment plans. In fact, a review of the literature confirms these success factors.[1] Hospitals that have tried to use clinical paths primarily as a nursing system found that the use and benefits of paths were minimal and often discontinued them.

The major reason use of clinical paths falls short of expectations is not only lack of participation of medical staff and other disciplines in path development but also a failure to integrate clinical paths into an overall process of continuous quality improvement.[2]

Gaining physician support and understanding of potential benefits of clinical paths became a primary goal in the early phases of clinical path development at NMH. In an era in which 80 percent or more of each patient's hospital costs is controlled by what the physician orders, changes in practice patterns that influence cost and quality can only occur with heightened physician awareness and multidisciplinary collaboration.[3]

The orthopaedic clinical path experience and outcomes were presented throughout the organization in various forums to increase physician and staff awareness and to generate enthusiasm for expansion of the project. The presentations used both concurrent and retrospective (prepath) data to identify trends, achievements to date, and opportunities to improve patient care.

Another key decision communicated to physicians and staff was that the primary goal of clinical paths at NMH was to improve the quality of patient care by redesigning systems and changing clinical practice with increased efficiencies and clear treatment goals. Reduced costs were realized as a secondary outcome.

The organization recognized the resources deployed to the orthopaedic project and quickly learned of the positive outcomes, thus realizing the goal of generating further interest in path development.

PATH DEVELOPMENT AND DESIGN

Selection of Case Types

The process for selection of case types was central to the short- and long-term success of the project. An extensive analysis process was undertaken by the director of case management in conjunction with members of the finance department. Data were reviewed to identify diagnoses that were high volume, high risk, or high cost or that had extended lengths of stay. Using the hospital's case mix information system, an analysis was conducted using variables such as average length of stay, average cost per diagnosis-related group (DRG), payer distribution, annual case volume, and distribution of cases by physician. The focus was on identifying opportunities to improve quality and reduce costs given the expansion of managed-care payers in the area.

The goal of this assessment was to identify 10 diagnoses for implementation in 1993 that met criteria. A checklist entitled "Diagnosis Selection Matrix" was developed by the director of case management that used key variables to assist in the diagnosis selection process (Exhibit 18–1). This document provided a structure and process to review and rank case types in a comparative manner. Although the matrix does not use a scientific approach, it provides ample information to identify selections as "best choices."

Another factor considered important in selecting appropriate case types is the predictability of the illness/treatment course. Predictability is the relative ease with which care throughout the continuum can be mapped for certain diagnoses. Surgical diagnoses, in particular, follow a more structured course. In contrast, medical diagnoses (e.g., congestive heart disease) do not adapt as readily to a clinical path format due to the degree of variation in predicting outcomes. In the first generation of clinical paths, it was decided to focus on surgical diagnoses to gain experience in using paths. This was a prerequisite before complex medical diagnoses could be selected.

Based on the analyses, the following 10 diagnoses were selected for implementation in 1993: spine and neck procedures, cardiac valve and bypass surgery, car-

Exhibit 18–1 Diagnosis Selection Matrix

Clinical Specialty:

	Net Revenue	% Mgd Care	Patient Volume	Interested Physician	Quality Issues	Orgztn. Oppty.	System Barrier	Case Type Predictable	#2 ALOS	N	Cost per Case
	1	2	3	4	5	6	7	8			

Time Period

DRG#

Legend:

1. Net Revenue/Full Cost
   0 = <0.95
   1 = 0.95–1.05
   2 = >1.05

2. % Managed Care
   0 = <1/3
   1 = 1/3–2/3
   2 = >2/3

3. Patient Volume (per year)
   0 = <25
   1 = 25–75
   2 = >75

4. Interested MDs
   0 = none interested
   1 = some interested
   2 = most interested

5. Quality Issues
   0 = no concern
   1 = concern, not yet verified
   2 = concern, verified (external or internal)

6. Organization Opportunity
   0 = limited opportunity
   1 = moderate opportunity
   2 = immediate major opportunity

7. System Barriers
   0 = nonperceived
   1 = some barriers
   2 = many barriers

8. Case Type Is Predictable in Its Illness Course
   0 = very unpredictable
   1 = somewhat predictable
   2 = very predictable

Scoring Instructions: If you have 3 or more 2s, this case type has potential for clinical path. Further analysis is indicated.

Approved: _____   Date: _____

Courtesy of Northwestern Memorial Hospital, Chicago, Illinois.

diac angioplasty and catherization, Caesarean section, normal vaginal delivery, major depression, and nonspecific cerebrovascular event.

Clinical Path Format

Decisions about the format and time frames for design and implementation of clinical paths at NMH required discussion and input from all disciplines. Agreement was reached that the clinical paths would use actions and expected outcomes as major categories. Actions included consults, tests, continuum-of-care planning, treatment, teaching, nutrition, activity/safety, and medications and/or IV. Expected outcomes were defined as the expected response to a specific treatment regimen. They were identified either by day of stay or by strategic points on the clinical path. Each discipline was asked to develop the content for its respective activity component. For example, under continuum-of-care planning, case management staff identified when they should be involved to initiate discharge-planning activities. They outlined both the frequency and the natures of those interventions. In addition, signatures were required by each nursing shift within time frames specified on the path. The decision to require signatures from professional staff was made by the clinical path work groups prior to implementation.

Time frames for clinical paths were formatted to organize the prehospital, hospital, and posthospital experience along a time continuum. Given the thrust to ambulatory care, there was acknowledgment that not all clinical paths should be organized according to days. For example, the Normal Vaginal Delivery Clinical Path was formatted according to stages of labor, delivery, and postdelivery. A protocol was developed to assist the work groups in deciding which format was best suited for the specific clinical population.

Each clinical path contains specified clinical criteria that identify patients who are appropriate for a particular path. If the patient meets the clinical criteria necessary for assignment, the patient is assigned by a staff nurse at the point of entry, which may be in the emergency department, on the unit, or in labor and delivery, depending on the whether the clinical path encompasses that clinical area.

Variance Record and Reporting

An integral part of clinical paths is the variance record. Variances need to be systematically monitored because of patient individuality. Variance analysis identifies and resolves issues concurrently and allows for trend reporting.

The development of the variance record occurred simultaneously with the development of the clinical paths. Input from all disciplines was solicited, with agreement that the variance record needed to be easy to use. It would be used to capture information that would identify opportunities for improvements in clinical practice and in systems. Each clinical path has a variance record that has four categories: patient/family, care provider, system, and community. Variances can be either positive or negative. For example, a negative patient variance is problematic blood sugar management of a patient with diabetes, resulting in an extra day of hospitalization. A negative care provider variance may occur when a physical therapist's final visit is delayed, such as over a weekend, resulting in extra days of care. System variances that are negative may include canceling of tests versus delay in diagnostic testing, lack of bed availability, or a lost medical record. Positive variances are also important because they point to clinical practices that facilitated the patient's recovery or reduced the length of stay. For example, a positive variance may include a patient's ability to tolerate physical therapy earlier than prescribed on the clinical path and for longer periods of time, allowing for discharge one day earlier than anticipated. As each clinical path work group established experience with using the clinical path and variance record, refinements were made in the categories to more effectively capture common variances occurring within a specific patient population.

All members of the interdisciplinary care team, excluding physicians, are responsible for concurrently monitoring variances or deviations from the clinical path on a daily basis. If a variance occurs, the care team member must not only document the variance but also develop a corrective action plan to resolve the variance.

Initially, the clinical paths and variance record were not a permanent part of the medical record. Traditional care provider documentation in the medical record was the primary method of capturing and storing patient information. In 1995, a decision was made to integrate the clinical paths into the medical record as a means of reducing duplicate documentation. A pilot project was initiated, and the variance record was renamed the "Clinical Path Quality Improvement Tool" (Exhibit 18–2). This quality improvement (QI) tool is not a permanent part of the medical record. When a patient is discharged, the QI tool is removed from the medical record and placed in a designated area for retrieval by the nurse patient care coordinator (PCC). This direct caregiver role was developed in an effort to manage effectively patients assigned to a clinical pathway. It also includes the responsibility for aggregating all variance information on a monthly basis and developing a report to be presented to the clinical path work group.

Two major issues are related to the use of the variance record. The first is the volume and diversity of information that is collected. Data must be acquired from multiple sources and linked by patient to identify variables. Access to financial and demographic data is more readily available in the current information systems environment. Clinical information, however, is primarily manual and therefore requires individual patient chart review. Currently there are no automated systems in house to support the clinical path processes except for the quarterly financial reports. The data collection and review is a labor-intensive, manual process that

Exhibit 18–2 Northwestern Memorial Hospital Clinical Path Quality Improvement Tool

Initial	Full Name

Prescribed LOS:
Admission Date:
Discharge Date:
OR Date:
Date Initiated:
Date Path Completed:
Time of Delivery:
Total LOS Hours:

Variance Code

Pt./Family
A1. Condition
A2. Decision
A3. Availability
A4. Difficulty Learning Skills
A5. No Support/ Assistance at Home
A6. Other

Care Provider
B1. Physician Order
B2. Decision
B3. Response Time
B4. No Documentation
B5. Other

System
C1. Bed/Appt. Time
C2. Information Delay
C3. Supplies/Equipment

C4. Unable To Schedule Test/Procedure
C5. OR Time Unavailable
C6. Patient Escort
C7. Consult Service
C8. Other

Community
D1. Placement/Home Care
D2. Transportation Delay
D3. Other

Date LOS/POD	Describe Variance	Variance Code	Describe Corrective Action	Note Written for Patient Condition/ Community Variance Y	Signature	Continue/ Suspend Path

Courtesy of Northwestern Memorial Hospital, Chicago, Illinois.

requires considerable professional time. In the first generation of clinical paths, the variance information was collected and reviewed by the clinical nurse specialists in conjunction with the respective director of nursing. Recently, the nurse patient care coordinator was assigned responsibility for collating variance information. This nursing role was developed as part of a comprehensive, professional nurse career model to provide leadership to the clinical path process. Information is collated, and a monthly report is developed to review with the clinical path work group. A second issue is incomplete documentation by nursing and other staff responsible for implementation of clinical path actions. The manual and redundant data entry processes present the potential for incomplete and/or missing documentation. Even though many of the clinical paths are now a permanent part of the medical record, the variance record is not. As a result, documentation on the variance record is sometimes neglected. Periodic staff education is done on all patient care units to assist staff in improving documentation. The goal for NMH is to implement a comprehensive clinical information system that is integrated with other transaction systems to support the clinical decision makers effectively. An automated documentation system would also support review and identification of missing data and provide rules-based alerts and reminders.

Variance Reports

Variance information is collated by the PCC and developed into a monthly report. Two reports are used for this analysis. The monthly variance analysis is used to track variances occurring in a specific category—for example, the number of patient/family variances (Exhibit 18–3). The monthly variance report (Exhibit 18–4) is used to identify

- actions taken at last month's meeting
- findings/conclusions related to quality indicators
- opportunities for improvement
- follow-up communication

A quarterly analysis is also conducted that uses financial information such as average cost per case and expected reimbursement, average length of stay, and volume. This report is completed by the department of management engineering, using data derived from the hospital's cost-based accounting system and the patient care information system. Personal computer software applications are used to store and organize this information. The analysis compares the patient population for the time period under study with a prepath comparison group that was constructed prior to implementation of the clinical path. The prepath comparison group is developed for each clinical path using patients with the same diagnosis-

Exhibit 18–3 Northwestern Memorial Hospital Clinical Path Project Monthly Variance Analysis

Clinical Path:

Date:

Month of Variance Analysis:

Number of Patients Assigned to Path:

Number of Patients Completed Path:

ALOS:

Patient/Family Variances: Number of Patients:

System Variances: Number of Patients:

Care Provider Variances: Number of Patients:

Community Variances: Number of Patients:

Quality Indicators/Outcomes: Number of Patients:

Privileged and Confidential under the Illinois Medical Studies Act

Courtesy of Northwestern Memorial Hospital, Chicago, Illinois.

Exhibit 18–4 Northwestern Memorial Hospital Clinical Path Project Monthly Variance Report

---

Clinical Path:
Date of Meeting:
Month of Variance Analysis:
Present:

    A. Updates on Action Taken Last Month:

    B. Findings and Conclusions Related to Variance Analysis:

    C. Findings and Conclusions Related to Quality Indicators:

    D. Opportunities for Improvement:

Action	Who	When

    E. Follow-up Communication:

	To	When
DON		
Unit(s)		
Medical Staff QM Comm.		
Other (identify)		

_____
Signature

Privileged and Confidential under the Illinois Medical Studies Act

Courtesy of Northwestern Memorial Hospital, Chicago, Illinois.

---

related groupings or ICD-9-CM principal diagnoses. Trends are tracked and reported at the monthly clinical path meetings.

BENEFITS

The clinical path project at NMH has been extremely successful primarily due to its interdisciplinary approach and focus on the continuum of care, which includes preadmission, the point of health care entry, and postdischarge settings. Clinical paths are perceived by the health care team as a patient-centered, outcomes-focused system that facilitates continuous improvement of quality and cost outcomes. They are used as integrated tools that serve as care plans for achieving desired outcomes as well as coordinating care. Moreover, they are important communication tools that promote collaboration and input among members of the health care team.

In 1995, there were over 44 clinical paths in operation. Savings of approximately $4 million in variable costs and 6,700 patient care days were directly attributed to the use of these clinical paths. Significant reductions have occurred in length of stay and cost per case, resulting in savings ranging from 10 to 50 percent. Numerous clinical and service improvements not only have benefited specific clinical path patient populations but have been generalized to other populations as well.

Since the inception of the clinical path project in 1992, physicians have become increasingly comfortable in using paths and have incorporated clinical practice guidelines to accompany many paths. They have provided the leadership necessary to ensure compliance with clinical paths among their peers and medical house staff, resulting in a diminishing variation in practice patterns.

Use of clinical paths facilitates early identification of problems or potential problems, which in turn increases satisfaction among caregivers, patients, and their families. Caregivers report improved satisfaction in using clinical paths that outline standards of care in an orderly and sequential manner. Patient-friendly paths have been developed for many clinical paths to allow a better understanding of the process of care. Use of the patient-friendly path thus facilitates patient and family participation in the treatment, recovery, and discharge phases. Once patients have shared and understood communication goals, progress is focused and enhanced.

Patient education is initiated at preadmission for the majority of clinical paths and is the responsibility of a multidisciplinary team that includes the case manager and both nursing and ancillary services staff. The clinical paths foster early discharge planning and allow the patient and family to begin making the necessary arrangements to ensure a timely discharge. Continued patient education is integral to successful use of clinical paths, because it ensures that the requisite time and resources are focused in this arena.

In summary, there have been numerous benefits from using clinical paths at NMH. The development of a focused department of case management served to build the infrastructure associated with clinical path development. Using an interdisciplinary approach to build the clinical path infrastructure proved to be the key factor in predicting success for this project. From the beginning, full participation and input from all health care team members ensured that the standards used on the clinical paths were appropriate and that changes in clinical practice occurred as a result of variance analysis. The outcomes achieved through this project resulted in improved quality care for patients as well as a reduction in the costs of care. Most important, the project has facilitated a continuous QI process that encourages examination of clinical practices in a collaborative manner. The clinical pathways are integrated into the QI processes at NMH. Each pathway has defined expected outcomes that are measured and reported on regularly at the clinical path work group meetings. Follow-up interventions and review of the pathway outcomes are the ongoing results of the process.

INTEGRATION WITH INFORMATION SYSTEMS

Clinical information systems capable of supporting the functional requirements of clinical paths are being implemented at many hospitals throughout the country. The goal of the clinical path project at NMH is to integrate the documentation processes with the use of clinical paths and the variance tracking, using technology as an enabler. The information systems department is developing an overall clinical information systems strategy for NMH's emerging integrated delivery system. The plans include clinical integration of order entry and order communication functions with the clinical path tools and processes, which will replace or enhance existing applications. This clinical information systems integration will create the foundation for an electronic medical record for NMH and will pave the way for the automation of clinical paths and variance tracking.

With this capability, a path would automatically be assigned to a patient on the basis of admitting diagnosis. Each day, the path (or phase of treatment) would be stored in the system as a standard order set. Physicians could then review and simply order the whole set or adjust paths as needed for an individual patient. Nursing and other health care team members would document against the clinical path, using charting by exception, noting only when the patient did not follow the appropriate path. These exceptions would be automatically captured and stored as variances to be used for variance tracking and analysis.

Use of technology to capture the patient information directly and store it in a database would allow for the tracking and managing of outcomes. The outcomes would include patient, functional, clinical, organizational, and financial outcomes, with future variables defined at a later time, as indicated. In addition, with

Table 18–1 The Clinical Path Project at Northwestern Memorial Hospital: Case Management Information Requirements

Clinical Process	Functional Requirement	Technology Requirement
Information access	Accessibility from all care portals, internally and externally	Network communications to support geographically dispersed locations
	Information captured once and available wherever needed, without reentry	Medical equipment device interface for data acquisition
	Data collection and review at the point of care	Mobile computing capabilities
	Ability to access external references from clinical workstation	Graphical user interface from a universal workstation
	Clinical dictionaries to define standard data definitions	Application interface engine
Information delivery	Ability to provide a dynamic clinical profile by patient according to minimum data set (industry standard with user modification capability)	Integrated data repository from multiple feeder systems
	Clinical pathway resource library for all pathways	Database reference library
	Ability to modify pathway(s) by patient	User-definable screen tools
	Ability to combine more than one pathway by patient	
	Standard order sets driven from the clinical pathway	Integrated order communication
	Table driven to define	
	• Clinical path templates	
	• Diagnoses	
	• Procedures	
	• Providers	
	• Actions	
	• Outcomes	
	• Variance definitions	
	• Preventive and wellness screening protocols	
	• Wellness screening protocols	
	• Research protocols	
	Support documentation against the pathway	Point-of-care access and retrieval of data
	Support charting by exception	
	Electronic signature capability	

continues

Table 18–1 continued

Clinical Process	Functional Requirement	Technology Requirement
	Ability to report variances	
	Ability to monitor and trend variances	
	Focus review of quality indicators	Standard query language (SQL)
	Ability to access and review health plan requirements by patient	Contract management data
	Access to utilization management criteria and patient documentation	Support industry standard formats
	Capability to access patient demographic and financial information from the workstation	Case mix data
	Rule-based logic	
	Alerts and warning capabilities	
	Comprehensive audit trail	
Information management	Universal patient identifier to allow linkage of patient records across multiple systems	Common user interface across platforms and applications
	Data repository—transaction based to support real-time data availability	Relational nonredundant database
	Data repository—analytic processing to support retrospective review and research	Long-term storage of patient information
	Security management to protect confidentiality and privacy of patient information	Security management to the data element level
	Data presentation tools to support graphics and trending	Screen design tools
	Management reporting	
	Ad hoc reporting and SQL	
	Integration of clinical and financial outcome data by patient	

Courtesy of Northwestern Memorial Hospital, Chicago, Illinois.

data stored across time by patient, diagnosis, and so forth, the ability to track variances and link them to the clinical path outcomes would support analyses and identification of potential problems or other variables. This process would support the continuous improvement and management of clinical paths and care guidelines by providing reasons that something did not occur. It would also more clearly identify the reasons for variability from one patient to another or from clinician to clinician. Automation coupled with appropriate statistical analysis would point to which interventions were particularly effective at certain points in time. Further, analysis would be focused on a select group of key processes and/or outcomes versus the total universe.

The science and art of using information from clinical paths and clinical practice guidelines to improve clinical decisions remains in its infancy stage. Automation of outcomes and variances will facilitate our understanding of how to use these tools and make the necessary changes to improve patient care.

CONCLUSION

NMH gained valuable experience in defining the processes and data requirements initially as a manual program. The project team invested time and resources in building the internal support and commitment to identify an effective program. Use of iterative steps and development of tools that could best support the data collection and organization requirements of the clinical processes allowed NMH to refine tools and techniques over time and use. Now that NMH has implemented the case management program using clinical paths, there is a clearer understanding of the process model that can drive the enabling technology requirements. NMH has also benefited from the management of change, with reorganized job roles and responsibilities and new documentation requirements. Given the experiences and lessons learned in the development and implementation of the case management program, NMH is better positioned to define the functional and technology requirements (Table 18–1) necessary to support the program as a result. With the evolving state of the software available in the market, variance tracking and management will be second-generation functionality. NMH has now defined the criteria to assess and manage variances and therefore will be better prepared to automate the processes, with technology as an enabler.

NOTES

1. V.A. Mahn and C. Heller, *Clinical Paths at Carondelet St. Joseph's Hospital: Clinical Paths Tools for Outcomes Management* (Chicago, IL: American Hospital Association, 1994).

2. Ibid.

3. K. Zander, "Defining Nursing . . . Roots and Wings," *Definition* 1, no. 1 (1985): 1–2.

CHAPTER 19

Group Health Cooperative of Puget Sound: A Population-Based Strategy

*Clayton Gillett, Alan Golston, Robin E. Johnson,
and Dorothy Teeter*

Chapter Objectives

1. To discuss the rationale for developing the concept of population-based care management.
2. To describe the implementation of a planned system of care.
3. To delineate the accomplishments of a population-based planned system of care for the heart care population.
4. To discuss technology applications to provide the information necessary to implement a population-based strategy.

Group Health Cooperative of Puget Sound (GHCPS) is a large not-for-profit health maintenance organization (HMO) serving western Washington with an enrollment of approximately 425,000. GHCPS owns and operates two hospitals and 32 clinics, has approximately 700 staff-model physicians, and contracts with an additional 1,500. The HMO is predominantly a staff model but in recent years has seen significant growth in its network and point-of-service products. The purpose of this chapter is to explain why GHCPS developed its concept of a population-based strategy for managing care, the implementation of a planned system of care, and the accomplishments in the heart care population.

The concept of a population-based strategy for managing and delivering care was developed in response to the convergence of three forces—increased pur-

---

chaser and patient demand for health plan accountability as it is related to clinical and service quality outcomes, increasing price pressure in the managed-care marketplace, and increasing organizational requirements for information systems to support the delivery of care.

As a result, this strategy was adopted at GHCPS as a way to improve concurrently its performance in clinical outcomes, customer satisfaction, and price position in the marketplace. It was also very important to support clinical practice teams with information as they redesigned their work to meet demands of an increasingly competitive managed-care marketplace. Several key factors and assumptions contributed to adopting this strategy. They were as follows:

1. Clinicians needed a way to organize the diffuse health care requirements of 425,000 GHCPS enrollees into more discrete population segments that have clinical significance. In other words, although the health plan tracked the number of its enrollees by payer source, the clinical team needed to know what its enrollees' health care needs were, regardless of payer source.

2. The manual systems that practice teams used to track patients' health care needs, care plans, and required follow-up care did not provide the needed clinical results reporting, reminder systems for appointments, or appropriate customized patient education materials.

3. To reduce cost and utilization, decrease practice variation, and ensure consistent high-quality patient care across all delivery sites and clinical teams, practitioners needed evidence-based clinical guidelines. These guidelines needed to be available on computers (clinical workstations) along with specific clinical patient information so that clinicians could have both guidelines and specific patient data at their fingertips for appropriate decision making.

4. Continuous improvement of care required the measurement of outcomes on a provider-specific basis. These outcomes needed to include feedback on clinical outcomes and the complete patient experience, including service quality and ease of access of care. These feedback systems required survey, database, and scanning technologies to provide the necessary information.

5. Enrollees were beginning to expect that the health plan would give them customized prevention plans based on health risk assessment. Such an expectation would require a lifetime health monitoring system to track the risks of various patient populations over time and to modify their care plans accordingly.

The following population-based strategy description represents the experience of GHCPS as it has developed its approach to care management. Components of the strategy, the technical and operational requirements, and an example using the heart care program are described.

THE COMPONENTS OF THE POPULATION-BASED STRATEGY, USING HEART CARE AS AN EXAMPLE

Population Identification

Population-based managed care is a systematic, planned approach to caring for patients who have predictable health care needs. The goal of this approach is to achieve the best health and satisfaction outcomes with cost-effective use of health care resources. This is accomplished by identifying resource-intensive, clinically significant, relatively homogeneous populations and developing a planned approach to their care based on clinical evidence and the reduction of variation in practice. As an organizational strategy for improving outcomes, it is critical to begin by identifying the populations where the greatest impact can be achieved.

What Is a Population?

A population is any group of patients who have predictable health care needs related to a characteristic that they have in common. The characteristic shared may be

- age (infants)
- age and gender (perimenopausal women)
- ethnicity (Native Americans)
- health risks (smokers)
- symptoms (low back pain)
- disease status (diabetics, depression)

Because resources are limited, populations need to be analyzed to determine where the greatest return for investment can be made. Detailed analysis of populations is a resource-intensive undertaking. Populations are selected on the basis of the following criteria:

- evidence that effective treatments will influence outcomes or disease progression
- the cost of caring for the population
- the size of the population
- risk management issues
- member, provider, and health care purchaser concern/interest in improving care for the population

Once the priority populations have been selected, multidisciplinary teams are organized to develop and implement planned systems of care. The strategy requires the participation of key process owners across departments and/or divisions. In the selection of the teams, it is critical that key players from departments with the authority to make organizational change be included. Selecting staff who have implementation expertise and clinical expertise is important. A team without both clinical and implementation expertise and influence will not be able to develop the consensus needed to "sell" the planned system of care and the changes in practice necessary to the practitioners and managers who have not been involved in its development.

The Clinical Roadmap

This population-based strategy at GHCPS is identified as "the clinical roadmap." It was launched in 1992 as an organizational strategy to develop systems of care for populations defined by disease or health risks. The clinical roadmap program began with work in four populations: heart care, diabetes, tobacco use, and pregnancy care. In 1994, the program expanded to include the depression and breast care populations, and in 1995, it began work in the areas of immunizations and asthma. These populations were selected on the basis of the criteria discussed previously. In each case, teams were developed with clinical and administrative cochairs. For example, the heart care services clinical roadmap team was cochaired by the director of specialty services and the director of the Center for Health Studies. Other members of the team included cardiologists, family practitioners, registered nurses, a pharmacist, a data analyst, and a specialty manager.

Developing a Definition for a Specific Population

The first work of a roadmap team is to establish a working definition of its population that serves to define the scope of the team's work. This can be fairly straightforward, or highly complex and controversial. For example, GHCPS's pregnancy care team defined its population as "all women with evidence of pregnancy in the system." By defining their population this way, they excluded women at risk for pregnancy, women planning for pregnancy, and infertile women. By contrast, the breast care team defined their population to include women at risk for breast cancer, women with breast problems, and women with breast cancer—a more global approach. There are positives and negatives with each approach. A narrow scope allows the team to focus its efforts and facilitate population identification, outcome measurement, and the development of improvements. In addition, a narrow scope may permit a team to avoid areas of controversy initially while building momentum and support for the work. A broader definition introduces complexity, which may slow the definition and measurement process; however, a more comprehensive system may be developed over a longer period of time.

Operationalizing the Definition

Operationalizing the definition is a critical step. All databases and measurement systems are driven by the algorithm. The quality of the algorithm determines the quality of the tools developed to support the clinicians and the effectiveness of the interventions. Therefore, each clinical roadmap team develops a methodology to operationalize the population definition and an algorithm used by the computer to identify members of the defined population. This methodology is refined as the team discovers nuances in the data sources and validates the methodology through chart audits and provider feedback. The data source to identify a patient as a member of a clinical population varies according to the population but typically includes information from the hospital information system, the pharmacy system, the lab system, or outpatient visit diagnosis codes.

Heart Care Example

The clinical members of the heart care team initially developed a narrative description of the population for use in the development of a computer algorithm to identify patients. The team chose to define its population broadly so as to understand better population demographics, cost, utilization, and satisfaction. A broader understanding of the population was believed to facilitate the identification of the clinically relevant subpopulations in which improvement efforts would be most successful and efficient. The description included patients with vascular heart disease, coronary artery disease (CAD), congenital heart disease, and cardiomyopathy.

GHCPS does not have a complete electronic medical record to collect clinical information. The team recognized that in the absence of complete clinical data, any algorithm would not match completely the clinical description. Therefore, the population had to be identified with the data that were currently available. The data at GHCPS were limited to the hospital system, claims, the pharmacy system, and laboratory results.

This first effort to develop an effective algorithm allowed the team to understand better the complexities of the population. This tool was effective in describing demographics, cost, utilization, and satisfaction for the heart care population. The population identification algorithm allowed the team to survey and conduct focus groups with the heart care population to learn about customers' requirements and their level of patient satisfaction. However, in an effort to develop an algorithm that was sensitive enough to capture the whole population, the ability was lost to identify a population that had a similar set of predictable health care needs. Therefore, a narrower definition was required.

Patients with CAD were identified as the largest population of heart care patients and the group in which evidence showed that effective treatments could improve outcomes (service quality, clinical quality, utilization, and cost) dramatically. The team developed a very specific algorithm to identify only those patients with CAD. It was clear from medical record reviews that the tool excluded some patients with CAD, but the population was relatively pure and could be used to capture specific data. The more specific algorithm enabled the team to find benchmark data in published research. This process led the team to begin to collect baseline performance measures and to set goals about what areas of clinical quality, satisfaction, and cost should be measured, tracked, and improved.

Outcomes Identification

Each clinical roadmap team identifies a list of health outcomes for the defined population to monitor and improve. These outcomes may include changes in disease progression, reducing or preventing complications and treatment side effects, improving functional status, or prolonging life. The team first defines the desirable outcomes on the basis of its ability to capture the data and the usefulness of the outcome. Long-term health outcomes such as blindness caused by diabetic retinopathy may be difficult to measure due to the long course of the disease. In such cases, it is important to measure and monitor a specific health care process that is known to have a causal effect in the outcome of interest. In the case of diabetes, an example might be annual dilated retinal exams. Other outcomes are immediate, and end points can be measured directly.

In addition to identifying optimal health outcomes, the roadmap team also conducts focus groups with members of the patient population to identify "customer requirements." Customer requirements are concise statements, in the patient's own language, that describe what patients want and expect from their care. These requirements are translated into survey questions that can be administered to measure how well customer needs are met.

The third area of outcome identification for a population is cost and utilization. For GHCPS's pregnancy care population, these outcomes are measured "on a per-episode-of-care" basis: that is, cost of a pregnancy. For chronic disease populations such as heart care, diabetes, and HIV/AIDS, total cost of care and total utilization may be critical outcome measures. Utilization of key procedures, such as angioplasty or coronary artery bypass graft, may also be used as outcome measures.

After specific health, satisfaction, and cost outcomes have been identified for a population, the organization's performance is measured to determine where "gaps" exist between desired outcomes and actual outcomes. The work of the clinical roadmap team is to identify health processes that will close these gaps and result in improved health, satisfaction, and cost outcomes for the defined population.

Heart Care Example

The heart care team identified four areas for health outcomes monitoring. Three of these areas were chosen on the basis of the large variation found in our organization and between internal data and external benchmarks. Due to the variation and difficulty in risk adjusting these three measures, goals have not yet been set. However, the measures have been captured over time to help understand our practice patterns and identify when significant change in practice occurs. These measures include rates of (1) coronary artery bypass graft (CABG), (2) angioplasty (PTCA), and (3) cardiac catheterization. These measures continue to be used in the descriptive analysis of the population. The fourth and last measure focuses on the smoking rate of this high-risk population.

The heart care team's customer service outcomes for customer requirements include (1) timely communication between primary care and cardiology, (2) satisfaction with the technical quality of care, and (3) the coordination of care planning between primary care and cardiology. These outcomes are routinely measured in the annual satisfaction survey of the heart care population.

Cost and utilization in the heart care population are tracked, and particular attention is paid to the total per-member-per-month (PMPM) cost for the population. Our semiannual analysis displays costs and utilization data, including inpatient and emergency room utilization, outpatient services, laboratory costs, radiology costs, home health nursing visits, and the use of skilled nursing facilities. This information indicates that a number of factors can greatly affect cost and points to meaningful strategies to reduce these costs.

Identification of Gaps and Variation

With the establishment of a base set of performance measures, the team then looks for gaps between current practice and the desired level of performance. This desired level of performance can be determined by the evidence in the medical literature, the performance expected by the consumers, or benchmarking with comparable organizations. It is important to choose the focus carefully to ensure the ability to build consensus within the team as well as individuals who will be affected by the changes that will result. If the changes needed to close a gap are large in scope, the team will need to justify the effort that will be necessary.

Heart Care Example

When the heart care roadmap team was identifying gaps and variations, research reports discussing the new lipid-lowering agents and other pharmaceutical interventions for patients with confirmed CAD were common. The team naturally focused on this issue, and a gap was found in the pharmacological management of patients using ACE inhibitors, beta blockers, and lipid-lowering agents. It also became clear that no systematic interventions were available to help patients change their unhealthy lifestyles. Research showed that intervention with high-risk individuals could reduce cardiac procedures and reduce mortality. The team decided that the focus of the first efforts would be on the treatment of patients with confirmed CAD.

Improvement Strategy and Tools

Improvement strategies may be driven by simple tools, such as the measurement of key customer requirements, or by evidence-based guidelines that include elaborate measurement systems with feedback. Once the performance gaps are identified, it is critical to choose an improvement strategy that will effectively address the underlying reason for the gap. If a gap suggests that the system needs to identify patients sooner who are experiencing a myocardial infarction (MI) and new diagnostic tests are available, the improvement strategy may be as simple as choosing and implementing a new laboratory test. However, if there is a gap in clinical practice compared with the current evidence in the literature, the improvement strategy may need to be coordinated over a larger number of people and diverse systems of care. If this is the case, a far more encompassing implementation plan is needed that includes effective education, feedback, and monitoring systems. Most clinical roadmap team initiatives focus on evidence-based guidelines as the primary driver of practice pattern changes.

Evidence-Based Guidelines

Evidence-based guidelines are a method to evaluate and improve clinical practice through an explicit evidence-based approach. This approach requires teams to evaluate all of the available data on the effectiveness of a clinical practice and to determine the effects of the proposed practice on all relevant outcomes. This rigorous evaluation informs providers about the current research on a given intervention and gives them the tools to provide the appropriate care to a specific patient. Evidence-based guidelines at GHCPS also provide feedback to providers about how well they are meeting the recommendations of the guideline. Due to the rigorous nature of the guideline process, expert opinion is clearly exposed, and recommendations derived from explicit evidence focus the team's effort on areas where improvement of outcomes has been demonstrated in the literature.

The process of developing and maintaining a guideline is shown in Figure 19–1. A clinical problem or potential gap may already be identified as part of the roadmap methodologies. The identification of these gaps may be scientifically based or developed through anecdotal evidence. Following the identification of the problem, enthusiasm for developing an evidence-based guideline needs to be tempered by the reality of the cost of development. As a result, a set of four questions is asked as a screen of suitability:

1. Is there an owner of the project?
2. Can the proposed change be measured?
3. Is adequate literature available to attempt an evidence-based approach?
4. Will the proposed practice change result in outcomes that will justify the efforts?

If the project does not meet these criteria, then another method or tool is chosen to share the evidence that has been gathered. If the project meets the criteria, the team moves forward with the development of internal data and the review of data from the literature.

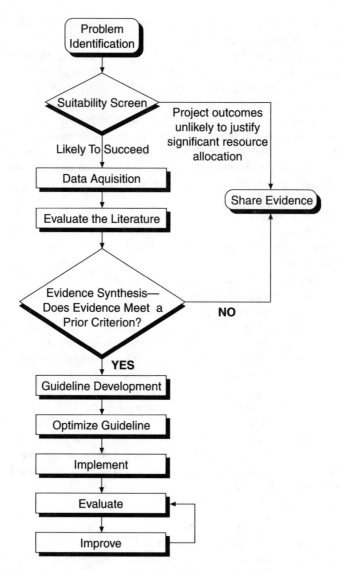

Figure 19–1 Process of Developing and Maintaining a Guideline

Once the literature review is complete and the data on internal performance are gathered, the information is summarized in a balance sheet. The balance sheet serves as the second suitability screen. It shows the current performance, the expected change in performance, and all the associated costs and benefits. If the project is cost-effective or if the quality gain is judged to be critical, the guideline development process continues.

The guideline is developed through a process of rigorous evaluation of the literature. The literature informs providers about the current research on a given intervention. These interventions are reduced to clear, concise recommendations when the evidence is clear. Implementation planning identifies ways to incorporate these recommendations into the daily practice of providers and identifies methods for feedback of performance to leaders and providers. The ability to reinforce the change in practice with better tools for patient education or tools for providers to identify high-risk individuals is critical to implementation. Providers must be able to identify patients to whom the guidelines apply, and have relevant patient-specific data available at the time they are delivering care.

Testing the guideline and the implementation methods is accomplished by piloting the guideline in a defined setting prior to full implementation. After the evaluation of the pilot, the guideline is revised for systemwide implementation.

Heart Care Example: Secondary Prevention Guideline Development. The heart care team was interested in the secondary prevention of CAD because evidence indicated that patients who had been diagnosed with CAD might not have been receiving the most beneficial care according to the most recent evidence. Providers were also voicing concern about the research about lipid-lowering agents in this population and their use in patients without evidence of CAD. It also was clear from an initial review that when providers had a number of options to manage a patient, providers did not always choose interventions that were most likely to reduce the risk of future events. This variation in practice provided a focus for the guideline team.

From the beginning, it was noted that greater consistency in the application of an evidence-based approach would improve patient and provider satisfaction and the quality of care. It was also believed that appropriate use of expensive lipid-lowering agents could reduce costs by targeting individuals who were most likely to receive benefit from the medication.

The roadmap team evaluated the evidence and developed a tool to guide both practice teams and patients in their decision making. The tool provided a prioritized list of interventions based on the evidence of their benefit. Recommendations were made on the following interventions in order of importance:

- tobacco cessation
- aspirin
- lipids
- beta blockers
- ACE inhibitors
- estrogen replacement for postmenopausal women
- sedentary lifestyle
- calcium channel blockers
- psychosocial factors
- antioxidant vitamins

The recommendations cite representative studies, including the number needed to treat, which gives the practice team and patient a clearer understanding of the potential risks and benefits of a particular practice or intervention.

Through use of the algorithm, patient registries were supplied to the practice teams. These registries identified providers' patients with confirmed CAD, their medication lists, and their most recent lab results pertaining to CAD. With this information, practice teams were able to identify patients who were outside the guideline recommendations and to take appropriate action.

Heart Care Example: Secondary Prevention Guideline Implementation. The guideline implementation plan contained recommendations on how to organize care to meet the targets stated in the guideline. Critical to the implementation plan was the selection of designated cardiac risk reduction teams consisting of a physician, a nurse, and a pharmacist in each clinic to receive training to become local resources for provider teams. These teams were empowered and accountable for the improvement process in their clinics. The implementation plan for the secondary prevention guideline included a description of how a practice team or a clinic may organize around this work. It also explained the results of two implementation methods that had been pilot tested.

Working with their managers, the expert teams were asked to decide if one of these two models would work best or if they wanted to use aspects of each. The result was that a number of implementation methods evolved. Evaluation of the implementation methods is continuing, and as one particular method emerges as the most effective, that information will be distributed to the expert teams and their managers.

Provide Measurement and Feedback

Measurement and feedback are critical components of any widely distributed clinical improvement effort. Practice teams are motivated to consider their practice patterns when timely evidence shows that their practice pattern does not meet reasonable goals or benchmarks. Measurement and feedback are part of the process to build support for, as well as evaluate and improve, any evidence-based guideline. Roadmap teams are responsible for creating key goals and targets for the delivery system. Practice teams, clinics, and regions are held responsible for their performance on the key goals and targets. The roadmap teams also provide support to the practice teams on "best practices" within as well as outside the organization.

Heart Care Example. In the first year, the measurement and feedback plan for the secondary prevention of CAD guideline focused on the management of lipids. Although smoking cessation and the use of aspirin are greater priorities than lipid management, measurement systems were difficult to develop. Data on smoking status are not captured effectively in any automated system at GHCPS, and many patients buy aspirin over the counter outside the GHCPS pharmacy system. These issues made it difficult to capture complete and reliable data about these key interventions. Again, this points out the necessity of good data systems and information to support this strategy. The expense of lipid-lowering medications and the ability to capture current information on lab results and pharmacy data made information collection easy and complete.

The three goals for 1995 and 1996 are listed in Table 19–1.

THE RESULTS OF THE STRATEGY TO DATE

Outcomes

GHCPS uses a common framework to identify improvement goals and measure the effectiveness of its population-based strategies. The framework includes the following:

- Identify the significant outcomes for the population and measure performance.
- Identify the care processes (supported by the medical evidence) that are effective in achieving the significant outcomes and measure performance.
- Design the tools, systems, and supports to ensure that the desired care processes are implemented in the delivery system.

Experience has shown that many years are required to measure health outcomes. Thus, annual performance goals for longer-term health outcomes are not appropriate. However, clinical roadmap teams are encouraged to set longer-term outcome goals

---

Table 19–1 Heart Care Team's Goals for the Management of Lipids, 1995 and 1996

Goal	1995	1996
Low-density lipoprotein (LDL) drawn within 12 months after hospitalization for CABG, PTCA, acute MI, or unstable angina	85%	95%
Total cholesterol/high-density lipoprotein (HDL) <6 within 18 months after hospitalization for CABG, PTCA, acute MI, or unstable angina	65%	75%
LDL <130 within 18 months after hospitalization for CABG, PTCA, acute MI, or unstable angina	60%	70%

for their populations. On an annual basis, each roadmap team sets performance goals around specific care processes that will result in improved health outcomes for their populations. Performance on these care processes is measured and fed back to practice teams to focus and guide their improvement efforts.

Overall, GHCPS's population-based strategy has shown improved performance of effective care processes, increased patient satisfaction, and reduced cost and utilization for the initial populations (heart care, diabetes, pregnancy care, tobacco cessation, immunizations). Ongoing measurement of care processes and outcomes will inform GHCPS of the effectiveness of this strategy.

Secondary Prevention Outcomes

The heart care team has produced several improvements through the implementation of its strategies. Lipid management goals have improved as much as 43 percent for the organization. Patient satisfaction in the technical quality of care and the thoroughness of treatment has increased significantly. These improvements are the beginning of the process, and greater improvements are expected as the guidelines become a more integrated part of each provider's practice. As better tools become available, patients at risk will be identified sooner, along with interventions to empower them to better take care of themselves prior to the manifestation of CAD. These interventions will reduce the impact of CAD on their lives in the future, improve functional status of the population, and reduce costs for late-stage intervention.

Technology Applications

The clinical roadmap teams at GHCPS are in the process of evaluating a number of new technologies to help in the improvement of quality, satisfaction, and cost of patient care. Below are a few examples with descriptions of how they will assist the teams to continue to improve value for our customers.

- World Wide Web applications
  1. *Internet.* Many applications on the Internet are designed as a resource to the general public and GHCPS members. These currently include marketing information, pictures and profiles of physicians, articles on patient self-management, an electronic version of our quarterly magazine, a question-and-answer section, and GHCPS's most recent HEDIS data-reporting set. All of these services help individuals understand GHCPS better or allow another alternative communication tool for patients who prefer to communicate through the Internet.
  2. *Intranet.* These applications resident on the internal web page have been designed to convey tools and information to employees at GHCPS. They

include current clinical guidelines, all standard internal publications, medical library resources, and various business information resources. The Intranet continues to expand, and the heart care team is evaluating its use to distribute patient educational materials and provide assistance to providers who educate patients.

- Clinical workstation
  1. *Problem lists.* Problem lists provide the practice team with a list of major diagnoses for each patient. This list is designed to provide reminders to practice teams at the time care is provided. Problem lists are currently available in the medical chart at GHCPS and are currently being developed for the workstation.
  2. *Lifetime health monitoring system.* The lifetime health monitoring system is designed to capture information about the lifestyle of patients as they enter the GHCPS system or as they come in for a physical exam. Data on all risk factors are collected and entered into the clinical workstation. The information is used to provide patients and practice teams with reminders about areas that need intervention. The tool is designed to support the practice teams with customized reminders of areas where patients may need support. This system might remind a provider that the patient he or she is about to see for a high fever is a smoker, is participating in high-risk sexual activity, or has a family history of premature CAD. This will help the practice team provide appropriate follow-up at every opportunity, reinforcing the need to change lifestyles.

CHALLENGES FOR THE FUTURE

A major challenge for GHCPS and for any organization implementing an evidence-based, planned approach to care is to assist front-line practice teams in making the transition from their current practice to this new way of thinking and organizing themselves to provide care. Support can mean relatively simple changes such as regular team meetings to discuss data about outcomes and to assign follow-up tasks or more major changes such as redesigning the role of the practice nurse from phone triage to population management. To assist in this effort, GHCPS recently launched a new initiative called "practice improvement" that is geared toward helping front-line teams with tools, coaching, and support.

Another major challenge is to build the patient care system with enough flexibility so that it can be adapted to respond to changes in technology, changes in how patients participate in their care, and changes in care delivery systems. It means anticipating that as more people routinely access the Internet in their workplace, at school, and in their homes, their requirements for electronic access to information and support about all aspects of their life, including health care, will expand. At the same time, many patients are taking a much more active role in participating in decisions about their care, which means that the information not only needs to be accessible but needs to be in language that patients can understand.

Finally, the ultimate challenge for any population-based system of care is to ensure that each individual within the population receives the benefits of the system, customized to his or her unique care needs. This means that the care of patients with multiple disease states or prevention needs is coordinated and integrated at the primary care level and as they receive care across the continuum. It also means having a process by which patient education material can be adapted to match an individual's learning style, reading level, visual acuity, and native language. At GHCPS, one approach is to use our data warehouse and clinical workstation as primary integrating tools. The data warehouse will allow the integration of patient reminders so that patients with chronic disease and prevention needs will receive one notice that informs them of both routine prevention screenings and routine chronic care. The clinical workstation will integrate all the information about an individual patient at the point of care so that if the patient is diabetic and has CAD, the relevant data will be displayed in a way that allows the provider to take both conditions into consideration.

CONCLUSION

The execution of a population-based strategy will continue to require organizational commitment from the senior executive team and the front-line practice teams. The success ultimately resides with the improved health status of the patients that GHCPS serves. GHCPS believes that population-based care is the strategy that will take us into the next century in developing tools for providers and patients for the delivery of care. The landscape of managed care will change during this time and require better reporting systems and more informed patients with significantly reduced resources. These patients will have different desires and needs than the patients we serve today. The population-based care strategy will provide us the tools to manage the extreme pace of change in the delivery of health care and allow us to improve outcomes in an environment of delivery system transformation. Without a systematic approach to the care of specific populations, provider teams will not be able to manage the aging demographics of our patient population in the future. GHCPS will continue to adapt to the changes in patient care and the delivery system environment, as it has for the past 50 years. No system or strategy will be robust enough to meet all of the needs of a system adapting to an environment that we cannot at this time predict. However, we believe that this system, population-based care, is the first step in the evolution of care into the next century.

PART IV

Thriving in Redesign

CHAPTER **20**

Meeting the Challenges of Never-Ending Redesign

Mickey L. Parsons, Carolyn L. Murdaugh,
and Robert A. O'Rourke

Chapter Objectives

1. To describe the individual and organizational impact of constant change.
2. To discuss the emerging requirements for new leadership, management structures, and roles.
3. To introduce strategies for organizations to thrive in the new age of process management.

Never-ending change! It seems invigorating or oppressive, depending upon one's perspective. But for today's organizations to compete with the ever-increasing Wall Street ownership of health care they must be committed to unrelenting improvement. The emerging "Columbia standard" is forcing traditional downsizing and radical redesign to achieve benchmark operating costs per unit of service and redesigned clinical processes to provide cost-effective care across the continuum. Charles Handy, the noted British business guru, calls these times the "age of uncertainty."[1] Vaill uses the metaphor of "permanent white water" to describe these times for organizations.[2]

Clearly, as the examples in this book of operational and clinical redesign reveal, the revolution in health care is gaining momentum. The days are gone when a director or manager could say, "Let's wait until after the first of the year, when activities settle down" (or "until summer vacations are over," or "until the new administrator or physician arrives"). Competition never waits, and perpetual anxiety and attention to the changing marketplace are new for the health care work force. Leaders, including administrators and physicians, must first grapple with

341

their own personal reactions to these changes and develop a personal and professional philosophy and practice for success in the environment. Only then will effective leadership be provided to facilitate and support staff in creating the kind of changes that are needed.

Workers are traumatized by downsizing, layoffs, and outsourcing. A recent *Wall Street Journal* article quoted Alan Binder, Princeton University economist, as saying that "capitalism is getting meaner."[3] Particularly in health care, employees are shocked at the changes, because they have not prepared to work in a process-focused organization. This pertains to many physicians who believe that changes in the health care process will necessarily reduce the quality of medical practice and unfavorably affect patient outcomes. However, as documented in several chapters of this book, the development of new clinical paths for managing specific diseases requires physician "buy-in" and the presence of data suggesting that the patient's outcome will not be compromised. In fact, several excellent clinical management strategies described in this book were championed by physicians cognizant of the need for more cost-effective pathways for obtaining similar or better medical results.

NEW LEADERSHIP REQUIREMENTS

Education and effective leadership have never been more needed. Along with the simple design of jobs in silos came a management philosophy of "People need to be told what to do." Direct supervision and a command-and-control form of management were prevalent. As organizations change to the process focus, the need for new leadership and management structures becomes readily apparent. The evolving new leadership will focus on data-driven decisions based on cost and eventually on clinical outcomes research. Administrators will no longer be able delay changes by challenging the benchmark operating comparisons, and physicians will no longer be able to use the excuse that "it's cookbook medicine." Benchmark costs and evidence-based care have become the new standard by which leadership is judged. Data-driven recognition is compelling the new competition.[4]

The evolving new leadership will also emphasize coaching and facilitation.[5] The elimination of numerous levels of management and the emergence of self-management and membership in a team-based organization will require new skills for leaders. To maximize the creativity and generation of new ideas and methods of doing work, every person must be fully brought into the process. In this new paradigm, both the leader and the staff member will be accountable. Staff members can no longer wait for instructions; they must be self-starters and problem solvers who actively perform the current process with feedback from multiple data sources and constantly seek new ways to improve. The leader is responsible for the performance of the process and for its constant improvement. To accomplish these goals, facilitation and coaching skills are essential. Knowing when to be patient and when to add pressure to the team is important. In the haste to reduce costs and make "something" happen, leaders may expect everything to be accomplished in two weeks. Slash-and-burn downsizing can be quickly accomplished. However, redesign of operational and clinical processes requires an organization-wide approach with multiple goals. Time and a comprehensive project plan are required. Change projects in health care can be more easily implemented than sustained, indicating the need for effective planning, implementation, and evaluation processes.

A case study report from Cedars-Sinai Medical Center in Los Angeles provides an example of a comprehensive clinical process redesign that is still needed across the country. Their ideal concept of managed care is disease management. With over 40 clinical pathways encompassing nearly 200 guidelines, the organization's progress has been dramatic.[6]

STRATEGIES FOR ORGANIZATIONS TO THRIVE

How are these type of accomplishments in operational and clinical redesigns possible? A phrase by Vaill that is the title of one of his books, *Learning as a Way of Being,*[7] best describes the ongoing change process for individuals and organizations. To be successful while "living in permanent white water," to use his metaphor, leaders must become very effective learners. "The practice of learning as a way of being is a process of becoming a more conscious and reflective learner, more aware of one's own learning process and how it compares to the learning processes of others."[8]

Learning needs to be addressed for all members of the organization. Practical strategies for learning and organizational change include the ongoing communication of the "case for action." The case for action can never be communicated enough and has been inconsistently communicated by leaders. Second, development programs for physicians and other clinical leaders are essential for effective team-based leadership. As the care delivery system is more fully redesigned across the continuum, collaborative leaders for specific service areas will continue to be essential.

As health care organizes around processes, staff development programs are needed for employees to enhance their role transition from responsibility for a task to accountability for an outcome. Technical training for the more complex components of new jobs and information on the use of data to measure performance will support new roles within the processes. Skill development in basic communication, specifically assertive communication, enhances the overall work of the team.

Last, there is a need for new organizational team members described as "change support agents." These persons will be employed in human resources, pastoral care, social services, and staff development. One aspect of their roles will be to listen, support, network, and assist leaders and staff through the permanent white water of change. Support becomes particularly important in health care. Hospital staff and physicians in particular are experiencing the anxieties and intensity of change; however, they must continue to provide high-quality services to a patient/client. Without receiving support, it is difficult to provide support to others. Other industries are challenged to provide excellent customer service, but not by the life-and-death realities that exist in health care.

In summary, the health care revolution has begun. Each of us must decide if we will participate in the revolution and grow or be quickly outdated and unemployable. This includes all parties involved in health care delivery. The opportunities to create the new health care delivery system of the future exist for those who are willing to face uncertainty and never-ending redesign.

NOTES

1. C. Handy, *Beyond Certainty: The Changing Worlds of Organizations* (London: Arrow, 1995).
2. P. Vaill, *Managing as a Performing Art: New Ideas for a World of Chaotic Change* (San Francisco: Jossey-Bass, 1989).
3. "The Outlook: Inflation Stays Low, with Aid of Some Luck," *Wall Street Journal,* 16 December 1996, A1.
4. J. Morrissey, "Reaching for the Clouds: High Standards, Efficient Management Spur Success for Top 100 Hospitals," *Modern Healthcare* 26, no. 50 (1996): 52–64.
5. F. Hesselbein et al., eds., *The Leader of the Future: New Visions, Strategies, and Practices for the Next Era* (San Francisco: Jossey-Bass, 1996); T. Porter-O'Grady and C. Krueger Wilson, *The Leadership Revolution in Health Care: Altering Systems, Changing Behaviors* (Gaithersburg, MD: Aspen Publishers, Inc., 1995); M. Hammer, *Beyond Reengineering: How the Process-Centered Organization Is Changing Our Work and Our Lives* (New York: HarperCollins, 1996).
6. K. Southwick, "Case Study: Cedars-Sinai, Los Angeles, Makes Progress toward Disease State Management as the Ideal of Managed Care," *Strategies for Healthcare Excellence* 9, no. 12 (1996): 1–9.
7. P. Vaill, *Learning as a Way of Being: Strategies for Survival in a World of Permanent White Water* (San Francisco: Jossey-Bass, 1996).
8. Ibid., 47.

Index